# Widows in African Societies

# Widows in African Societies
## Choices and Constraints

EDITED BY BETTY POTASH

STANFORD UNIVERSITY PRESS
STANFORD, CALIFORNIA
1986

Stanford University Press
Stanford, California

© 1986 by the Board of Trustees of the
Leland Stanford Junior University
Printed in the United States of America


CIP data appear at the end of the book

# Preface

ALTHOUGH WIDOWS constitute as much as 25 percent of the adult female population in many societies, they have been a topic of little interest to researchers. The available literature on widows focuses almost entirely on cultural norms of widow remarriage. The emphasis is on how such patterns contribute to the survival and reproduction of groups. Little is known about widows themselves: their interests, the strategies they employ to realize such interests, the forces that determine such strategies, and the quality of their lives.

The papers in this book offer a corrective to the group-centered, norm-centered bias of the older literature. They also offer a corrective to more recent feminist literature that takes as its model the adult married woman even though many women spend much of their lives uninvolved in conjugal relationships. Finally, this volume suggests that many anthropological assumptions about social organization look different when examined from the perspective of widows and should be rethought. The nature and extent of communal support, the quality of in-law relationships, the relative importance of conjugal and maternal ties, the significance and durability of marital alliances, patterns of household and community development and dissolution, and the importance of women's ties to their own natal groups are some of the issues requiring reexamination.

This volume is an outgrowth of a symposium I organized for the 1980 meetings of the American Anthropological Association to obtain comparative data on African widows. My own field-work among the Luo of Kenya raised a number of issues that the literature did not address. Thus I asked participants to examine the options and constraints affecting widows and to consider in particular the following issues, a procedure that gives the contributions their unity:

1. What is the incidence of widow remarriage? How does re-

marriage relate to widows' other interests? What factors affect its occurrence? (Consider, for example, land rights, modes of economic support, religious beliefs, marriage rules, and rights over children.)

2. What are the similarities and differences between initial marriage and remarriage?

3. What happens to widows who do not remarry? Do they return to their natal group or remain in their husband's community? Why? Who is responsible for their care and economic support? How are they treated by the community? What role do children play in such treatment?

4. What are the household arrangements for widows?

5. To what extent have the options of widows been modified by changes in marriage and inheritance laws, new economic institutions, missionary activities, or other structural transformations?

All of the symposium papers—which did indeed comment on these issues—have been revised and expanded for publication here. Additional papers were solicited to add historical perspective and broaden the geographic coverage. Although not a representative sample, the collection does cover a broad spectrum of societies in different parts of the continent, societies where one finds varied kinship systems and patterns of economic and political organizations, as well as diverse adaptations to modern conditions.

None of the contributors other than Jane Guyer had focused on widows as a major research interest in the field, and the analyses were done from field notes gathered for other purposes. Only Enid Schildkrout had an opportunity to return to the field in the course of writing her paper. This volume must thus be regarded as a preliminary attempt to understand African widows. It is our hope that it will stimulate research on a much-neglected topic.

Mariam Slater has been an enthusiastic supporter of this work since its inception, serving as one of the discussants in the Symposium on African Widowhood held during the 1980 meetings of the American Anthropological Association. She has given generously of her time and skills, often acting as an unofficial coeditor of this volume. My papers, in particular, have benefited from her critical mind, her clear thinking, and her great sense of style, even though I have not always had the good sense to take her advice. All of us involved in this book owe Professor Slater our gratitude for efforts that go far beyond the assistance one normally expects of a colleague or friend.

Mona Etienne, Jane Guyer, Enid Schildkrout, and Christine Gailey read earlier drafts of the Introduction and contributed valuable suggestions. Judith Mendell and Ann Fagan assisted with some of the editing. I am grateful to them for their help. I would also like to thank Robert A. LeVine for his insightful comments as a discussant in the symposium, some of which are reproduced in Slater's Foreword, and for the hospitality he and Sara extended to me in the field.

Finally, I must note with sadness the death of Dorothy Dee Vellenga, one of the contributors. Her enthusiasm for this project was such that she continued working on her paper even in periods of severe pain, and never complained. Her cooperativeness, her unfailing good humor, and her dedication to scholarship were unusual, and I am grateful that I had the opportunity to collaborate with her.

B.P.

# Contents

# Contributors

MONA ETIENNE is research associate at the New School for Social Research, New York. She has taught in France, Ivory Coast, Canada, and the United States. In Ivory Coast, she also served as a consultant and as a UNESCO expert for various development projects. In collaboration with Eleanor Leacock she edited *Women and Colonization: Anthropological Perspectives*, and she has published extensively on the Baule. She received her doctorate from the University of Paris in 1985.

JANE I. GUYER is Associate Professor of Anthropology at Harvard University. Her principal research interests are social history and African household organization. She has published on Beti cocoa farming in Cameroon, where she did research, and has also written a review article on African household organization for the African Studies Association. She received her Ph.D. from the University of Rochester in 1972.

PAMELA LANDBERG, after completing fieldwork on the Swahili coast of Tanzania, received her doctorate from the University of California, Davis, in 1977. She has taught at New York University and presently holds an administrative position at New York Law School.

JEAN-CLAUDE MULLER, a professor at the Université de Montréal, has published extensively on the Rukuba of the Jos Plateau area of Nigeria. His most recent work, *Du bon usage du sexe et du mariage*, is a comparative study of Plateau marriage systems. He received his Ph.D. from the University of Rochester in 1970.

CHRISTINE OBBO, a Ugandan anthropologist educated at Makerere University, received her Ph.D. from the University of Wisconsin, Madison. Her interests include rural and urban planning, development, rural and urban migration, and the effect of social change on gender relations. Her book *African Women:*

*Their Struggle for Economic Independence* is based on her research among poor urban women in Kampala, Uganda, and in the rural areas of Uganda and Kenya. She is currently an assistant professor at Wheaton College, Massachusetts.

REGINA SMITH OBOLER has done fieldwork among the Nandi of Kenya and in the urban United States. She received her Ph.D. from Temple University in 1982, and is currently teaching anthropology and sociology at Kutztown University, Kutztown, Pennsylvania. She is the author of *Women, Power, and Economic Change: The Nandi of Kenya*.

BETTY POTASH spent five years in Africa, teaching and doing research at the University of Nairobi and Lagos University. She received her Ph.D. from New York University in 1970 and has also been a Fellow of the African Studies Program at Boston University. She received an M.A. from the University of Chicago. Her research on the Luo focused on women and their role in development. She has taught at Syracuse University, Lehigh University, and Medgar Evers College of the City University of New York.

FRANK A. SALAMONE is Chairman of the Social Sciences Department of Elizabeth Seton College, Yonkers, New York. He received his Ph.D. in 1973 from the State University of New York, Buffalo, and he has taught at SUNY Brockport, St. John's University, and the University of Jos, Nigeria. He has done fieldwork in northern Nigeria and published on the Dukawa and the Hausa. His research interests include ethnicity, religion, and anthropological theory.

ENID SCHILDKROUT is Curator of Anthropology at the American Museum of Natural History. She has done research in Ghana and Nigeria. Her book *People of the Zongo* is a study of ethnicity and cultural change in Kumase, Ghana. Most recently she has published on children's economic activities in Kano, Nigeria. She received her Ph.D. from Cambridge University in 1969.

MARIAM K. SLATER, a professor of anthropology at Queens College, City University of New York, has published on both Africa and the Caribbean. Her Ph.D. dissertation at Columbia University, completed in 1958, was published as *The Caribbean Fam-*

*ily: Legitimacy in Martinique.* Her research among the Nyika of Tanzania formed the basis for her book *African Odyssey.* Currently she is doing research on the evolution of human sexual behavior, with particular reference to the incest taboo.

DOROTHY DEE VELLENGA at the time of her death in 1984 was a Scholar in Residence at Muskingum College, New Concord, Ohio, where she had previously been an Associate Professor of Sociology. She first went to Ghana in 1961-63 with the Peace Corps, returning in 1968-70 to do research on women and the law for her doctorate in sociology, which she received from Columbia University in 1975. She went to Ghana again in 1975-76 on a postdoctoral grant from the Social Science Research Council to study women cocoa farmers. She had been working on a number of papers based on this research at the time of her death.

# Foreword:
# Sons and Levirs

MARIAM K. SLATER

PERHAPS THE MOST famous widow in Western literature is known for her marriage to her dead husband's brother. The new husband is not strictly a levir, for the children of the pair would not be raised as if they belonged to the deceased. Nor was theirs what the Nuer call a "ghost marriage," a practice in which a man takes a wife in his dead brother's name. If the play in which this famous widow is immortalized were told from her own point of view, its title would be "Gertrude, Queen of Denmark." Instead, of course, the drama unfolds through the eyes of the widow's son, Hamlet, who was traumatized by Gertrude's anomalous choice of spouse. An even more disruptive marriage of a widow is also portrayed in our literature from a son's-eye view: it is Oedipus, not Jocasta, who has entered our mythos.

Except for the occasional "merry" ones, widows of the West tend to be kept off stage in life as well as in fiction and in sociology, playing out their lives in the wings. The reasons for this marginality are various, and they influence our perceptions of widows elsewhere, who may play different roles. As we shall see, although African widows may upon occasion have a hard time, in no society are they marginal—and in some they are freer than wives.

The very visibility of a hitherto invisible status is a serendipitous discovery of this volume, which takes a new empirical look at widowhood in Africa. The ten societies sampled display diversity without being formally representative of the sub-Saharan continent. These close-ups range from the matrilineal Akan and cognatic Baule of West Africa to the patrilineal Luo in the East, from urban Hausa and Swahili to Rukuba subsistence cultivators on the Jos Plateau of Nigeria.

Each paper presents the widow's angle, emphasizing her options, choices, and strategies. This is a transactional approach; the focus is on process as opposed to the emphasis on stable group relations found in functional-structuralist analysis.

Anthropology at its best is the "Mirror for Man," as Clyde Kluckhohn called it (1949), that allows us to escape from ethnocentric interpretations of other cultures and at the same time see our own in a deepened perspective. Since the distortions of self and other are mutually reinforcing, this volume makes a double contribution. And one of the most striking findings is that stereotypes about widowhood are just that—stereotypes.

Once revealed, the African patterns also invite us to look again at Western widowhood. In the Bible, which permeates our Western worldview, widowhood seems alien. It is the Biblical widow's fate that introduces us to that institution called the levirate, a concept involving a widow and her husband's brother in a relationship whose ambiguities will be explored in this volume. The vignette in Genesis (38:1) about Onan—known, it seems, for the wrong sin—dramatizes possibilities open to the levir if not the widow: "Then Judah told Onan to sleep with his brother's wife, to do his duty as the husband's brother and raise up issue for his brother. But Onan knew that the issue would not be his; so whenever he slept with his brother's wife, he spilled his seed on the ground so as not to raise up issue for his brother." Again, the woman is offstage in our consciousness. Indeed, she might well be referred to as "What's-her-name?" But the full Biblical story reveals the widow, Tamar, to be quite assertive.

What of the African widow? It is common wisdom in comparative ethnology and sociology that kin-based societies offer a corporate safety net for widows and orphans. Such societies reabsorb a widow by allowing her to marry within her husband's lineage, or they force her to do so by means of the levirate, widow inheritance, or some other form of remarriage. Before seeing how this stereotype is challenged by the papers in this volume, let us examine a genuine case of widow remarriage.

One of the ironies of Gertrude's crime, sin, or tragic flaw in *Hamlet* is that she exercised an option that many of the world's peoples would applaud if not insist upon. Laura Bohannan dramatically makes this point in her classic exploration of relativism, "Shakespeare in the Bush" (1966). Testing the much-vaunted universality of Shakespeare, which a British colleague had told her could be really understood only by the English, Bohannan tried to translate the main elements of *Hamlet* for the Tiv of Nigeria, who are expert storytellers. One of the elders began cross-examining the anthropologist about why Hamlet's zombie—they did not believe in a ghost, or insubstantial double, but only in a dead body animated by the witches—consulted Hamlet, a mere junior.

"Had the dead chief no living brothers? Or was this son the chief?"

"No," I replied. "That is, he had one living brother who became the chief when the elder brother died."

The old man muttered: such omens were matters for chiefs and elders, not for youngsters. . . .

". . . The dead chief's younger brother had become the great chief. He had also married his elder brother's widow . . . a month after the funeral."

"He did well," the old man beamed, and announced to the others, "I told you that if we knew more about Europeans, we would find they really were very like us. In our country also . . . the younger brother marries the elder brother's widow and becomes the father of his children. Now, if your uncle, who married your widowed mother, is your father's full brother, then he will be a real father to you. Did Hamlet's father and uncle have one mother?"

His question barely penetrated my mind: I was too upset and thrown . . . by having one of the most important elements of Hamlet knocked straight out of the picture. . . . I said that I thought they had the same mother . . . the story didn't say. . . . Determined to save what I could of the mother motif, I took a deep breath. . . . "The son Hamlet was very sad because his mother had married again so quickly. There was no need for her to do so, and it is our custom for a widow not to go to her next husband until she has mourned for two years."

"Two years is too long," objected the wife. . . . "Who will hoe your farms for you while you have no husband?"

"Hamlet," I retorted without thinking, "was old enough to hoe his mother's farms himself. There was no need for her to remarry." No one looked convinced. I gave up. . . . While I paused, perplexed at how to render Hamlet's disgusted soliloquy to an audience convinced that Claudius and Gertrude had behaved in the best possible manner, one of the younger men asked me who had married the other wives of the dead chief. (Ibid.)

Tiv and Western widows have little in common, and few would try to compare such apples and oranges. What we must rigorously guard against is making an unwarranted projection of the Tiv model of widowhood onto the entire preliterate or kin-based world, as textbooks tend to do. Actually, the levirate is present in only three of the ten societies in this sample, and in two of them the actors distinguish this arrangement from marriage. In one of the other seven, the practice of widow inheritance is contradictory to the rules of the kinship system, according to Mona Etienne in her analysis of the Baule of the Ivory Coast. Although the practice does take place, it involves kinsmen more distant than brothers and is considered quasi-incestuous, requiring purification by a ritual act of adultery.

Betty Potash hypothesizes that Westerners distort patterns of widowhood because ours is a conjugally structured society; descent and alliance theorists are paradigm-bound; androcentric analyses make women's roles invisible; and theorists assume a sort of *communitas* in non-Western societies that is likely to be chimerical.

In the symbolic-structuralist paradigm, many conclusions are also counterindicated by the African material. Assuming the ubiquity of marriage, in his version of alliance theory Claude Lévi-Strauss (1971) makes the following generalization: "There are no bachelors in primitive society." Unlike bachelors, unmarried women are not even dreamed of, for females are thought to be too valuable as scarce commodities to remain widows. They are immediately repossessed, as in the Tiwi model presented by Hart and Pilling (1966), in which a widow is remarried at her husband's funeral; even the unborn female is betrothed.

To the contrary, as case after case shows, the single status of the formerly married is not necessarily transitional or anomalous. Potash's data suggest that among the Luo, for example, marriage, rather than single status, can be an epiphenomenon. It may be a minor punctuation point in the life span of some women—depending, of course, on the stage in the reproductive cycle at which the husband dies. In some societies, a woman, although not divorced, lives singly even while her husband is still alive. This frequently happens when she reaches menopause, a pattern called "terminal separation."

One frequently finds that menopause frees a female from many taboos she has been obeying, and that she sometimes gains political decision-making power at this phase. Among the Bantu Nyika (or Nyiha) of Tanzania, whom I studied, the word for menopause is derived from the notion of a woman's becoming a man (Slater 1976a). No longer sexually desirable—or dangerous—the menopausal woman has options that resemble those of the younger widow or divorcée. The older woman and the widow can remain in her husband's compound, move back to her natal lineage, or move in near a son, who usually remains in his father's area. Like a wife, she has a house of her own. If there are grandchildren, they keep the older woman company, for children are excluded from a young wife's house. A young widow has sexual rights and can demand a kinsman of her husband to "scratch her back."

Whether sex rights and duties coincide with marriage, remarriage, or co-residence is an open question, depending on many variables in each specific society. The legitimization of children also does not follow any one generalized pattern. Neither Nandi nor Luo effectively permit remarriage, but childbearing can continue without negative sanctions. Widows in some societies may take not only new husbands, but lovers or consorts.

Options and constraints vary with such factors as life cycle, demography, marriage systems, residence rules, and the division of labor. Such supposedly independent variables as colonial penetration, universalistic religions, and cash economies do not have the monolithic influence so often attributed to them *a priori*. Furthermore, social change, we discover once again, is not unidirectional. Solidarity, for example, neither breaks down in the aftermath of colonialism nor automatically supports the widow.

For many reasons, we see, African widows tend not to be the passive objects of rules governing rights that men allegedly have to transfer women from group to group. In none of the cases does the widow aim to be reabsorbed into her husband's lineage. If she remains single, becoming a household head—whether in her husband's community or elsewhere—she does not (with few structural exceptions) risk the isolation that afflicts so many Western widows. Nor does she experience the impoverishment of identity or economic status.

Why have these papers brought to light regularities that were previously hidden? Some of the reasons have already been discussed, but Robert A. LeVine, one of the discussants who took part in the symposium that led to this book, commented on the advantages of the transactional approach used in the symposium papers. A life span model, he stated, one that allows us to study widows "by living their lives," is particularly fitting. For this model is part of the emic view—the way the actors involved perceive their careers. Even very young wives, he observed, must adopt a strategy for maximizing their well-being in their later years, as the papers demonstrate. LeVine finds that Frank Salamone's minimax model of widows' decisions among the Dukawa is an apt illustration of what we might see as a congruence of formal method and social reality. Finally, LeVine pointed out that the transactional model helps eliminate male bias in reporting on widows, a bias manifested in the structuralist assumption that only male dominance establishes norms.

The fact that African women in traditional ecologies are now recognized as having more independent identities than was previously thought may be related to events in the recent history of the West. The feminist movement, which reflects a number of changes in our society, has brought increased awareness of the multiplicity of women's roles. Feminist anthropologists have shown women elsewhere to be more economically independent than when they disappeared into the functionalist forest.

So, too, the fact that the African widow as single woman has suddenly become more visible, particularly in these studies, may relate to a generally increased awareness of women in nonmarital situations. The Western woman has emerged with more of an independent identity than before. In her role as a single person, whether before or after marriage, she has become more of what used to be called a "bachelor girl" than a stigmatized spinster or a widow with a leftover half-life. Now that 60 percent of nonfarming American women work outside the home, with many entering the labor force at higher levels than before, widows may become less peripheral.

The upper-class widow has always been different, because she is the repository of significant wealth, but the middle-class mainstream Western widow who is old today is a social victim. Her desolation has a dimension that is missing in Africa, and the contrastive demographics of the two areas help to explain why. In America today, the typical widow is a victim of ageism, and of age itself. Different life expectancy rates tell a large part of the story. Today, Americans live 16 years longer than they did at the turn of the century—and even then the chasm between Africa and the modern world in terms of health and mortality was wide, the average African life expectancy being 30-35.

As for the gender differential in American vital statistics, females are 60 percent of America's elderly, and there are six widows for every widower. In the United States, 15 million women are over 65, 3½ million of them over 80. The gerontological problems such facts present are exacerbated by the fact that a third of these women rely on Social Security for 90 percent of their income.

Another new trend already visible in America but not yet reflected in census analyses is not widespread even in modernizing Africa. Care for the upper-middle-class elderly by children—or grandchildren—has been complicated by the geographical mobility of younger and older generations. The long-distance caretaking made necessary, says Dr. Eugene Litwak, a professor of sociology and social work, is part of "an evolving new family structure in America . . . the modified extended family" (*New York Times*, Nov. 29, 1983). Stepchildren further complicate the kinship duties, which have been so reversed as to be described as "parenting your parents." A psychologist of aging, Dr. Stanley Cath, states that "The myth of the abandoned elder is just that— a myth."

In Africa and in America, then, it is the children who protect the widows. But American widows are more isolated by community dynamics; they are also more marginal in their society. In subsistence economies and rural settings, the woman who is young enough to work as a cultivator has a place in the labor force. At a later stage she is fortunate if she has grown sons. The importance in a woman's life of the levir or other liaison after the first husband is outweighed in this sample by that of a woman's sons. Only among the Swahili do mothers generally not live with sons. Both emotionally and economically, mother-son bonds supersede wife-spouse bonds.

Perhaps only observers of the Caribbean or Afro-American

family have seen women in nonconjugal contexts playing roles as socially strong as those of some of the African widows seen here. For among the New World non-elite, the female household head predominates in the developmental cycle of the household and in the network of kin relations. The dynamics involved are usually referred to as matrifocality. In such social arrangements the conjugal ties—whether cemented by formal or by consensual marriages—are not primary in a woman's life.

Rather, a woman's children provide for her after the marginal father-husband or string of lovers moves off. Some of these men have never joined the household, and women in these subcultures usually give birth to their first offspring while still living in their mother's household. As in Africa, children provide permanent bonds, although in the New World it is daughters rather than sons who are co-residents. Often, a three-generational "grandmother family" occurs, with a woman, one or more illegitimate daughters, and the children of the latter.

In a study of such communities in Martinique, in the French West Indies, I interpreted this development in terms of the absence of what Malinowski called "the rule of legitimacy" (Slater 1976b). By this he meant that differential status devolves on legitimate and illegitimate children, those born to parents formally joined, on the one hand, and more casually joined, on the other. One distinctive feature of such value systems is a social structure in which there is no necessary congruence between child-rearing and child-producing units. Moreover, residence with either unit is not articulated in a predictable manner. All arrangements generated are equally acceptable by the non-elite. One unexpected discovery in this present volume is that matrifocality, so defined, is also an integral aspect of the kin-based, more traditional societies of Africa. In Africa, as well as in Martinique and some other parts of the Caribbean—and occasionally elsewhere—the woman is more dependent on children than on mates.

Finally, it is noteworthy that a kind of marriage-ism has dulled our lens for studying single women in Africa and in Afro-America. By looking at how widows in African societies actually live, we avoid this perceptual bias and deepen our insights into the way society and reproduction operate.

# Widows in African Societies

# Widows in Africa: An Introduction

BETTY POTASH

WIDOWS CONSTITUTE a quarter of the adult female population in many African societies, yet widowhood has not been subject to systematic investigation by anthropologists. Such research is necessary for understanding the important modifications that women's relationships, rights, and powers undergo during the course of their life cycle. Moreover, the demographic characteristics alone suggest that our understanding of community organization and social processes is necessarily incomplete without a proper appreciation of the role of widows. When examined from the perspective of the widow, many social processes look different: the extent and nature of corporate kin group responsibility, the significance and durability of marital alliances, the differential importance attached to conjugal and filial bonds, patterns of affinal relationships, processes of household and community development and dissolution, and the nature and continuity or discontinuity of women's different ties to a community. Although the ethnography of widowhood is the primary concern of this volume and this introduction, I shall examine some implications of the research for understanding other features of social organization as well.

## A Closer Look at the Lives of Widows

Not only have widows been neglected as a major topic in the anthropological literature, but the limited treatment given to widowhood in Africa has focused on the wrong questions. A common misconception is that most widows are involved in conjugal relationships. The reality is that many widows live without spouses, and not as marginal elders. The factors influencing widows' lives, the options available to them, and the multiplicity of interests that affect their behavior—including, but by no means limited to, marital decisions—have not been systematically examined. This neglect and the distortions in the literature are related; they stem from three primary sources.

First, the concentration by anthropologists almost entirely on widow remarriage may come from an unconscious ethnocentrism of Westerners, who live in a conjugally structured society. There are, after all, other aspects to widows' lives. Even the sexual and procreative relationships that widows enter in some societies are misrepresented by most anthropologists as forms of marriage. Thus the celebrated levirate, in which a kinsman of the deceased becomes a consort of the widow and sires children to the name of the dead husband, should not automatically be conceptualized as marriage. This type of relationship between a widow and her dead husband's kinsman may, from an emic point of view (the perspective of the people concerned), be distinguished from marriage. In many groups it is the deceased, not the levir, who is regarded as the woman's husband. Etically (from the perspective of the outside observer), the levirate can manifest important differences in rights and obligations from those pertaining to the original husband and wife. By grouping such practices with other forms of marriage, we ignore the fact that in many cases widows involved in such relationships live alone and may have greater independence and responsibility than wives have.

A second distorting mirror is created by an androcentric interpretation of the role of women in general, and widows in particular, in economic and political activities. Little attention is paid to the economic role of widows, whom anthropologists often regard as dependents who must be provided for. On the contrary, widows may control adequate resources to support themselves.

Finally, the treatment of widows suffers from the complex influence of an outworn paradigm, namely British structural-functionalism (hereafter referred to simply as functionalism). This approach stresses the rights of kin groups in marriage and tends to treat widows as passive pawns. These essays show that, in reality, widows make decisions about their own lives. In many cases, they have the freedom to live alone and manage their own affairs, to form relationships with consorts, or in some systems, to marry again.

## Widows in the Literature

As Mariam Slater dramatically shows in her Foreword to this volume, widows in Western tradition are not regarded as central to the drama of life. This backstage role is also reflected in sociological studies of Western societies. Despite such research on widows as that of Peter Marris (1958) and Helena Znaniecki Lopata (1979), the relative paucity of data on widowhood, in comparison with the voluminous body of literature on courtship, marriage, and even divorce, is striking. Such neglect, I would argue, relates to the anomalous position of widows in Western societies, which are conjugally structured. Western systems emphasize companionate marriage and common conjugal funds; widows are regarded as somewhat peripheral and hence of little interest.

This emphasis on conjugality has also affected the study of widows in non-Western societies where domestic life is organized on a different basis. The focus in the literature, as noted, is almost entirely on widow remarriage and widow-consort relationships. This focus, which neglects other aspects of widows' lives, reflects, as I have suggested, an unconscious cultural bias. Not all societies are conjugally structured. Moreover, even where conjugality is important, relationships do not have identical meanings or significance cross-culturally.

Furthermore, although marriage is a universal or nearly universal experience for women in African societies, African women are not necessarily involved in marital relationships throughout their adult lives. In some West African societies, for example, as women approach menopause they leave their husbands and return to their natal kin. This practice has been described by Meyer Fortes (1949b) and Esther Goody (1973) as "terminal separation." E. E. Evans-Pritchard, in his study of the Nuer of the Sudan (1951), discusses unmarried women and widows in concubinage relationships. A number of studies describe divorced women who live alone, as for example, that of Abner Cohen of the Hausa of Ibadan, Nigeria (1969).

In some societies widows also spend much of their lives uninvolved in marital unions, but they are not necessarily marginal in their communities. Yet there is little discussion of the other options available to widows, the factors affecting their decisions about remarriage, the organization of widow-headed households, the nature of widow-consort relationships, or the social, economic, and other relationships and interests that widows have.

Despite the primacy the literature gives to widows' marital and consort arrangements, I would argue that such ties are of minimal importance in many societies. The widow who remains in her husband's community generally does so because of the structure of property rights, because of ties to children, or because she finds other advantages in remaining. The interpretation of this behavior simply as the exercise of corporate group rights to inherit widows is wrong. Marriage to a deceased husband's kinsman (termed "widow inheritance"), or leviratic relationships, which may be optional and are often temporary and short-lived, are usually determined by the woman's place of residence and her desire to continue sexual relationships and/or childbearing. The woman's age and her childbearing history also affect such marital and consort decisions. In some societies rights to residence with natal kin provide widows with alternatives to marriage and/or to remaining in their husband's community. In others, widows may enter new marriages elsewhere. Sometimes they have no right to remain.

The range of options available to widows varies, but widows in most societies have choices and exercise them. There are systems, however, in which marriage is used for political manipulation, to acquire clients or a large female labor force. In such societies widows may indeed have few options and become objects of male transactions. Here the term *inheritance* may be truly appropriate.

The papers in this volume demonstrate that contrary to commonly held views, there is generally no communal support for widows. Many widows are self-reliant, living alone and heading their own households. They may receive occasional gifts, but concepts of communal support and corporate group responsibility are largely idealized. Access to land and housing are important factors affecting widows' marital and residential decisions. In old age widows depend on children, sometimes on natal kin. The maternal-child bond is central to widows' lives and affects their behavior in many ways. Concerns with maintaining ties to children are important influences on remarriage and residence. Not surprisingly, the childless widow may be in difficulty.

The second factor that contributes to the paucity of data on widowhood, male-centered bias, leads to discussing women only in relationship to men—primarily in terms of marriage and motherhood. Other interests are largely ignored. In spite of the fuller treatment of women during the last decade, there is still a tendency to ghettoize research on their behavior, so that findings from such studies have had less impact than they should on anthropological theories and concepts. Even when mainstream theories have been called into question and reformulated on other grounds, statements about women based on such theories persist unless challenged by feminist scholarship.[1] Thus textbooks often reproduce unacceptable concepts of widowhood that derive from functionalist analyses of the 1940's and 1950's, even as that paradigm is questioned elsewhere. Available ethnographic data, although incomplete, suggest more variation and choice than these concepts indicate, but such data are not used to question these generalizations.

All the comparative statements anthropologists make about widowhood use perspectives derived from this functionalist paradigm. Neither Marxists nor symbolic structuralists deal with widows per se. But functionalists have no interest in the multiple roles of the widow, only in the institutional arrangements governing the "inheritance" of widows. The emphasis is on how these institutions contribute to maintaining the social system, and the focus is on corporate group rights. Since marriage is seen as an arrangement made by men, which transfers rights over women from the woman's group to the husband and his group, such institutions as the levirate and widow inheritance are interpreted as enabling the husband's group to retain these rights.

1. This issue was addressed in a session of the 1982 annual meeting of the American Anthropological Association, "Worlds in Collision: The Impact of Feminist Scholarship in Anthropology."

For descent theorists, the functions of these institutions are the physical reproduction of the group. Marriage gives the husband's group rights over any children born to his wife; the levirate and widow inheritance merely continue these rights and ensure reproduction of offspring. For theorists emphasizing alliance, marriage is seen as an institution that creates affinal links between groups. The "inheritance" of widows perpetuates such ties by ensuring that affinity does not end with death. In both descent and alliance approaches, widows are discussed under the rubric of inheritance, and it is the widows themselves who are seen as the objects to be inherited.

Much attention has been given in the literature to developing a taxonomy of marital and consort relationships. Distinctions are drawn between the levirate, in which children are filiated to the deceased, and widow inheritance, in which the genitor, or biological father, is also the pater, or social father. Such formalistic distinctions are not consistently followed, as Max Gluckman notes (1971). More important, they tell us nothing of the relationship between a widow and her husband's successor; they speak only of the filiation of children.[2] Nor does the terminology indicate anything about the diverse processes by which such relationships are established.

This lack of attention to process is a particular problem in those theories that seek structural correlates for the levirate or patterns of widow remarriage. The best-known of these approaches, the hypothesis developed by Max Gluckman, associates patrilineal descent with a complex of traits including the levirate, marital stability, high bridewealth, and a mode of property transmission termed the house property complex, in which each group of full brothers inherits a share of their father's estate through their mother. This hypothesis was subject to much criticism in the 1950's by scholars who showed that the correlation did not work (L. Fallers 1957; Leach 1957; Stenning 1959; and see R. Cohen 1971, who summarizes some of these critiques). The hypothesis was subsequently reformulated to suggest that it

---

2. Distinctions between adelphic and filial succession, i.e., inheritance by brothers or sons, may also indicate important differences in descent group organization and the rights and obligations of agnates. But this has little to do with widowhood.

was the house property complex, and not descent per se, that was associated with the levirate and marital stability, but the data do not support this reformulation either (Abrahams 1973).

Let us take examples from this volume. The Dukawa have the levirate but no house property complex. The Luo have both, but acceptance of the levirate relates to a complex of factors, including lack of residential alternatives and a desire for children. Regina Oboler's analysis of the Nandi suggests the reverse of Gluckman's thesis: her conclusion is that the security Nandi widows have through house property makes the levirate unnecessary for them. The difficulty with Gluckman's hypothesis, and with similar attempts at correlating structural variables, is the lack of attention to process or organization. There is no consideration of the complex of factors that affect behavior. We do not know how property systems influence action. Nor do such approaches explain variation.

The issue of form and process is important in understanding the limitations of the distinctions conventionally made between the levirate and widow inheritance. These terms do not distinguish two discrete and uniform types of relationships between a widow and her husband's successor; they concentrate only on structural form. Leviratic relationships have in common only three characteristics: they are usually with a husband's kinsman (although non-kinsmen and maternal nephews may sometimes be levirs with the permission of the kin group); they are socially recognized as legitimate; and children are considered to be the descendants of the deceased and not the levir.

The practices by which a levir is chosen vary. In some societies a younger brother may be the automatic successor; in others the choice may rest with the widow, who is free to select any member of the lineage, but sometimes requires formal approval of the elders. A council of lineage elders or the lineage head may determine who shall take over the widow or who shall make her an offer. Leviratic relationships may be optional or mandatory. Emically they may be regarded as an exercise of lineage rights or they may be viewed as an obligation to the widow. They may also be seen as necessary inducements to secure the widow's agreement to remain, if the husband's kin want her and her children to stay.

the interests affecting widows' decisions but generally present little information on the social and economic consequences following from such decisions. We know little about widows' lives.

The scattered references in the literature do not provide a comprehensive picture of widows. So scant is the literature that the only comparative volume dealing with African widows is a work by a Maryknoll sociologist who is concerned with the attitude of church members and leaders in four East African societies toward the levirate (Kirwen 1979). Some additional comparative material is found in *The Family Estate in Africa*, edited by Robert F. Gray and Philip Gulliver (1964), which discusses widows in relationship to different modes of property inheritance, and in Lucy Mair's article surveying African marriage (1953).

*A Social Process Approach to Widows*

This book seeks to fill some of the gaps in the literature by examining in more detail the options available to widows, the interests that affect the decisions they make about their own lives, and the consequences of such decisions. Despite the proliferation of "new" theories of social process, I continue to find Raymond Firth's distinction between social structure and social organization the most useful general approach. *Structure* refers to the principles underlying the forms of social relationships; *organization*, to behavior (Firth 1951: 28, 36).

As actors, widows make choices from among the possibilities available to them. But alternatives vary from system to system. Although behavior cannot be explained by such abstract principles as descent, affinity, or sibling solidarity, and conformity to norms is not automatic, it is clear, nonetheless, that some norms have strong institutional support and others do not. Rules concerning marriage and child custody, rights of residence, access to productive resources, the sexual division of labor and the labor requirements of productive technologies, moral values, religious beliefs and supernatural sanctions, the basis by which prestige is accorded, and available channels for meeting sexual and emotional needs are aspects of the structure that influence, but do not determine, what widows do. By identifying the possibilities available to widows, the constraints under which they operate, and the factors affecting choices, we can both understand behavior and relate it to the larger system. This approach is not new, of course; it is common ethnographic practice. But it has not been applied to the study of widows.

Similarity of structural form does not indicate similarity of content. Let us again consider the levirate, which is present in several of the societies described in this volume. A comparison shows quite different factors influencing the formation of leviratic relationships.

For the Nandi, Regina Oboler shows that the levirate is a cultural ideal that is seldom practiced. Widows reside alone or with adult sons and take over the management of the husband's estate. Most widows are under no pressure to continue childbearing. Although a levir is normatively expected to act as adviser to the widow, in practice many widows manage their own affairs. Control over resources through the house property complex enables a widow to refuse the levirate. Should she desire to continue her sex life, she may either accept a levir designated by her husband's kin, who will visit, or choose a lover outside the husband's lineage. In either case, the deceased and not the genitor is socially recognized as father or pater. Since a community includes men of different lineages, a number of possible consorts are available.

Luo widows, as my own fieldwork demonstrates, also reside alone and manage lands transmitted through the house property mode of inheritance. However, they choose levirs from their husband's lineage, according to my study. Communities are organized on a segmentary lineage principle, and the few non-agnatic or stranger groups reside there by virtue of past favors granted by lineage members. If a non-agnate consorts with the widow, this is considered adulterous. Women are expected to continue bearing children, and some widows desire to do so. A woman's status and her security in old age depend on having many sons. Widows with no children, or with daughters only, may bear children after the death of a husband; widows with sons sometimes do not. The levir is not a husband and has few rights or obligations. Typically he is not a husband's brother but a more distant kinsman. Neither the Luo nor the Nandi effectively permit remarriage, although some interethnic marriages occur in modern urban settings.

Among the Dukawa, according to Frank Salamone, leviratic unions are similar to marriage except for the filiation of children. The widow resides with the levir. In this society several options are available to widows. Although a younger brother of the deceased is expected to offer the widow a leviratic relationship in order to induce her and her children to remain, a widow is free to reject this offer and make other arrangements. She may remarry or return to her father's home, often taking children with her. Salamone describes the factors affecting widows' decisions in terms of a minimax model. The organizing factors affecting widows' behaviors—the options and the constraints—clearly differ in these three systems, as do the ensuing relationships.

The Rukuba of Nigeria, as Jean-Claude Muller shows, practice a form of polyandry and permit consort relationships for those widows who choose to remain in a deceased husband's home. Women are simultaneously married to several men who live in different communities. On the death of a spouse, a widow may reside with one of her other husbands, remarry, or remain in her deceased husband's community. In the last case she may accept a lover. He is not necessarily an agnate of the husband; the only restriction is that he comes from the same marriage-regulating moiety. Moreover, widows may have several lovers simultaneously, as well as engage in more casual affairs.

Such relationships may be regarded as leviratic with respect to the filiation of children; in other features they appear to resemble more closely what Evans-Pritchard (1951) termed widow concubinage. In the Rukuba arrangement, there is no co-residence between widow and consort, and lovers have no formal obligations to each other. Sometimes, however, such relationships are close and partners may offer each other assistance. Muller analyzes the range of factors that affect widows' choices from among the options available to them. The difficulty of farming alone is one factor that may induce a widow to leave and join another husband or remarry. Her age and the age and residence of her children are other considerations.

As options and constraints within a system change, so too do behaviors. Jane Guyer shows how transformations of the political economy of Cameroon relate to modifications in the position of widows at various periods of Beti history. When power and wealth were based on trade, and later on political clientage, widows were valuable resources whom men wished to inherit. By acquiring widows and wives, men acquired valuable affinal connections and clients. Widows had little choice. Women were also important sources of labor for producing the food necessary to feed retainers. When cocoa farming was introduced, the political economy changed again. Once wealth came to be based on plantations, widows ceased to be desired resources and became competitors for valuable land. Men no longer wished to inherit widows. Although complexly caused, the abolition of the legal provisions for widow inheritance was consonant with these changes in the political economy.

Dorothy Dee Vellenga's data also show how changes in the larger society modified the position of widows. Colonial changes in Akan inheritance laws gave some widows access to property. But such inheritance rights exacerbated strains between the widow and her husband's matrilineage, and the husband's heir ceased to take responsibility for the widow. However, widows' acquisition of cocoa farms by inheritance, gift, or purchase has placed them in an advantageous position. Today widowed farmers in rural Ghana are economically better off than either wives or divorced women.

Enid Schildkrout's analysis of Hausa data shows how widows' choices depend not only on the options available in the society, but also on the widow's life cycle stage. Hausa women depend on sons for support in old age, and a new marriage may jeopardize that support. Younger widows and divorced women who expect to be able to bear and raise children to maturity will generally remarry; older widows will not. Muller similarly analyzes the importance of life cycle stages and children to Rukuba widows' choices.

Among the Baule, widows' marital decisions are also affected by ties to children, but the strategic considerations are quite complex, as Mona Etienne demonstrates. A woman's status, as well as her security in old age, depends on her establishing a following of junior dependents whose production and reproduction provide her with wealth and with additional dependents in the next generation. Women receive children from kinsmen in adoption and also give their own children for adoption, retaining ties to both. Such relationships are generally formed with members of a woman's cognatic descent group. A major consideration for women is to maintain these links with junior dependents, her own and adopted. If a widow has dependents in her natal community, she may prefer to go there. Alternatively, if a widow's position is more secure in her husband's community—as it would be, for example, if her sons are established there, or if she has no dependents in her natal home—she may prefer to accept marriage with a cognatic kinsman of her husband. These complex strategies of widows show that Baule widow inheritance is anything but automatic.

Both Christine Obbo and Pamela Landberg describe how widows' access to resources allows them to manage their own lives. Landberg shows how having the right to inherit houses enables several women to form a cooperative residential and work group. Swahili widows and divorced women often join households of female uterine kin, which provide temporary residence for those who wish to remarry and permanent shelter for others.

Obbo shows how control over property rights enables women to violate cultural expectations and determine their own future. She calls our attention to personality factors and argues that it is the ingenuity of widows rather than cultural ideology that influences behavior and enables them to find ways around societal rules. Widows who are less enterprising or who are suffering from loneliness or bereavement may lose control over economic resources and over their own lives.

The papers in this volume show clearly that widows are not passive objects of male transactions. Nor do they conform automatically to cultural norms. Widows have interests and options, and make choices affecting their own lives.

## Some Characteristics of African Widowhood

Let us examine some of the factors relating to the varying position of widows in different African societies. Drawing on the case studies, we shall look first at the demography of widowhood. Then we shall examine some of the factors that structure the options available to widows. In particular, we shall consider rights of residence and access to productive resources, claims on natal groups, custodial rights over children, rules of remarriage, and the political uses of marital ties, all of which are important variables that affect the strategies available to widows. These and other interests influence the decisions they make. The economic position of widows will then be described. Finally, we shall examine some of the complex effects of societal transformation.

*Demographic Patterns*

In Western societies widowhood is largely associated with aging, but this is not necessarily the case in Africa. Demographic patterns vary. The stage in the life cycle at which women become widows depends on the marriage system. Where there is a wide age disparity between spouses, many women will be widowed at a relatively young age. This is particularly true of second or third wives in polygynous systems. The Luo data show how great this age disparity can be. In those societies where remarriage is not possible or likely, widowhood is a status rather than a phase between marriages. Some women may spend the greater part of their adult lives as widows. In some groups widows constitute up to 25 percent of the adult female population. Such women either head their own households or are incorporated in the homes of children, affines, or natal kin. Although we have no data on the emotional meaning of widowhood in these systems, it seems likely that the psychological adjustment will be different from that which obtains in societies where the loss of a spouse is less foreseeable.

In contrast to this demographic pattern, in other groups there is little age disparity between husband and wife. Such societies are likely to have a lower percentage of widows, and the widows will typically be older. Men are almost as likely as women to experience the loss of a spouse. This volume does not treat widowerhood, a topic also ignored in the literature, but Jean-Claude Muller does discuss the similarities between widowers and widows among the Rukuba.

Age disparity between spouses is not the only factor involved in demographic variation. Patterns of divorce and remarriage are also important. Enid Schildkrout shows how widowhood clusters at two different periods of the life cycle, depending on prior marital history. Hausa women who remain married to their first husbands will be widowed at a relatively young age. Those who divorce and remarry may not be widowed until late in life, since second husbands tend to be closer in age to their wives. The time of life at which a woman becomes widowed affects her subsequent marital behavior. For older women widowhood may be a permanent status.[3]

As marriage patterns undergo transformation, the demography of widowhood reflects these changes, although statistical data that would allow comparisons of past and present are not available. These transformations are complex and their implications poorly studied. At the simplest level, in those societies where there has been an increase in the age of marriage for women and/or a reduction in the incidence of polygyny, the number of women who become widowed early in life is probably declining. In such situations widowhood may increasingly become a phenomenon of old age if life expectancy increases, but research is needed to establish the extent of this trend.

More complex is the impact of various structural changes on the status of widows. In some systems where widowhood was once a phase between marriages, it has now become a permanent status for some women, either because they are freer to reject such marriages or because affines no longer wish to marry widows. In others, widows who formerly could not remarry may now do so. A host of structural factors are implicated in these transformations: new marriage and inheritance laws, the impact of Christianity and Islam, the possibilities of interethnic marriage, new modes of economic support, cash cropping, land shortages, the availability of hired labor, and new bases of prestige and status. But the manner in which widows and others respond to new possibilities and/or adapt to new constraints is complex and variable. There are no automatic concomitants of such structural changes and no uniform trends that cut across societies. This complexity can be unraveled only on a case-by-

---

3. Ronald Cohen, in his study of the Kanuri, also provides data showing how widowhood is related to divorce and remarriage. Cohen notes that in high-divorce societies widowhood is infrequent, a finding supported by Landberg's Swahili material (Cohen 1971: 116-17).

case basis, a point we will discuss in more detail later in this introduction.

*Widows' Options: Residential and Marital Possibilities*

Societies differ in the formal options available to widows. Among the Beti, the Nandi, and the Luo these options are limited, and widows generally have little choice but to remain in their husband's community. They may have nowhere to go and departure usually requires leaving children behind. Once widowed, a Nandi or Luo woman remains in that status for the rest of her life. However, widows may have greater independence than wives and more control over their own lives.[4] In other systems described in this volume, widows have more options, including remarriage and—except for the Rukuba—rights to return to their natal home. They can, with the exception of the Hausa, take children with them. The availability of options depends on a configuration of rules, including rights to residence and access to productive resources, custodial rights over children, and rules of remarriage.

African women typically have no rights of inheritance in their husband's estate. In patrilineal descent systems property goes to a man's sons or brothers; in matrilineal groups, to a sister's son or other uterine kin. Except where colonial or postcolonial changes in inheritance systems have given widows a share of their husband's estate, most women gain access to productive resources only through some kinship relationship. Islamic societies are an exception because wives and daughters receive a small share of the inheritance, but usually this is not enough for self-sufficiency. Under modern conditions women sometimes purchase land or receive property through testamentary disposition, although such wills do not always go unchallenged, as Obbo's examples indicate. For the majority of African women, access to land and housing still depends on some kinship connection.

4. Even though Beti widows can return to their natal kin, doing so sometimes jeopardizes their sons' inheritance rights. Most widows remain. A few Nandi women may also establish temporary residence with their kin, but since children have no rights there, the children usually remain in their father's home. Very few wives or widows leave; many of those who do eventually return to their sons.

In some groups women acquire residential rights and access to land only through marriage. If widows have no possibility of remarriage elsewhere, and no rights to return to their natal group, they will necessarily remain in their husband's community. Sometimes even widows who do have other options find it advantageous to stay. Those widows of childbearing years who reside in their husband's community typically have the chance to form some type of socially recognized sexual and procreative relationship. This is rarely mandatory, but it is sometimes, as among the Mossi, a prerequisite for remaining (Lallemand 1977). The choice of the partner often rests with the widow. These relationships may constitute marriage, they may be leviratic, or they may fall into another category, as in systems of positional succession where an heir assumes the social position of the deceased and becomes not only husband to the widow but father to the children of the deceased. Such relationships often have secondary importance to widows' lives, as the data on the Nandi and the Luo indicate. They may also be impermanent.

Several patterns of household arrangements exist for widows who remain in their husband's community. In some societies widows live alone and head their own households; consorts visit for sexual and procreative purposes but have no other responsibilities. In such situations, characteristic of the Luo, the Nandi, and the Rukuba, widows typically manage their own affairs. A consort does not take on the role of husband.

In other groups a widow resides with the husband's successor. This was formerly the case among the Beti, where inherited widows formed part of the labor force that produced food for a man's dependents. It is also the case among the Baule, although Etienne notes that in many marriages, including widow inheritance, the spouses may reside separately during much of their union. Of the societies covered in this volume, only the Dukawa have a pattern of widow-levir co-residence. Some accounts in the literature also report such residential arrangements, but the data are usually insufficient to determine whether widows are fully assimilated to the household and have a role similar to wives. Widows in some of these groups may shift residence again as sons mature, but such residential shifts are not confined to widows.

The factors that underlie these different modes of residence merit examination. Different degrees of economic interdependence between men and women stemming from the sexual division of labor and the means by which women have access to male labor may be factors, but our sample of societies is small. Among the Beti, the Luo, and the Nandi, widows reside alone and largely support themselves. By contrast, in several societies where widows reside with the husband's successor, men appear to be responsible for providing specific types of subsistence goods that women do not control, as in pastoral societies, or else male labor is a necessary precondition for women's work, as among the Tiv. In these cases widows may not be economically self-sufficient. Where economic activities are organized cooperatively within a compound, it may be necessary to continue to reside with a group, as among the LoWiili (J. Goody 1967).

Patterns of allocation of managerial authority over the deceased's estate may also influence residential arrangements. Among the Nandi, the Luo, and the Rukuba, widows themselves have effective control. Oboler suggests that it is the secure rights Nandi widows have through the house property complex, as well as the availability of hired labor, that allows them to manage their own affairs—although widows with mature sons may prefer to cede responsibility to them. The husband's brother, who normatively has a supervisory role, does not exercise this in practice. In some other systems with house property, however, widows are not reported to have such managerial rights, as among the Shambala (Winans 1964).[5]

Although male guardianship is reported for a number of societies with and without house property, it is not always clear what powers guardianship entails. In some systems it appears to involve little more than advice to the widow or assistance in legal matters (LeVine 1964; Mair 1934; M. Fallers 1960). In others the guardian appears to have effective control over the estate and its disposition (Gulliver 1964; Klima 1970).[6]

5. Among the Shambala, a male guardian is appointed to manage the estate if there are any immature sons. The widow and children move in with him. He may be a husband's brother, in which case a leviratic relationship is established, or a mature son of any of the widows of the deceased.

6. Robert Gray (1964) suggested a connection between patterns of widow remarriage and the transmission of family estates. Where the estate is kept intact for ultimate division among a man's sons, according to Gray, the guardian acts as

Older widows who remain in their husband's community or return after residence elsewhere usually reside with mature sons. Either the widow or the son may be regarded as the household head. In some societies the households are separate but linked for specific purposes, such as economic cooperation. Childless older widows who remain in their husband's community are sometimes isolated and may suffer serious economic deprivation (Lallemand 1977).

Not every society offers widows durable rights in the husband's community; in some the rights of residence terminate on his death.[7] In those systems where widows must leave, as among the Hausa and the Swahili, remarriage outside the husband's kin group is usually a jural possibility. It may also be an option in societies where widows have the right to remain, as among the Dukawa, the Baule, or the Rukuba. The decision to remain—or to remarry outside—will depend on the widow's perception of what will be most advantageous. Ties to children are often an important consideration.

*Importance of Natal Group Ties*

An option available to widows in some societies is the possibility of returning to their natal group. One of the most important variables affecting the options and power of women is the

the husband's successor and the family maintains its identity as a separate unit residing on the family estate. "Husband succession" includes all instances of the levirate, as well as some arrangements in which the successor and not the deceased is pater (which is termed "widow inheritance" in other schemes). But among the Luo the levir neither controls the estate nor acts as husband; among the Nandi there may be no successor to the husband's position. Even where the guardian is a husband's successor, as among the Arusha, the extent to which families maintain their separateness varies (Gulliver 1964). Gray contrasts "husband succession" with "widow inheritance" where the estate is divided among heirs and the widow moves in with an heir. But widows are not inherited in all systems. Among the Ganda, for example, the heir does not establish a conjugal relationship with the widow (Mair 1934; M. Fallers 1960).

7. Gonja widows must leave. They remarry if they are young and they return to their natal community if they are old (E. Goody 1973). Hausa widows may remain if they have sons in the home or may return to their sons later; Gonja and Mossi widows do not acquire residential rights through sons. Among the Mossi, although the widow has other options, the only way she can remain in her husband's community is to enter an actual or a nominal marriage with an affine. She may do so if she has sons there, since sons provide economic assistance (Lallemand 1977).

extent to which natal group ties offer alternatives to marital and
affinal ties. If women have rights to return to their kin and are
welcome there, they have some leverage as wives and are less
subject to a husband's control. Widows with this right may also
be in a good negotiating position, requiring inducements to
remain in the husband's community. Salamone's data on the
Dukawa and Etienne's on the Baule support this view. Dukawa
widows have several options: they may accept the levirate, return to their natal home, or remarry. Their decision is affected by
the sexual attractiveness of the levir, the generosity of affines,
and the treatment they previously received as wives. Such incen-
tives are not necessary in societies where widows have more
limited options.

Karen Sacks is one of the few anthropologists to discuss the
significance of a woman's role in her natal group, for which she
uses the term *sister* as a convenient shorthand. She suggests that
sisterhood confers important rights in all African societies except where processes of state formation or class formation have
destroyed these rights (Sacks 1982). However, such rights are
not universal in all societies termed *stateless*. Luo widows, for
example, have no rights to return to their natal community. I
found no instances in my census of married women or formerly
married women residing with fathers or brothers. Among the
Rukuba, who are organized into chiefdoms, such residence is
equally rare. Muller found only two elderly women who were
residing with natal kin because they had nowhere else to go. The
Rukuba regard these situations as anomalous. In a few societies
women may occasionally return as dependents whose acceptance is more a privilege than a right, as is the case for the
Arusha (Gulliver 1964). Such women are sometimes marginal in
their natal communities. The presence or absence of natal group
rights is a major source of differentiation in the position of women
in African societies and needs more attention.

The specific character of widows' rights in their natal group
also shows variation. A particularly interesting contrast can be
found in the accounts of the Swahili and the Hausa. Under Islamic law, widows and divorcées return, at least temporarily, to
their natal kin. In neither of these societies are most women self-
supporting. Swahili women in Kigombe, however, can inherit

houses. Several female uterine kin may join together to form a viable economic unit, providing a temporary or permanent alternative to marriage. Hausa women in Kano, by contrast, could not inherit houses until recently. If they do not remarry, most rely primarily on fathers, brothers, or sons for support, although all women earn something and a few are self-supporting. Some women, not represented in Schildkrout's sample, lead independent lives as prostitutes (Pittin 1983). Hausa widows and divorced women who return to their brother's home are frequently pressured to remarry; Swahili women are not. Ultimately most Hausa widows depend on sons in old age; Swahili on mothers, daughters, or other female uterine kin.

Although natal group rights are present in some societies characterized by patrilineal and cognatic descent, such rights take on particular importance in matrilineal systems. In many of these societies a woman's ties to her own uterine kin may have greater importance than ties to affines. The different modes of residence associated with matrilineal descent, only a few of which we can give here, have diverse implications for patterns of family and community development (Richards 1950) and for the position of widows.

In some groups, such as the Yao of Malawi, residence is uxorilocal. A community is formed around a group of women. Men reside in their wives' communities almost as outsiders. Although authority and village headmanship are formally vested in men, women have considerable power and a man's ability to exercise leadership depends on their support. A brother who wishes to establish his own village must convince his sisters to move. It is brothers and mothers' brothers who look after the interests of women and children, not husbands. Widowhood in such systems does not alter a woman's position in her natal community or affect the rights and influence she exercises there. A widow may remarry or not as she wishes. In either case, she continues residing near her sisters and children, turning to her brother for the same type of assistance as before.

A few Yao women whose husbands are headmen reside virilocally in their husband's community. On the husband's death, either the widow may return to her own matrilineal community, assuming the role she had before, or she may remain. She is particularly likely to stay if her children are mature and have established themselves in their father's village—often by marriage—and do not wish to leave. The widow may accept the husband's heir as husband, or not, as she prefers (Mitchell 1951, 1956).[8]

In some other matrilineal societies, uterine kin are not concentrated in a single community but are dispersed. This is true for the Tonga of Zambia (Colson 1951) and for the Suku of Zaire (Kopytoff 1964, 1977), although the residence rules differ. In such systems widowhood may entail residential shifts, though not to any particular kin-based community. The Suku, for example, combine virilocal residence with uterine descent. Although there is a matrilineal center, few members reside there. Women live with their husbands for the duration of the marriage; divorced or widowed women either remarry or join a brother, mother's brother, or other matrilineal kin. Since sons are expected to live with their father until his death, male uterine kin are also dispersed. On a father's death, sons join some male uterine kinsman wherever he happens to be residing. Occasionally they may remain with a father's brother.

The pattern of the Ndembu of Zambia, by contrast, leads to the formation of communities based on matrilineally related men. Women leave to reside with their husbands, but eventually return to their natal group. The movements of widowed and divorced women are important to the growth and survival of uterine communities, since children accompany their mothers. Although residence of a nephew with his mother's brother is commonly termed avunculocal, this may be an inappropriate term for situations such as that of the Ndembu. Turner makes it very clear that it is the mother's residence that determines the movement of children, not the maternal uncle's. Mature sons will reside with their mother, wherever she is. On her death, however, if she has not returned to her natal community, they may take up residence in their uncle's village. Brothers move as a group (Turner 1957).

8. Since the Yao practice positional succession, in which a uterine heir assumes the social position of the deceased, he becomes husband to the widow and father to the deceased's children. The widow may agree to act as his wife, a relationship that does not necessarily involve sex, or he may free the widow from any obligations toward him once the installation ceremony is completed.

In both the Yao and the Ndembu situation, widows are not merely dependents exercising claims on their natal group, as is the case among the Hausa and the Arusha. Rather, a woman's movements and her influence over children are crucial to the reproduction of the community. Her support is necessary to her brother's or son's ability to exercise leadership.

This pattern, common to matrilineal systems, is not exclusive to them, as Etienne's account of the Baule shows. The Baule have a cognatic descent system with a matrilineal bias. Women have rights in their mother's cognatic descent group—including rights to chieftainships—and strong attachments to uterine kin. Where a widow settles with her children, her own and adopted, is important to the survival and growth of the community. Thus both the husband's cognatic kin and her own kin group may wish the widow to stay with them in order to retain the children. A brother not only welcomes his sister, but has obligations to her, such as preparing fields for cultivation, that take precedence over those he has to his wife. Yet a widow's decisions are influenced by her own strategic considerations, as we noted earlier. Etienne spells out the complex interplay of interests that affect the behavior of the husband's group, the widow's group, and the widow herself.

*Widows' Interests and Attitudes Toward Marriage*

It should be evident by now that factors other than a desire to establish marital or consort relationships influence a widow's matrimonial and consort decisions. Residential and property rights and rules of remarriage set limits on what is possible, but the choices widows make within these limits are influenced by their own interests and their notion of what is possible and appropriate behavior. Some of these values and interests predispose widows to accept marital or consort relationships. A desire for children (Luo), sex and companionship and the sanctions against non-marital sexuality (Dukawa), the lack of economic self-sufficiency (Swahili), fraternal pressure (Hausa), loneliness and the possibility of interethnic marriage (Obbo), and the burden of farming alone (Rukuba) are examples noted in this volume. Other factors may operate against the establishment of conjugal or leviratic relationships: the advantages of residing with uterine kin and interests in maintaining links to dependents (Baule), concern with support in old age and the desire to maintain ties to children (Hausa), a wish to be independent of male control either temporarily (Swahili) or permanently (Nandi), the presence of hired labor to reduce dependence on affines (Nandi), and the availability of other outlets for sex and procreation (Nandi and Swahili).

This is a complex interplay of interests, and the fact that widows sometimes opt not to marry or establish consort relationships raises questions about the meaning of marriage for African women. One issue is the importance of conjugality compared with other relationships in meeting a woman's emotional and social needs. It is sometimes suggested that companionate marriage is not a characteristic of African societies except among a small number of Western-influenced elites; that women and men rely on other relationships for companionship and emotional gratification. If this is true, widows should be well integrated into communities and ought not to experience the degree of isolation and loneliness reported for women in societies more conjugally structured (Marris 1958).

Obbo's paper raises important questions about this perception. She describes a number of cases in which widows are extremely lonely and have difficulty adjusting to living without husbands. Indeed, some of the widows in her sample are so emotionally vulnerable that they allow themselves to be exploited by unscrupulous men and women. Obbo suggests that this problem is common to widows in East Africa. Her cases, though few in number, are drawn from several different societies.

Other accounts of East African systems, such as Oboler's study of the Nandi, suggest that widows are well integrated into the community and prefer their independence to establishing a leviratic relationship. Luo women do accept a levir, but such relations appear to offer little emotional or practical support in the community I studied. Rather, widows rely on children to meet these needs and on other women for sociability. Swahili widows and divorced women are sometimes reported to prefer taking lovers and residing with uterine kin to marriage, if this is economically feasible. How do we account for these diverse views of East African societies? Cultural variation undoubtedly exists, but this can only be part of the answer, and it evades some of the important issues raised by Obbo's paper.

One possible explanation is that anthropologists have paid too little attention to how widows perceive themselves and are perceived by others. We may not have attended sufficiently to the emotional aspects of widows' lives, concentrating instead on structural arrangements or economic interests.

Another possibility relates to the nature of Obbo's sample. All of the widows she interviewed come from the more affluent strata of their societies. Some are urban or periurban residents. To what extent has socioeconomic differentiation affected the integration of such women (and men) in their communities? Have they distanced themselves from kinsmen, or do the jealousy of kinsmen and neighbors and conflicts over property lead to a diminution of the importance of these ties and an intensification of the conjugal bond?

I knew only a few affluent people in my research community, but my contacts with these few may be revealing. Although several men were respected for the contributions they made to funerals and other community activities and for the assistance they provided to people seeking jobs, others were resented and considered to be "proud." Two women I knew well told me of the jealousy they encountered. In both cases the women's economic circumstances had declined, one through her husband's illness, the other on his death when the husband's brother took most of the cattle, cash, and other property. Both told me that when they were experiencing hardship, neighbors came to gloat and to express satisfaction that now the women were no better off than their neighbors.[9] I have no way of knowing how typical these situations are. If, however, economic differentiation produces rivalry and tends to isolate the more successful, it might well be that the more affluent wives and husbands come to rely more on one another. In such circumstances it would not be surprising if widows experience the extremes of loneliness that Obbo finds in her sample.

9. By the time of my research, the formerly affluent widow, now poor, was highly regarded in the community. Since her husband's death some 30 years earlier, she had become a leader in church and community activities, known for her helpfulness to others. In a most unusual gesture, people collected funds and built her a house.

The availability of sexual outlets other than marriage is another source of variation among societies. Sexual behavior and attitudes have been poorly studied in Africa, sometimes because women are reluctant to discuss such matters—like the Luo, who consider questions about sexuality to be "bad questions"—and sometimes because the issue is simply ignored. The limited data available, however, suggest that there may be important differences in the amount of sexual activity women engage in, and possibly in the importance sex has for them.

Helen Ware's analysis of West African data indicates that in high-fertility societies with long postpartum sex taboos, women are sexually active for only a limited portion of their lives. In a typical life cycle for some societies, a woman marries at 16, bears six children and has one stillbirth, and becomes a widow at 41. Such a woman would spend more than 15 of her 25 married years abstaining from sex (Ware 1983: 23). Sex may not be an important motivation for widow remarriage in such systems. In other groups, such as the Dukawa, sexual needs and the attractiveness of the levir are important factors influencing widows' decisions. Here there are no acceptable outlets for sexual gratification other than marriage, and sex is important to women. By contrast, Swahili, Rukuba, and Nandi widows are free to take lovers if they desire and many do so. Sexual motives may enter into marital decisions, but other factors may be more important in determining a conjugal or leviratic commitment.

## The Economic Position of Widows

One of the most consistent findings in this volume is the degree to which widows are economically self-reliant. Since African women generally contribute substantially to the household economy and often provide most or all of the support for themselves and their children, this should not be surprising. But it does run counter to perceptions of widows as dependents who in preindustrial societies are provided for by communal kin institutions. Generally widows support themselves, sometimes with the assistance of children. Older women rely on sons, co-wives' sons, occasionally daughters. In those societies where rules of seclusion (Hausa) or limited access to resources (Swahili) prevent women from being self-sufficient, widows depend partly on natal kin or enter a new marriage, although all women work.

A growing body of literature documents the importance of women's economic activities in Africa.[10] In some societies women are the primary subsistence producers; in others men are. The type and degree of female and male economic interdependence relate to labor organization, the requirements of the productive technology, and to patterns of income distribution. Unlike Western marriages, in which conjugal funds are combined, many African marriages involve no pooling of resources. Men and women control their own incomes and make independent contributions to the household. One or both may also have outside obligations (Mullings 1976; Robertson 1976). These differences in types of income control have implications for widows.

In Western societies with common conjugal funds, the death of a husband sometimes leaves the widow in reduced circumstances (Marris 1958; Lopata 1979). This does not necessarily happen in African societies; widows continue to produce goods much as they did before. In some societies, such as the Nandi and the Luo, the widow acquires effective managerial control over the husband's estate. Whether widows experience economic difficulties depends on the nature and importance of the husband's contribution. The position of Nandi widows is much the same as when their husbands were alive; Beti widows are poorer; and Akan widows are better off than wives since they are free to pursue their own activities and need not provide assistance on their husbands' farms. The degree and type of economic assistance provided by kin is also variable. Distinctions should be made between the provision of goods and income, labor assistance, and access to productive resources.

In none of the societies described in this volume do affines take responsibility for providing goods or income. Occasional gifts may be made if relationships are good, but there is no expectation of support as such. In those societies where women produce the bulk of the subsistence goods and earn cash through farming, as among the Nandi, widows are largely self-sufficient.

10. Some of the more important collections of essays are Hafkin and Bay 1976, Bay 1982, Oppong 1983, and Steady 1981. Individual articles in journals and monographs on African women are too numerous to cite here. Some of the general collections of writing on women that include papers on African women are Rosaldo and Lamphere 1974, Schlegel 1977, Reiter 1975, and Wellesley Editorial Committee 1977.

Such self-sufficiency may not be the case in societies where men and women produce different types of goods, as in pastoral societies, or where male labor is essential to women's activities. In these situations, although reciprocal exchanges and cash payments sometimes enable women to acquire male goods and services, a major means of access is usually through sons or through attachment to the household of an affine or a woman's own consanguineal kin.

Dependence on children is particularly important, as many of the papers in this volume show. Guyer and Muller both give examples of the difficulties faced by widows without sons. Such widows do not starve, but their lives are difficult. Such dependence is often a factor affecting widows' residence, marriage, and childbearing decisions, according to Etienne and Schildkrout. Among the Baule, adopted as well as own children are important to a woman's wealth and to her support in old age.

Some of the published literature suggests a greater degree of affinal responsibility than is indicated in our sample. Tallensi men in Ghana are reported to have a moral obligation to provide for their brother's widow and children. This responsibility is reinforced by a fear of supernatural reprisals (Fortes 1949a).

It is difficult to determine from the published literature how much support is actually given. Clearly, when men control the food resource, as in pastoral societies, aid must be provided. However, those few studies that focus on widows report little actual support (Lallemand 1977).[11] Perhaps my experience with the Luo may be instructive. Toward the end of my fieldwork I conducted a household census that included questions on the levirate and on the support of widows. Men regularly reported that they helped the widows they "took over." Having previously been told by a number of widows that levirs never provided support, I instructed my research assistants to probe further. The aid turned out to be occasional gifts of food, cash, or clothing, and sometimes help with house repairs or with plowing. Some men could not specify the type of help given, but reported only general aid. With one exception, there was no responsibility for

11. Mossi widows may marry affines and move into the new husband's home if they are young. Older women live alone and rely on sons for some income. The childless widow is poor and must do without.

regular provision of cash or food, or payment of school fees, even for children sired by the levir, but sometimes a non-leviratic husband's brother helped with educational expenses. Do the differences between the cases cited in this volume and previously published accounts reflect ethnographic variation? Or are they the product of reliance on different informants and/or interviewing techniques?

Labor assistance is sometimes more readily available to widows than income support. Among the Dukawa, however, women are self-sufficient and need no help except in case of serious illness. They produce shea butter and beer, which they sell, and maintain kitchen gardens. Luo widows are also self-sufficient, but must hire labor for plowing. Sometimes affines provide this service—if they own a plow—but most women prefer not to rely on in-laws, whose assistance may be late or not forthcoming. To meet this expense, which is usually met by a husband, widows have to work harder to earn additional cash.

In those societies where some farm tasks are organized cooperatively, widows may continue to be involved in the communal work parties that were available to them as wives. This is the case for the Nandi. But a Mossi woman's participation terminates at her husband's death. She may participate in a work group only through her new husband's household or with a son (Lallemand 1977). In some societies, reciprocal labor groups have disappeared or are so modified that they exist in name only. Luo weeding parties today consist of women who are hired to work for three shillings a day. Formerly the only obligation was to feed such groups. Widows and other women with limited access to cash may be unable to secure such assistance, but they are still able to support themselves. Swahili widows and divorcées in Kigombe also work cooperatively, but their pattern involves female uterine kin.

Where farming is a joint enterprise between spouses, or where male labor is a necessary precondition for women's work, the death of a husband may increase the labor burden for widows. Among the Rukuba and the Beti, affines help, but not much. Labor difficulties may influence a Rukuba widow to leave and join another husband. Baule widows who do not accept marriage with a husband's kinsman rely on their brothers or on children, own or adopted, to clear land for them. The Nandi who have access to cash can hire labor. Akan widows are even in a privileged position relative to wives. They have land of their own, and access to hired labor, which they pay for from cash crop earnings. They no longer need to devote time to their husband's farms.

The third type of economic dependence, access to productive resources, has already been discussed in terms of residence rights. Even where widows have rights to property in their husband's community, however, such rights do not always go unchallenged. Whereas Oboler reports that property rights are secure among the Nandi, Obbo provides a number of examples from other East African societies where widows find it necessary to protect themselves from affinal exploitation. Land conflicts between widows and affines are also reported for the Beti and the Akan. Land shortages or particular types of cash-crop farms, such as cocoa plantations, may be implicated in such conflicts.

As the data in this volume show, concepts of communal support for widows are more a Rousseauian ideal than an ethnographic reality. Such concepts—reinforced by theories of sibling equivalence and group interests in marriage—fail to take into account the importance of women's economic activities and the large number of societies in which women are not economically dependent. Thus an oral tradition has developed among anthropologists that interprets the levirate and widow inheritance partly as mechanisms that provide for the support of widows and their children. An informal survey of colleagues suggests that many anthropologists believe that this interpretation comes from classic volumes on social organization. It does not. Nor does it generally appear in introductory texts. Only Kottak (1974), among a number of texts I consulted, mentions economic support, and he does so almost in passing. Yet so pervasive is this oral tradition that it has been picked up by sociologists whose contrast between Western and non-Western mechanisms for the support of widows is based partly on such anthropological "findings" (Kirwen 1979; Lopata 1979; Marris 1958).

As we have seen, the situation is more complex than a simple notion of communal support indicates. There are variations in the amounts and kinds of assistance from various support sources that are available to widows. The case studies in this volume suggest that apart from the help given by children and sometimes natal kin, widows generally receive little or no income support, but they may receive some labor assistance and they generally have access to productive resources.

*Effects of Societal Transformation*

Some readers may be tempted to attribute the lack of communal support to a breakdown of kinship institutions resulting from the penetration of colonialism, monetization of the economy, and capitalist expansion, but such an interpretation would be unfounded. Certainly these developments have transformed all societies, modifying social structures, but change has not been unidirectional. There has been a varied impact on the organization of kin groups, different types of adaptation to a cash economy and labor migration, and different implications of such adaptations for the lives of widows. Two of the case studies in this volume, Guyer's and Vellenga's, provide detailed historical data on some of these processes. These studies and others show the complexity of societal transformation. There is no indication of a general transition from communal to more individualistic systems, although this has occurred in some places.

Guyer's account of Beti transformation is particularly revealing of such complexity. She shows a decline in what can legitimately be considered widow inheritance that coincides with a growth in the importance given to patrilineal descent. Both processes result from changes in the political economy. The patterns of widow inheritance that developed at one period of Beti history were not a matter of communal support for widows; rather, women were an important means of obtaining political and economic power. As cocoa farming replaced "wealth in people" as a major source of economic and political status, widows lost their value as resources and were no longer inherited. With cocoa farming, land increased in value, residence stabilized, and the interest in inheriting land, combined with residential stability, brought about a strengthening of patrilineal descent. The complex transformation of social relationships that resulted and the implications for widows are spelled out by Guyer in a careful and intricate analysis.

Vellenga's discussion of Akan history shows a different pattern of transformation. Strains related to the competing claims of matrilineage and conjugal relationships were further exacerbated by colonial changes in inheritance laws. As widows began receiving shares of their husband's estate, they found the matrilineage heir to the property unwilling to accept responsibility for them. Conflicts over inheritance escalated, leading to agitation for additional changes in the law to protect women. Distinctions among the legal rights of widows in different types of conjugal relationships became an important issue in court cases, particularly in polygynous arrangements. Such conflicts continue to occur today, as Akan women resort not only to the courts and the legal system to secure their rights but also to informal mechanisms. Yet Vellenga shows that contrary to the popular view of widows as disadvantaged, rural widows are in fact economically better off than wives.

Landberg's account of the Swahili of Kigombe reveals interesting relationships between inmigration and marriage patterns, on the one hand, and the strength of women's ties to their female uterine kin, on the other. Kigombe has experienced considerable inmigration of men who become established in the community through marriage. Although women have little say in first marriages, which are generally endogamous within a cognatic descent group, they have freedom of choice in subsequent marriages. Many widows and divorced women prefer to marry migrant husbands, who exercise less control over their wives. Such marriage allows for the maintenance and possibly the strengthening of uterine bonds, sometimes at the expense of marital stability, and frees women to visit and farm with female uterine kin.

As new laws, courts, and religious and economic institutions become part of the social structure, they change the available options for widows. But individuals react in diverse ways to new possibilities. An excellent example is found in widows' contrasting responses to modifications in inheritance laws among the Akan and the Baule. Widows of government workers in the Ivory Coast receive a pension on their husband's death. But some Baule consider such pensions to be part of the deceased's estate, which properly should go to his cognatic kin, not to his widow. Etienne cites the case of a widow who agreed to marry a maternal uncle of her late husband so that he could get the pension. Such a marriage would normally be considered a violation of kinship rules, since a husband's uncle is too close a relative to marry. The difference between the responses of this widow and the Akan widows described by Vellenga could not be more striking. The Baule woman agreed to a marriage that violated kinship rules in order to circumvent new inheritance laws and preserve the rights of her husband's kin group, but Akan widows took advantage of new possibilities, using the courts and even the Labour Department to secure a share of the husband's estate.

Christianity too has evoked varied responses. Most mission churches, as discussed by Kirwen (1979) and Spencer (1973) for East Africa, preach against the levirate and widow inheritance, urging that widows be free to remarry, but one of the greatest difficulties they have encountered is in modifying marriage practices.[12] Despite the inroads of Christianity, Nandi and Luo widows do not remarry except in rare instances in urban settings. Most Nandi widows are not involved in the levirate, but we do not know if missionary influence is a factor here. Age and economic self-sufficiency may be more significant. Among the Luo, many of whom are Christians, the levirate continues. Although I was told that some "saved" Christian women refuse such relationships, the census data do not bear this out. The difficulty missionaries have had in changing marriage practices is not simply a matter of ideology or incomplete acculturation to new beliefs. Rather, the interests of the widow herself, her desire for children, the need to remain in the husband's community, concern with social prestige, and concepts of proper behavior continue to operate, conflicting with Christian theology.

Karla Poewe's study (1978) of the effectiveness of Jehovah's Witnesses and Seventh-Day Adventists in modifying behavior among the Luapula of Zambia shows some of the intricacy of the issues. Both churches preach against widow inheritance, but SDA, which is more loosely organized, has had little impact. Under prevailing social and economic conditions, the desire for community acceptance appears more important to widows than church doctrine. By contrast, Jehovah's Witnesses, because of a theology that stresses the imminence of Armageddon, a greater

12. The mission instituted Christian churches among the Nandi and the Luo, but not all Luo independent churches take this position.

separation of converts from the community at large, and a more effective social organization, have been more successful in modifying marital behavior.

Although Christianity in theory "frees" widows to remarry and/or avoid leviratic and widow inheritance relationships, there is considerable variation among the responses of widows in the groups we have observed. Even among the Beti, where the termination of widow inheritance was partly due to missionary influence, such influence was relatively ineffective until reinforced by economic and political transformations.

Economic transformations have also had diverse effects on widows' options. In some situations widows have gained control over resources through changes in inheritance laws, the purchase of land, testamentary disposition, or involvement in new forms of economic activity. These changes have made it more feasible for them to control their own lives. Obbo shows how widows who control resources are able to resist the demands of affines and/or avoid unwelcome consort relationships, but not all widows take advantage of these possibilities even when they are available.

But modern economic conditions are not always beneficial to widows. Scattered reports from a number of African societies suggest that in some societies widows are becoming vulnerable to economic pressures. A Kenyan newspaper account in February 1984, for example, describes a speech by the Director of Social Services of Nyanza Province, the Luo homeland, complaining that older widows were being driven from the land by their husband's kin. The fact that this was considered newsworthy suggests that such occurrences are not yet socially acceptable. But they are happening. I have since learned of one women's organization that built a dormitory for homeless widows near Kisumu, the major city in that area. Although the Luo have long experienced land shortages, at the time of my fieldwork (1973-76) widows' rights were still secure. But land registration had just been completed, changing the system of tenure from one of use rights to a private property system in which land could be sold. The combined effects of land shortage, the commoditization of land, and possibly the absence of sons in town probably help explain these recent developments. Achola Pala Okeyo

(1980) predicted that women would lose land rights with the change to private property and the sale of land.

There are also reports of the formation of widows' organizations in a number of other African societies. In Burkina Faso, for example, a Widows and Orphans Association was established in 1977 to help widows and their children who were being driven off the land by husbands' brothers. The association is reported to have a multiethnic membership of 1,500, with branches in several parts of the country. It trains widows in job skills to provide them with a means of support.

Landlessness is not, of course, universal in Africa. There are areas where land is not scarce and widows' rights seem relatively secure, and societies where widows now are able to inherit land or purchase land during their marriage. Both patterns are represented in this volume. The Nandi, the Rukuba, and the Dukawa are examples of the first situation; the Akan of the second. Nonetheless, the growing scarcity of land in some places, and the differential value of farms devoted to certain cash crops such as cocoa, may create or exacerbate conflicts with affines over resources.

## Widows and the Rethinking of Anthropological Concepts

The discussion thus far has sought to contrast the reality of African widows' lives with anthropological folklore about their situation. But the ethnographic data in this volume also raise questions about other anthropological theories. Many aspects of social organization look different when examined from the perspective of widows, and many of our concepts and methods accordingly warrant rethinking. In this section we will consider some of the implications of the new data presented in this book for other issues in anthropology.

### Alliance and Descent Theories: A Reevaluation

Many of the studies in this volume emphasize the control widows have over their own lives and show that women are not objects of male transactions. Even in societies that limit a widow's range of choice and restrict her to residence in her husband's community, she still has certain options. But as Guyer's analysis shows, not all societies allow her a choice.

Women's productive and reproductive roles are important in all African societies, but there are significant differences in marriage systems and in the degree to which marriage is used as an avenue for political power. Meillassoux (1981), Bledsoe (1980), and Guyer (this volume) show the different ways in which marriage is used. Whereas Meillassoux discusses generation and gender differences in power, which he relates to elders' control over marriage, both Bledsoe and Guyer focus on individuals and show how powerful persons manipulate marital transactions to secure clients, wealth, and labor. Among the Kpelle (Bledsoe 1980), the various strategies used by aristocratic men include wife lending, creating indebtedness for bridewealth, and securing labor in bride service. Women of aristocratic lineages who are linked to powerful men also use their control over young female initiates in the Sande (the women's secret society) to collect payments from those who seek wives. Kpelle marital manipulations appear to center primarily on the disposition of wives as a means of securing male labor and clients, although some men are interested in wife accumulation. The reverse holds true for the Beti, where wives and widows were themselves used for labor, although clientage was also a factor.

From a methodological point of view, there are important differences between these two analyses. Guyer integrates ethnographic and historical material to analyze societal transformations in the context of a changing political economy. The historical data, however, do not lend themselves to a discussion of marriage among the less powerful who presumably were not in a position to accumulate widows or wives. We know only about power holders. Moreover, since behavior cannot be observed retroactively, we learn much about systemic factors but not about the actions or attitudes of individual women. Bledsoe's analysis, by contrast, does not tell us how the marriage system developed. Nor does it relate such development to other questions about the political economy. As an observer of an ongoing system, however, Bledsoe is able to describe the strategies women use to gain some control over their persons and is also in a position to report on the marriage system of non-elites.[13]

13. Unfortunately, Bledsoe does not deal with widows except for a brief reference to the levirate (p. 82).

Both of these studies as well as Meillassoux's raise important points about the nature of marriage. Where the disposition of women is used as a means of political control, marriage plays a different role from its role in societies where men merely wish to have many wives as a means of securing descendants or acquiring prestige. Elsewhere Guyer raises questions about the conditions under which politically manipulative marriages emerge (1981: 94-96). But where marriage does not have such political significance, or where the woman herself is the strategist regarding her own marriage, as among the Baule, even if options are limited, women have more choice. Widows are not disposed of in the manner formerly common among the Beti. Luo widows select a levir and can send him away; Nandi widows may choose a consort or not, as they please. Widows in both societies manage their own lives. In neither group does the consort acquire rights to the widow's labor or services, as occurred among the Beti.

The approaches to marriage represented in the works cited above or in the recent collection of essays on marriage prestations edited by Comaroff (1980) show the inadequacies of older theories. Although a Kpelle or Beti marriage could be regarded as an alliance, it is not groups that are allied, but individuals, who secure personal benefits from marital transactions. One difficulty in explaining widow "inheritance" in terms of the maintenance of marital alliances is the failure to specify the nature and content of such alliances. Another is the lack of correlation between the significance of affinal relationships and their perpetuation. Affinity is an important basis for organizing activities in some societies, such as the Dukawa. In others, such as the Luo, the main basis for mobilizing people is not affinity but descent. Yet Luo widows have little choice but to remain in their husband's community and generally are involved in leviratic relationships. Dukawa widows are free to reject the proposed leviratic union and leave.

Descent theory is similarly inadequate as an explanation. It is tautological. When the widow remains in her husband's community and continues to bear children, the husband's group acquires more descendants. But this is the result of behavior, not an explanation for it. Moreover, we do not even know the extent to which widows continue reproducing, since there are virtually no data on widows' fertility. Sometimes the husband's kin are indeed interested in having the widow remain, particularly if her departure means the temporary or permanent departure of children. Such is the case among the Dukawa and the Baule. But even where such group interests are reported in the ethnographic data and not merely assumed, there is still the question of how group interests in alliance or descent translate into the behavior of individuals.

Some of the factors influencing widows' decisions have been noted elsewhere in this Introduction and are more fully explored in the individual case studies. Less is known about the motives of the consort. Cohen reports that the Kanuri know of the levirate but do not practice it. Since men have custody of their dead brother's children, they see no point in assuming responsibility for the widow (R. Cohen 1971: 75). Fortes, by contrast, describes the strong sense of moral responsibility Tallensi men feel toward their brother's widow and offspring (1949a). Muller notes that Rukuba men with no wives in residence seek relations with widows for sex and companionship.[14]

One of the most detailed discussions of the differences between group and individual interests is provided for the Baule. Elders of the cognatic descent group are those most interested in having the widow remain in order to retain the children, but such men are often too closely related to the deceased to inherit his widow. More distant kin, including those connected by paternal links or those of slave descent, are acceptable marriage partners, but such men may be less interested in promoting group interests because they are unlikely to succeed to group leadership. Etienne examines the complex interplay of interests and the difficulties elders have in finding a man to offer marriage to the widow.

Earlier theorists used the principle of sibling equivalence in discussing the levirate and widow inheritance. Since brothers occupied a similar social position and might have joint interests vis-à-vis other groups, it was held that they could substitute for one another in certain areas of behavior. We know from the eth-

14. Within the Orthodox Jewish community in Israel, a practice has developed of extorting large sums of money from widows who wish to be free of the obligation of marrying a husband's brother or of waiting until a younger brother reaches marriageable age. I am informed that this practice has become quite profitable and is regarded as scandalous by some non-Orthodox Israelis.

nographic literature that sibling rivalry is often as characteristic of a relationship as shared interests. The Luo are a case in point. But the literature generally does not tell us why men agree to become consorts or why they are willing to sire children in the name of the deceased. Abrahams (1973), reviewing some studies of the levirate, suggests that "ambivalence" of siblings might be a more appropriate term than equivalence. He reminds us of the biblical story of Onan, who spilled his seed rather than raise up issue for his dead brother.

It is perhaps unfortunate that many of our ideas about the levirate and agnatic responsibility were shaped by early studies of the Nuer. The Nuer practice not only the levirate but also ghost marriage, in which a man will take a wife and sire children in the name of a deceased kinsman. Whereas Evans-Pritchard was careful to distinguish ghost marriage from the levirate (1951), some anthropologists tend to discuss these together to emphasize group interests in marriage. In some ghost marriages men do not take wives of their own, but depend on others to marry for them after their death (1951: 110-11). In such situations there can be no conflict between a man's interest in providing for his own legal wives and children and his interest in supporting an agnate's legal wives and children; he has no wives or children that are legally his.

In many leviratic relationships there may be just such a conflict of interest, if men are involved in both leviratic unions and marriage. Such leviratic unions coupled with marriage also occur among the Nuer. Data in this volume show that levirs do not necessarily take on the role of husband or father. Among the Luo they are not involved in socialization or support of children they sire; among the Rukuba they have no economic responsibilities; and sometimes they misappropriate property, as several of Obbo's examples show.

*Mother-Child Bonds*

The importance of mother-child bonds is evident in the papers in this volume. Several studies, most notably Lallemand's monograph on the Mossi (1977), show the difficulties childless women face in some societies. One mechanism by which a barren woman acquires parental rights is to become a female husband (Obbo 1976; O'Brien 1977; Oboler 1980). Another solution is fosterage or adoption (E. Goody 1971, 1982; Etienne 1979). Parental dependence on children for support in old age is cited to explain continued high fertility in Africa (Caldwell 1976).

Such parental dependence may apply not only to adult children, but to immature children as well. Child labor is common in subsistence societies. This was also true of preindustrial Europe and the United States. Detailed research is now beginning to demonstrate the nature and significance of children's economic roles. An important example is Schildkrout's (1978) study of children's trading roles, which shows how Hausa women depend on children for the pursuit of their own economic activities.

There is an evident connection between dependence on children and a widow's marital decisions and residential shifts. Luo women say there is no point in leaving a husband's community, since women will always return to their sons, who will build them a house and look after them. In a number of societies marital decisions relate to anticipated needs for future support and the desire to secure such support. Schildkrout in this volume shows how such factors affect Hausa women's marital decisions. Rukuba widows with mature sons do not leave the husband's community. In many societies women who do leave eventually return to join or follow their sons. This is true of the Nandi, the Rukuba, the Hausa, and the Luo.

An even more intricate interdependence between children's and women's movements may exist in societies that practice fosterage or adoption. Although Gonja fosterage patterns separate mother and child and do not affect a woman's marital decisions, the mother's natal home, to which she retires, becomes the visiting place for her children of different marriages (E. Goody 1971, 1973). Among the Baule, however, a woman's strategies to maintain ties to her own and her adopted children do influence marital and residential decisions. She must weigh the relative merits of remarrying in her husband's community and returning to her cognatic kin in terms of the residence of her children. Their current and predictable future residences are important considerations, since her power and wealth depend on the number of junior kin she controls. Landberg's paper on the Swahili also suggests a relationship between a woman's ties to her uterine kin and the practice of fostering children with them. A woman maintains strong attachments to a uterine-based household in which her children may be reared and to which she returns between marriages terminated by death or divorce. The details of the interrelationships of fosterage and adoption, children's residence, and women's residence require further study.

### Household and Community Organization

Widowhood is one source of diversity and complexity in household and community organization. The key relationships that tie a woman to domestic groups change with marital status and age. Conjugal bonds may be central to a woman's integration into household and community during marriage, but widows who do not remarry either head their own households or are incorporated in other units through natal, affinal, or filial links. In old age the important ties for a woman may be ties through sons; in a few societies, through daughters. As patterns of integration change, so, too, may women's rights and responsibilities.

We know from several decades of research on residence rules and household organization that membership of domestic groups fluctuates, and that household members have varied relationships with one another and with members of other household units.[15] Esther Goody's (1973) study of Gonja provides an exemplary analysis of the types of complex relationships that obtain within and between households. Accounts that merely discuss where widows are domiciled or how consorts are chosen are inadequate. We need to know how the allocation of rights and responsibilities changes when widows head their own households, attach themselves to those of natal or affinal kin, or reside with children. Do widow heads of household play the same role as male heads in representing domestic group interests to other households and to the community? Are the allocation of responsibilities and patterns of authority between brother and sister or consort and widow similar to those between husband and wife when they form a household? The failure to address such questions, particularly when investigating societies with a high incidence of widows, may result in an oversimplified picture of both community organization and women's roles.[16]

15. Yanagisako (1979) and Guyer (1981) review this literature, the latter with special reference to Africa.
16. The failure to consider widows may also affect the collection and comparability of data on the incidence of polygyny. Ethnographic accounts are not

## Conclusion

It is apparent from the rich body of ethnographic data presented in these papers that both the inadequate research on widows and the distorted picture that has emerged from inappropriate paradigms suggest the need for a more careful examination of widowhood. Such an examination has implications both for understanding the position of widows cross-culturally and for a more general understanding of social process. The nature and extent of kin group solidarity, patterns of affinal and consanguineal relationships, variations in household and community organization, the relative importance of female and male economic contributions, the significance of natal group rights, and the nature of marital alliances are but a few of the issues that are illuminated when examined from the perspective of widows.

Such a perspective is also necessary for understanding the transformation in women's roles in the course of the life cycle. Too frequently discussions of a woman's position in society center on the adult married woman. Life cycle data are often provided, but they are not always integrated into the analysis. Yet the key role relationships in women's lives change over time. Conjugal bonds may be central to a woman at one stage of life; a widow or divorced woman may be an independent household head and manager when young, and dependent on children in old age. Affinal and natal group relationships also change in character, as may residence. Insofar as there is transformation of roles and responsibilities, it is inappropriate to talk of a woman's position in static terms. Rather, we may need to concentrate more on the changes in the configurations of a woman's relationships and responsibilities to see how these affect the diverse positions she occupies during her life span.

---

usually clear on this point, but presumably most ethnographers do not count among a man's wives those widows he has "taken over" in the levirate. Children he has sired with such women are probably also not included among his offspring since he is not their social father. It is less clear what criteria are used in determining who is a "wife" in situations where a man takes over a widow to whom he is regarded as husband. How these factors are treated affects the data provided on the incidence of polygyny, numbers of children sired, and the like.

# Wives of the Grave:
# Widows in a Rural Luo Community

BETTY POTASH

THE LEVIRATE is widely practiced among the Luo, but in many respects leviratic relationships are of secondary importance in the lives of widows. Although anthropologists commonly treat the levirate as a continuation of marriage and regard the consort as the husband's successor, among the Luo such relationships are different from marriage.

The levir is usually a married man who lives in his own home. His responsibilities and interests are directed primarily to his wives and legal sons, who are part of his descent line. These sons will inherit from him and carry on his name. By contrast, the widow's children, including natural offspring sired by the levir, belong to the deceased husband's line and will inherit there. The widow is interested in safeguarding her children's property and must provide for their economic support. Leviratic relationships are characterized by separate residence and widows will typically continue living in their deceased husband's home. Widows have no domestic responsibilities to the levir; the levir has no responsibility for support or socialization.

Funding for my research was provided by a University of Nairobi Faculty Research Grant. I would like to thank the university and particularly Professor Philip M. Mbithi, then chairman of the Department of Anthropology and Sociology and now Vice-Chancellor, for their support and assistance. There is no way that I can express my gratitude to the many women and men of the community I studied for their hospitality, patience, and help. It is impossible to name here all of those who assisted me, but I must express particular thanks to Mr. Kabasa, an education officer, who not only took time to explain many intricacies of Luo culture, but also provided much practical assistance. To him and all the women and men of the community I dedicate this article in the hope that it will help others to understand the customs and ways of the Luo.

Duolocal residence and the separation of sexual-procreative functions from other responsibilities is striking. Indeed, these arrangements are reminiscent of such "unusual" forms of marriage as that reported for the famous Nayar, of South India, where a lover visits a woman but does not reside with her or have responsibilities toward the offspring. Among the Nayar, however, the economic and socialization functions are vested in the woman's brothers; among the Luo it is the woman herself who takes on these responsibilities. Although Luo widows do not have the sexual freedom of Caribbean women—and normatively are not expected to remarry or take lovers other than the levir—there are parallels between Luo leviratic unions and the Caribbean type of matrifocal family with respect to the limited male role. Indeed, some of these marriage patterns that have been regarded as atypical may be more common than we suppose.

Luo widows are not inherited; it is the woman who chooses a consort. She may if she wishes refuse to form such a relationship. Few do. In some instances, however, the levirate appears to be more nominal than real. To understand why widows accept the levirate, we must first understand why they remain in their husband's community. Several factors influence that decision, especially ties to children, who must remain in their father's community, and the fact that Luo widows have no right to return to their natal home. Parents or brothers may refuse to shelter a separated widow.

Cultural values also play a part. Women who leave are apt to be treated as loose women or poor mothers who abandon their children. They have no way of knowing what treatment they will encounter in a new home, in contrast to the known relationships and position they have in their husband's community. Furthermore, marriage cannot be legally terminated without a return of bridewealth. So most widows do remain and are likely to accept a levir. But this is not the central relationship in a woman's life.

Ties to children and the responsibility women have for their own and their children's support influence their behavior far more. Widows who head their own homes have the sole responsibility for household management and child rearing. In old age women depend on sons and sons' wives for financial and labor assistance. Widows without sons, or widows whose sons and sons' wives are working outside the community, may find themselves alone. These relationships and responsibilities have been much affected by changes in the economy during the colonial and postcolonial periods. In this paper we will examine the nature of leviratic relationships and the impact of socioeconomic transformation on widows' lives. Since there is so little actual documentation in the literature on how the levirate works—though much theorizing about its importance—I shall describe the institution in some detail and show why it does little for Luo widows.

## Research Methods

The research on which this paper is based was undertaken in a Luo community in western Kenya during several periods adding up to a total of eight months, between 1973 and 1975. In addition to using techniques of participant observation, I collected life histories from 45 women and 14 men. Some were widows or levirs, and some had been reared by widowed mothers. General insights into widowhood, marriage, and maternal-filial ties come from these materials. I also conducted a household census of two of the four lineage neighborhoods that make up the community. Three students from the University of Nairobi did the interviewing.[1] This census included 46 widows, who constituted 18 percent of all women married into the two lineage neighborhoods—including those women who were living with their husbands but temporarily outside the community. All the statistical data come from this survey. Ages, when unknown, were estimated by the interviewer through discussion with the informant. Widowhood was not a major research interest, but the data are adequate for a preliminary account.

## The Luo

The Luo, a Nilotic-speaking people, are the second largest ethnic group in Kenya. They occupy the areas of South and Cen-

1. Betty Obonyo, Fenno Ogutu, and Barak Owuor, formerly students at the University of Nairobi, conducted the census. Obonyo and Cliopas Omulo, a local school teacher, acted as my research assistants and interpreters. I would like to thank them all for an excellent job.

tral Nyanza around the northeastern shores of Lake Victoria Nyanza. Kenya Luo are part of an extensive migration of Lwoo-speaking peoples who moved from their original Sudan homeland into Uganda and Kenya, arriving in the Nyanza area between 1490 and 1600 (Ogot 1967; Crazzolara 1950-54). Territorial expansion characterized Luo settlement patterns until the onset of British colonial rule, which began with the establishment of the East African Protectorate in 1895. Attempts to colonize the Luo were not made until 1899. The end of territorial expansion and the growth of population in the colonial and postcolonial period have led to serious land shortages today. Cultivation practices have changed from a system of fallowing to a more continuous use of plots, which reduces yields, and the plow has replaced the hoe in the preparation of fields.

Colonial rule also coincided with a marked decline in cattle herds resulting from rinderpest epidemics that broke out in Nyanza between 1880 and 1900. Herds were further reduced as animals were sold to pay taxes. Pastoralism gave way to labor migration, first as forced labor and/or temporary seasonal work on the Uganda Railroad, in gold mines, and on European settler farms. Today wage employment is the dominant male activity. Thus most adult men work outside the community throughout their productive years. Those who remain at home either fish, or engage in small crafts, or trade. Women produce the food supply.[2]

*Monetization of the Economy*

Today no Luo family can survive without cash. The prestige activity for men is no longer pastoralism but wage labor. Social position, and particularly the opportunities available to children, depend primarily on a man's success in the urban areas, which is rarely achieved. Although subsistence needs are met by women, women also contribute some income beyond subsistence requirements. Formerly, grain surpluses were exchanged for animals; today women engage in a variety of activities to earn cash, but such opportunities in the rural areas are limited. The monetization of the economy has markedly changed rural

2. Changes in the Luo economy have been described in various sources: Stichter 1982, Okeyo 1980, Hay 1976, Fearn 1961, and Whisson 1964.

life. Cash payments have replaced barter and exchanges of communal labor. Today money is needed to purchase food items and clothing, to pay school fees and medical expenses, and to hire plow teams if one does not have a plow. In the past, communal work parties were organized to help with weeding in return for similar assistance, but now it is necessary to hire women to weed. Only women with cash to hire weeders can secure assistance in farming; feeding a work party is not enough. All women earn some cash to meet household expenses by cultivating small amounts of cash crops or by petty trade, beer brewing, weeding, or the sale of surplus grain. Many pay school fees and meet other expenses as well. Remittances from migrant men are important for meeting major expenses, particularly school fees and land preparation costs. Widows and women with nonworking husbands—or whose husbands do not provide—must meet these needs themselves. The ultimate responsibility is the woman's. If necessary, she must add more income-producing activities to the already onerous burdens of subsistence cultivation and household work.

## The Economic Position of Widows

Widows have secure land rights[3] and are able to ensure sustenance for themselves and their children, but rights to movable property are more problematic. Here we must distinguish between rules of inheritance (cf. Ocholla-Ayayo 1976: 129-32) and actual practice. Sons inherit their father's estate through their mother in the house property complex. If there are adult sons, they inherit and widows generally suffer no hardship; a son would not deprive his mother of assets and might well be willing to have her manage household affairs. Otherwise, property including cattle, but not land, should legally go to the husband's brother, who is expected to act as guardian. Eventually the estate should be passed on to the biological sons of the deceased and any legal sons sired after the husband's death. Where brothers exercise their rights of control, widows may be deprived of

3. See the Introduction to this volume for a discussion of recent developments among the Luo indicating that some widows are being driven off the land. I do not know if this is occurring in the community I researched. This chapter reports on events as I found them from 1973 through 1975.

assets, as in the case of Doreen, described below. Even household furnishings can be taken, although I know of only one instance where this occurred.

It sometimes happens that a brother who takes over the management of property appropriates it for his own use, and nephews can do little in this situation. But brothers' rights are often not exercised. The widow frequently retains control over the property, either by force of personality or because the brother does not wish to make a claim. This is more likely when there are sons who are not yet mature, or when personal relationships are good. Today some men also leave instructions that their property should go to their wives.

Clearly, the economic impact of a husband's death is not uniform. Although widows generally have a difficult time earning enough cash, particularly if there are young children to educate, the extent to which the loss of a spouse modifies a widow's standard of living varies. It is the more affluent wife who is most likely to suffer relative deprivation. If the husband was a good provider, the widow's income will often decline unless there are adult sons to make up the difference. There is also the possibility of conflicts over property and loss of assets to a husband's brother. Less affluent women who carried a greater burden of support as wives may find their position as widows difficult but unchanged.

*Kinship and Marriage*

The Luo have a segmentary system of localized patrilineages. The core of the community is a group of agnatically related men who reside with their wives in dispersed compounds in a lineage neighborhood (*gweng*). The settlement pattern shows a general correspondence to the genealogy. A few non-agnates or strangers (*jodak*) also reside in the community by virtue of present, or more often past, attachments to local men. Men experiencing difficulties in their own lineage community due to quarrels or witchcraft, land shortages, or emergencies such as war or famine, may approach affines, uterine kin, or friends and ask for permission to settle, permanently or temporarily. They and their descendants constitute the jodak. Although their land rights are relatively secure, these people are in the community by sufferance and find it necessary to maintain a good public image. Since most men in the community are agnates of the deceased, both jurally and practically, widows who remain in the community and wish to form a consort relationship are effectively restricted to choosing a man from their husband's lineage, not an outsider.

Marriage is exogamous—i.e. it occurs outside the lineage. Bridewealth transfers rights over children as well as uxorial rights to the husband, who is socially recognized as father to any children born to his wife or widow. Residence is with the husband in his father's community. Polygyny is practiced and each wife in a compound (*dala*) has her own house (*ot*) and her own plot of land. On marriage the bride moves into her husband's father's compound and initially cooks and farms under her mother-in-law's supervision. Later she is given her own lands from her mother-in-law's holdings and the right to farm and cook for herself. Formerly this occurred after the birth of two or three children. Today it happens sooner. In some cases, particularly if a wife has been married for some time and lived with her husband outside the community, she may work for her mother-in-law for only a year or less, after which she will be given her own land. The land a wife acquires is regarded as part of her husband's estate, but she controls its use and produce for the duration of her marriage. If she leaves and later returns she can reclaim this land, provided she has left sons behind. A husband would not normally reallocate plots, taking land from one wife for the use of another, but occasionally a man with several wives does so. Eventually a woman gives these lands to her sons and sons' wives as they marry.

With the passage of time a son will establish his own home apart from that of his father. Formerly this was done when the son had a son of seven or eight. Today such moves may be postponed, since men who are working outside the community may prefer to leave their wives in their father's compound. However, a new home must be established by the time a man's children reach marriageable age because they cannot be married from their grandfather's house.

Sons are expected to establish homes in strict order of seniority. Violations do occur, particularly if a younger son is more successful financially than his older brother, but such violations are supernaturally sanctioned. The youngest son and his wife or wives are expected to continue to reside in the parental compound. These wives are expected to cook and farm for the mother-in-law. When the parents die, the youngest son takes over the remaining land and becomes the head of his own home. He makes a new entrance to the compound facing his first wife's house, symbolizing this transfer of authority. It is unlikely that parents will still be living by the time the youngest son's children reach marriageable age, but should this occur, I suppose the youngest son would establish his own compound. (I do not know of any such cases.) If all married sons have not yet established their own homes, the death of the parents will bring about the division of the home. Unmarried sons will remain temporarily in the compound, the oldest acting as head until all marry.

This pattern, which formerly assured elderly women of assistance from youngest son and daughter-in-law, has been modified by labor migration. Many sons work outside the community. They are expected to provide financial assistance to parents and usually do so. If married, they generally leave their wives behind. But sometimes a wife accompanies her husband; sometimes a son has no wife. It is not unknown today to find an elderly woman living alone in her compound. Although such women are not socially isolated, they appear to bear the sole responsibility for their own affairs. I have no specific information on the nature or extent of interhousehold assistance, if any.

Marriages are highly stable and few divorces occur. This stability is related to several factors.[4] Women have no rights to land or residence in their own patrilineage and are dependent on marriage for access to housing and farm land. My census data show no instances of widows or separated women residing with fathers or brothers. The only woman I knew who made use of consanguineal connections was a divorced woman working as a servant for a wealthy maternal cousin, her mother's sister's son. Women may have affectionate ties with their natal family, may visit, and may sometimes send money to parents, but they cannot really turn to them for residence or economic support. In

4. A fuller account is available in Potash 1978.

cases of separation, women have nowhere to go unless their parents consent to their return and are willing to repay the bridewealth.[5] The custody of children is vested in men. Women are reluctant to leave children behind, both for emotional reasons and because they depend on children for support in old age. Men are reluctant to marry formerly married women who have sons because they know that such women are likely eventually to join their sons. Finally, a woman's reputation suffers, since she is regarded as a bad mother, a loose woman, or of stubborn or difficult temperament.

These stabilizing factors characteristic of marriage continue to operate after the death of a husband. Most widows remain in their husband's community. Of the 46 widows in the census, 42 remained.

## Characteristics of Widows

Twenty-eight percent of the widows in the census were under 40 at the time of their husband's death; 60 percent were under 50 (see Table 1). The significance of such figures depends, of course, on life expectancy. I have no specific data for the Luo, but the life expectancy at birth for all of Africa was 45.9 for the years 1970 to 1973 (Economic Commission for Africa 1974: 16).

In polygynous marriages, most second and subsequent wives are much younger than their husbands. The mean age differences between husband and first, second, and third wife are 8.58 years, 18.5 years, and 22.8 years, respectively, as shown in Table 2. In addition to the general impact of polygyny on widowhood, there is also a small incidence of young adolescent girls married to wealthy elders who are willing to pay high bridewealth. These arrangements may be polygynous or the husband may be a widower.

5. Return of bridewealth is not an important factor in stabilizing marriage. In the community I studied, bridewealth payments were seldom completed in under five years and generally took ten. Thus, in cases of separation, there would often have been little bridewealth to repay. There are some marriages, however, where such payments may act as a stabilizing factor. In cases where young girls from poor families are married to wealthy older men to secure high bridewealth, payments may be made quickly. Parents often use the bridewealth to meet other expenses such as school fees, marriage payments for a son, or even subsistence needs. In such situations they may not be in a position to repay.

TABLE 1

*Age at Which Luo Women Become Widows*

| Age | Number | Percent |
|---|---|---|
| Under 20 | 4 | 8% |
| 20-29 | 5 | 10 |
| 30-39 | 5 | 10 |
| 40-49 | 15 | 32 |
| 50-59 | 1 | 2 |
| Over 60 | 5 | 10 |
| Unknown | 11 | 23 |
| TOTAL | 46 | 95% |

TABLE 2

*Age Difference Between Husband and First, Second, and Third Wives for All Marriages Where Age Is Known or Estimated*

| Age difference in years | First wife | Second wife | Third wife |
|---|---|---|---|
| Under 5 | 31 | — | — |
| 5-9 | 92 | 6 | 2 |
| 10-14 | 41 | 18 | 3 |
| 15-19 | 13 | 15 | 3 |
| 20-24 | 1 | 12 | 5 |
| 25-29 | — | 4 | 4 |
| 30-34 | 1 | 4 | 3 |
| 35-39 | — | 4 | 1 |
| Over 40 | 1 | 2 | 1 |
| TOTAL | 180 | 65 | 22 |
| Mean age difference | 8.58 | 18.5 | 22.8 |

## The Levirate

Most widows are—to use a Luo term—"taken over" in the levirate by an agnate of the husband. Of the 42 widows who remained in the community, 37 report such a relationship. Another woman had only recently been widowed. Given this high incidence of reported leviratic unions, I suspect that some of these may be nominal rather than real relationships. Several women in the census who report having been taken over were in their fifties and sixties when their husbands died. It is difficult to know what the content of their leviratic relations might be, since according to Luo custom a woman's sexual life terminates with the onset of menopause. The custom was reported by several married women I knew. Paul Mboya, a prominent elder who was considered to be an authority on Luo custom by local and expatriate scholars, states that Luo fear intercourse with a menopausal woman, believing it might cause death (Mboya n.d.: ch. 8). I did know two elderly widows who bragged about their ability to seduce young men after giving them a few drinks of local gin, but one told me that she terminated her leviratic relationship when she reached menopause since she "no longer needed a man." It would seem, then, that some leviratic unions are purely ceremonial.

In a typical situation, the widow chooses a man following the final mourning ceremony for her husband, usually about a year after his death. Although Mboya states that the levir is usually a brother of the deceased, my data suggest that the widow's consort is seldom a brother or half-brother, as Table 3 shows.

The choice of levir is for the widow to make, subject to the consent of the chosen and of the lineage elders. A widow is theoretically free to choose any man from within the lineage, but the census data indicate that choices are not random. As noted, distant agnates are chosen more frequently than brothers. Men who act as levirs are usually middle-aged married men who head their own households. These patterns need some analysis.

The tendency to choose a more distant agnate over a brother may reflect tensions in fraternal relationships. The Luo say that brothers should love one another, but they expect that men will grow apart and become envious of one another as they found their own separate families. Each man desires wives and children so that he may become the founder of an imporant lineage segment. Once married, he will concentrate his resources on building his own family, not his brother's. The Luo frequently blame this on wives. Thus, although brothers are expected to show solidarity, they are likely also to be jealous. Brothers' wives too may be envious of one another. Possibly the strains in relationships among brothers and even brothers' wives lead widows to choose more distant agnates.

Only a minority of men are involved in leviratic relationships.

TABLE 3

*Relationship of Levir to Widow's Husband*

| Relationship (if any) | Number of widows |
|---|---|
| Brother | 2 |
| Half brother | 1 |
| Half brother's son | 1 |
| Common grandfather | 24 |
| Common great grandfather | 2 |
| Same lineage neighborhood (gweng) | 1 |
| Different lineage neighborhood | 2 |
| Relationship unknown | 4 |
| Left levir and community | 1 |
| Left community | 3 |
| Not "taken over" | 5 |
| TOTAL | 46 |

As we noted, these are typically middle-aged men who have already established their own households. Of the levirs in the census, 54 percent were over 40 at the time they accepted the levirate, and 25 percent were over 50 (see Table 4).

Whereas 25 percent of men who are household heads are levirs, only 2 percent of married sons who have not yet established their own homes take over widows (see Table 5). The two levirs who are still residing in their father's compound are both 49 years old; one is divorced and had lived with a widow in her home for three years before they, too, separated. Apparently younger men who are engaged in establishing their own homes and families are less likely to accept leviratic relations than are household heads.

Labor migration may also play a role in the age distribution of levirs, but I do not have detailed information on this. Although many of the levirs in my census had been labor migrants, they were not asked whether they were working outside the community at the time they took over widows. Men who work outside the community typically do so throughout their adult years. They retire to the rural community when they are too old to work, usually when they are past 50. Although some men of all ages reside in the rural community, the male population is heavily weighted toward older retired men and young men who have

TABLE 4

*Ages of Luo Men at the Time They Accepted the Levirate*

| Age | Number | Percent |
|---|---|---|
| Under 30 | 1 | 3% |
| 30-39 | 5 | 18 |
| 40-49 | 8 | 29 |
| 50-59 | 4 | 14 |
| 60-69 | 3 | 11 |
| Unknown | 6 | 22 |
| TOTAL | 27 | 97% |

TABLE 5

*Involvement in Levirate of Household Heads and Married Sons Still Resident in Father's Compound*

| Number of leviratic relations | Number of men | Percent |
|---|---|---|
| Household heads: | | |
| One | 13 | 16% |
| Two | 6 | 8 |
| None | 55 | 74 |
| TOTAL | 74 | 98% |
| Married sons: | | |
| One | 2 | 2% |
| None | 78 | 88 |
| Unknown | 9 | 10 |
| TOTAL | 89 | 100% |

not yet started labor migration. I have no historical data on levirs' ages in the period before labor migration. Whether it is
demographics or a differential willingness on the part of younger
and older men to enter leviratic relations is not clear.

There are no reports of unmarried levirs in the census, although three of the life histories I collected involved unmarried
men acting in this role. In all three instances the men lacked sufficient bridewealth. One moved into the widow's home until she
reached menopause, whereupon she gave him cattle, and he left
to marry. Another, Samuel, was a full brother to the deceased.
He resided in the same compound as his father and the widow.
After his brother's death he took over the widow. Subsequently

she gave him bridewealth to marry, presumably from his brother's herds. He brought his wife to the compound. This was an unusual arrangement in that the widow acted as senior co-wife to the bride. The bride farmed and cooked under the widow's supervision until the bride had a child. Samuel took turns visiting the houses of both women and both cooked for him. This arrangement persisted for fifteen years. Then Samuel decided to establish his own homestead and moved there with his wife. The widow was taken over by another man.

Although these examples involve co-residence, in most situations the levir is married already and resides with his wife or wives in his own or his father's compound. Since widows generally continue living in their husband's homes, leviratic unions are characterized by duolocal residence (see Table 6). When a widow moves into the levir's homestead, the move is temporary. Only three widows report residing with the levir; 6 of the 27 men involved in leviratic relations report co-residence. In all but one of these cases the widow returned to her husband's home.

This pattern of residential separation relates to property rights and patterns of inheritance. Women acquire access to land only through their husbands or their children. If women are to provide for themselves and their children, they must maintain cultivation rights on their deceased husband's estate. Children inherit only these lands. Thus a woman is unlikely to move. In one life history the widow explained that she had moved into the levir's home because she had not yet had any children. If a woman does reside with the levir, he usually lives within the same neighborhood, so she can continue to farm her land. In rare instances (I know of two cases), widows may accompany levirs who migrate outside the community for wage work. One childless woman eventually left the levir. Widows who move from their husband's estate eventually return, either moving back into the deceased husband's home if he had his own compound, or moving into a new house. Building a new home for a widow whose husband had not established his own compound is one of the few obligations a levir has. Indeed, Luo claim that some men refuse the levirate because they do not wish to undertake this task.

The levir has few responsibilities to either the widow or her

TABLE 6

*Residence of Widows in the Levirate*

| Residence | Number |
|---|---|
| Remained in husband's home | 34 |
| Went away with levir: | |
|     Returned to husband's home | 2 |
|     Left levir but did not return | 1 |
| Left home, returned, and then took levir | 1 |
| TOTAL | 38 |

offspring. His role is primarily sexual. He is expected to visit the widow regularly for purposes of sex and procreation. Unfortunately, I did not obtain data on widows' childbearing. By comparing the age of children with the time of the husband's death, I can ascertain which children were probably sired by the levir, but such data do not provide an adequate picture of widows' fertility. I do not know, for example, which widows had already reached menopause. Nor do I have data on widows' attitudes toward childbearing, on the incidence of miscarriage and abortion, or on the frequency of levirs' visits and how this relates to fertility. Some of the widows in my sample may yet bear children. Since many anthropologists assume the levirate to be a mechanism for continued childbearing, the absence of data on widows' fertility is a serious drawback to testing this hypothesis.

Although my data are limited, they suggest areas for further study. If we arbitrarily take 40 as the age of menopause, eight of the fourteen widows under 40 bore more children after their husband's death, five did not, and one left the community. But patterns of childbearing appear to be slightly different for those widows who had previously borne sons. Only two of the seven widows with sons bore more children, compared with six of the seven widows who had no sons. Apparently the absence of sons is a factor encouraging further procreation. Of the nine widows who had no children by their husband, four left the community. These were the only widows to leave. These data suggest that although the levirate may afford women the opportunity of continuing their reproductive career, the extent to which they do so

TABLE 7

*Levirs' Reports on Paternity of Widows' Children*

| Paternity of widows' children | Number of widows |
|---|---|
| Husband only | 12 |
| Husband and levir | 9 |
| Levir only | 3 |
| No children | 2 |
| Paternity unknown | 1 |
| TOTAL | 27 |

depends on their childbearing history. Women need sons to support them in old age. Unfortunately, the data do not permit further analysis.

Specific questions on biological paternity were asked only of men who were levirs (see Table 7). These data are more accurate, since they are based on actors' reports. However, they provide no information on age of widow or sex of children.

Children born to the widow are legally children of the deceased regardless of biological paternity. The genitor is always accorded some recognition, but the degree of recognition varies. In theory, he is entitled to some of the animals given as bridewealth for any daughter he has sired. In practice, I found, there were cases where such animals are given and cases where they are not. The bridewealth goes to the girl's brother or her mother—sometimes to the brother of the deceased, if there are no sons. Some adult children visit their natural fathers and give them occasional gifts; others do not. Some children take their genitor's name. Much depends on the quality of the relationship between a man and his natural children. Several factors may have a negative effect on this relationship: residential separation of genitor and offspring; the lack of economic, nurturant, and socialization responsibilities; and the likelihood that a man will show greater interest in his legal children, who constitute his own descendants, than in natural children who count as descendants of the deceased.

*Economic Aspects of the Levirate*

The absence of economic responsibilities is clearly shown in the various life histories. Widows make this claim and cite detailed stories as proof. Achola, for example, said she sent the levir away because the relationship was too costly. "When he comes, he likes good things to eat, like tilapia." This is the favored local fish and is more expensive than other varieties. "He doesn't help in any way," she reported. She added that the relationship cost too much.

Similarly, Doreen reported that she received no economic help from either the levir or her husband's brother. Yet she maintained the relationship for many years. One of five co-wives of a wealthy man, Doreen was left with one daughter. On the husband's death, his brother took his cattle and much of his wealth, a right we noted. After selling a few things, he gave the widows a little money for food but kept most of the wealth. Each of the widows was taken over by a different man. Doreen's choice, an unmarried man by whom she bore three daughters and a son, continued to reside in his own house. Doreen, remaining in her husband's old house, managed to pay for most of her children's education. Not only was the levir poor, but as she said, "The man who takes you doesn't help. The only thing he does is give you children." He did help a little by repairing her kitchen. Yet he likes the children, and if he has something, he will give it to them. The children use his name even though they are considered to be the children of the deceased husband. Now that the children are adult, they usually go to see him as well as Doreen, bringing him sugar and soap. He is also entitled to part of the bridewealth.

Another widow, Rose, was left with three children to support. She too had no economic assistance. Her mother helped pay the school fees for one son and Rose paid for another son and daughter. No one in her husband's family provided assistance, nor did the levir. Today Rose's two sons are married adults who work on distant plantations and send her a small amount of money monthly. The only life history I have in which a levir supported or paid school fees for children is that of Samuel, the man who took over his brother's widow.

A different picture emerges from the accounts of the men in the census who were levirs. Only 5 of the 27 claim that they have no responsibilities. Others say they provide assistance of some kind, such as house repair or plowing or occasional help with food or money. Although various kinds of aid are reported, when the reports are analyzed it is apparent that where assistance is given it is an occasional reflection of goodwill rather than a formal duty. Only Samuel, who is a full brother, claims that he helped pay school fees. Levirs are usually married and concerned with the growth of their own family and the education of their legal children.

When the levir is a more distant agnate, he may be expected to have only a limited interest in the deceased's children, but what of closer agnates, the brothers of the deceased? Here we need to distinguish between ideal and practice. Luo believe that brothers should help one another, and men regularly do provide assistance in educating younger brothers or helping with bridewealth payments. But there are also strong competitive and individualistic tendencies in Luo culture. Thus it is regarded as a good thing if a man helps his brother, but men are not really blamed for concentrating their resources on building their own families.

To return to the cases just cited, not only did Doreen's brother-in-law fail to provide aid, but he appropriated her husband's wealth for his own use. Achola, however, the widow who had rejected the levir because of his expensive taste in food, reports that her husband's brother gives her food and money when she is short. She pays for the education of her children. Only a wealthy man might suffer a loss of public esteem for neglecting a sibling's needy children. In one household, for example, two surviving brothers, both wealthy men, jointly took on the responsibility of educating their dead brother's six children and providing them with clothing. Another man, a jadak or stranger, temporarily withdrew his own son from school so that he could pay school fees for a deceased brother's son. He says that his brother had educated him and he would not want people to gossip and say he was sending his own son to school and not his brother's.

Modern economic conditions have probably exaggerated competitive tendencies between brothers, but differences in wealth are not new. Luo genealogies are full of stories of father's brothers misappropriating a nephew's estate. Indeed, the wicked uncle is not an unfamiliar figure. Reports of limited assistance come also from some of the adult men and women who had lost their fathers during childhood. Many state that their uncles provided no assistance. Such accounts go back only to the 1920's or 1930's, when labor migration was already on the increase. Although contemporary economic conditions are different, these accounts do suggest that the limited help provided today is nothing new. Finally, although elders decry their loss of influence and blame individualism on the concern for cash, David Parkin's (1978) study of Luo in Nairobi shows that lineal authority persists. Men are not lost to kinship control; the arena has merely shifted from the rural to the urban locale.

*Economic Responsibilities of Widows and Sons*

The main responsibility for support rests with the widow herself. In some respects this is an extreme form of the usual family arrangement among the Luo rather than a departure from it, since a woman is always responsible for feeding herself and her children. However, widows may have an added problem because they do not have husbands in town who send them cash. Women manage by raising cash crops and engaging in petty trade. If they have mature or even adolescent sons, such sons usually provide some assistance. Take, for example, Barak.

Barak's father died when he was fifteen, leaving eight children. Barak had previously dropped out of school, planning to return. On his father's death, however, there was no money to pay school fees. His father's brothers did not provide assistance to help support the family, so he tried fishing, trade, and raising bananas. He also began cultivating some unused land his father's brother had bought in a new settlement scheme. Barak and the other children traveled half a day between the two communities to farm. After several years Barak decided that farming was not bringing in sufficient income. There was not enough money for school fees or clothing. He left the community and went first to Uganda and then to Tanzania, where he worked at fishing, trade, and most recently, smuggling. Between trips he returns home to visit. Now 26, he recently married and brought his bride home. The brother closest in age to Barak did not enter school until he was 15. He attended for only a year or so. When Barak left for Uganda, the brother left school and began to work on a plantation. Both sons send money to support the family. Their mother's levir provides no assistance, nor do the father's brothers. The mother herself has become a heavy drinker and apparently is not very productive.

Let us now turn to young widows who do not have supporting sons. If a woman is widowed at a young age, she may continue for many years to bear children for whom she has sole responsibility. The most extreme case I encountered was that of a young girl who was married before puberty to Rege, a man in his late sixties who was ill and near death. Rege married her to have descendants. He expects that when he dies, his elderly brother will act as levir to the widow and sire children in Rege's name. Since women do not marry more than once, and since most levirs are old or middle-aged, this girl of twelve or thirteen is likely to have a succession of consorts, with the result that she alone will have to support children all her life.

*The Levirate and Marriage*

Leviratic relationships, as should be clear by now, are different from marriage. In the first place, the widow has no uxorial obligations to the levir: she need not cook for him or perform other services. Furthermore, she does not perform agricultural labor that he can control. Second, widows have greater freedom than wives. They determine their own domestic routines or extra-domestic activities. They alone make decisions about their children. They are free to visit friends. This is not so in most marriages, where a woman is constrained to please her husband. Although he seldom exercises it, a husband has the power to send her away and deprive her of children. Levirs have no such power.

Leviratic relationships are also impermanent. No specific questions on duration were asked in the census, but several widows and levirs volunteered that their relationships were short-lived. The life history material shows a considerable range of duration. Some relationships lasted a few days; others endured for as long as fifteen years. Widows are free to send the levir away; they may also seek another levir. Sometimes the relationship ends because the man grows tired of visiting. If the man leaves the community to seek employment, the widow rarely accompanies him. This contrasts with marriage that is very stable.

Finally, household composition differs considerably from that in marriage. If the deceased was a polygynist the widows may continue to reside in the same compound, but each will be attached to a different man as levir. In these circumstances some of the rivalry of co-wife relations is reduced. Each woman manages her own affairs. Neither is there rivalry between a widow and her levir's wife, since they are not in competition for resources and do not share a compound. If sexual jealousy is present, it is not given overt expression. I heard no gossip about widow-wife conflicts and none of the women I spoke with ever complained of husbands favoring widows, only other co-wives. The quality of relations between levir and widow or levir and children is, as we have already noted, different from what transpires when a man is husband and father.

## Conclusion

The levirate has been examined in detail here, not because of its importance to widows themselves, but rather because of the attention it has received in anthropological discourse. Of greater importance to Luo women are economic issues; their significant emotional and social relations are ties to children, particularly their sons. I have no information on the importance women attach to sex. As we have noted, men and women work hard to support themselves in a cash economy and to educate their children. They hope that by having many sons, they will be in a position where one or more will succeed financially and be able to provide for them in old age. Increasingly, this hope is difficult to realize.

Ambitious men and women look to labor migration as the path to achievement. Many women prefer husbands to work outside the community. Such women report that having a husband at home would make little difference in their lives, although there might be some economic hardship. Only one woman I spoke to expressed a preference for having her migrant husband at home. Husbands do, of course, visit the rural home; sometimes wives take turns residing with husbands in town. Many women visit during the nonfarming season. But such women do spend most of their married life apart from their husbands, as de facto if not de jure heads of households.

Similarly, labor migration has affected mother-son relationships. Migrant sons send cash, but they too are away. Married sons may leave wives behind who help the mother-in-law, but sometimes sons are unmarried or wives accompany their husbands. Formerly an older woman might live surrounded by children and grandchildren in her own or neighboring compounds. Today this may not be the case. In earlier times the grandmother's house was also the home for young unmarried girls whom she educated. Today such living arrangements have disappeared, a casualty of both labor migration and formal schools.

One of the interesting developments in the contemporary setting is the increasingly important role daughters play in assisting parents. Daughters often send small amounts of cash, particularly to their mothers. Educated, salaried women, although few in number, help pay school fees for younger siblings. They may also build their mother a house, something normally considered a son's obligation. If the husband objects, the woman continues to provide, but surreptitiously. Women cannot reside with daughters, since exogamous and virilocal rules place them in different communities. Daughters visit but are not able to provide the labor assistance that is normatively expected of a resident daughter-in-law.

Luo women are hard-working and self-reliant. Many do not need help, since widows are normally middle-aged rather than elderly. But many of the sacrifices women and men make to advance their children's position will go unrewarded. Unemployment in Kenya is high, and increasingly, secondary-school graduates and others cannot find work. Only a few can realistically expect to succeed, and they are primarily sons and daughters from more affluent families who have the education and the connections.

# Nandi Widows

REGINA SMITH OBOLER

IN NANDI, unlike many other African societies, women have a strictly limited number of options in their marital careers. First marriages traditionally were arranged and usually still are, though a girl's personal preference now plays a larger part in the selection of her future husband. Marriage is viewed as a once-in-a-lifetime event for a Nandi woman, who is to remain forever the wife of the man who first married her. Though there was a traditional divorce procedure, divorce used to be so rare as to be commonly regarded as impossible. True divorce with return of bridewealth could only occur if a woman was childless. The rate of divorce is now increasing somewhat, but it is still very low. A woman may leave her husband, but she is not considered divorced. A separated or widowed woman cannot remarry, and any children she bears are descendants of her original husband.

However, as I will argue below, the fact that Nandi widows do not have many formal options does not necessarily mean that they are more constrained than widows in other East African societies. The corollary to the absence of divorce is the existence of extraordinarily strong property rights for wives. The extremely prosperous local economy, which is well integrated into the national cash economy, means the average Nandi family is affluent by rural Kenyan standards. These two factors—affluence and secure property rights—underlie the economic autonomy of the

My research was funded by grants from the National Science Foundation and the Woodrow Wilson National Fellowship Foundation, as well as a National Institute for Mental Health Predoctoral Training Fellowship. I wish to thank my research assistants Jennifer Jeptoo Kosut (Maindi), Peter Kipserem Bungei, William Kipsellem Sang', and Joel Kibiwot Tuwei, as well as my husband, Leon Oboler, for their part in the research.

typical Nandi widow, which in turn gives her a great deal of free-dom of action.

I have argued elsewhere (Oboler 1985) that commoditization of economic resources has undermined the economic position of Nandi women as wives. Somewhat paradoxically, it has also con-tributed to increased autonomy for these same women as wid-ows. Like other Kalenjin societies, Nandi is marked by the in-stitution of house property (Gluckman 1950). This means that a woman, at marriage, receives a kind of marriage settlement. A share of her husband's property is assigned to her and her de-scendants in perpetuity. This share can be added to during the marriage, and along with certain types of property in which a woman's rights predominate, forms her house property. A woman's rights in her house property are never lost, and she has the right to pass it to her sons regardless of who begets them.

The importance of the house-property complex and the pros-perity of the local economy are closely related to the incidence of the levirate, which according to informants of both sexes is pre-scribed by Nandi custom. (I use the term "levir" to mean a close agnate of a widow's dead husband with whom she has a formal sexual relationship.) If a widow is still of childbearing age, it is the duty of her husband's brother (or classificatory brother) to enter a sexual relationship with her and give her children. Eco-nomic aid is also seen as part of the relationship. When such an arrangement occurs in fact, it is viewed by the community with approval. Yet today the levirate is rarely practiced. Widows fre-quently enter sexual relationships, but usually lovers are not levirs. For reasons discussed below, younger widows are rather more likely than older ones to form leviratic relationships, but even then it is uncommon. Why?

House property means that a widow can have secure property rights without maintaining an ongoing relationship with any members of her husband's family. Prior to commoditization, male labor needed by a widow for such tasks as clearing land for cultivation was (at least normatively) provided by a levir, unless the widow could make a less formal arrangement, such as an ex-change of services, with some other kinsman or neighbor. Today, because of general affluence—land holdings that are large by Third World standards, along with almost universal cash-cropping—widows normally can hire whatever male labor they need. Older widows with grown sons may rely on these sons for labor and economic aid.

A widow in Nandi has a great deal of sexual freedom, and if she decides to take a lover he may be any man of her choice. Her husband's agnates cannot effectively interfere. (Though it is sometimes said that people can be "cursed" by community elders for various violations of social norms, no one ever told me that a widow could be cursed for refusing to accept a levir.) Since the local community is not agnatically structured, it is likely that a lover a widow chooses purely on the basis of personal preference will not be one of her dead husband's agnates. Children a widow bears inherit her house property in any case, since it is the identity of the mother, not the genitor, that is crucial in the transmission of house property.

The role of wife in Nandi is rather constrained. Nandi wives display great public deference to their husbands. For example, they may not manage significant property independently, and must in theory ask their husbands' permission to leave their homesteads for more than a short time. The role of widow, however, confers on a woman personal autonomy approaching that of a man.

## The Nandi

The Nandi, a Nilotic, Kalenjin-speaking people of western Kenya, numbered 322,200 in the 1969 census. They were traditionally semipastoralists with a strongly cattle-oriented ideology, though cultivation has always played an important role in their economy. Today they have a prosperous mixed farming economy in which cattle are still of major importance. Nandi was historically an area of low population density. The Nandi are still land-wealthy by comparison with other ethnic groups in Kenya. Most households produce cash crops, especially milk, maize, and tea, as well as subsistence crops. Modern Nandi is deeply enmeshed in the national cash economy. Cash is necessary to the average lifestyle and easily accessible through cash-cropping, local contract labor, and entrepreneurial activities. There is very little migration of Nandi men to other areas for wage labor, in comparison with patterns in neighboring ethnic groups such as Luo or Abaluhya.

Nandi social organization is based on patrilineal extended families, whose members usually live contiguously, and dispersed patrilineal clans of very little importance. There is a system of rotating age-sets for men but not for women. The latter take their age-set identity from their husbands. The settlement pattern is one of scattered homesteads. Each local community also has a Centre, a collection of shops, grain mills, beer clubs, etc., and site of community meetings and elders' courts. Each local community is made up of members of various extended families and clans. Neighbors are likely to be connected to one another by a dense network of affinal ties. Sisters try to marry into families that live close to one another, and it is common for young men who are friends and age-mates as well as neighbors to cement their bonds to one another by marrying sisters.

The community in which I conducted most of the research reported in this paper is located in the north central part of Nandi District. Neither the most "traditional" nor the most "modernized" community in Nandi, it may be considered fairly representative of the district as a whole. The average household/compound contains 8.1 people and 9.1 adult cattle and holds 20.6 acres of land. 16.8 percent of ever-married male household heads are polygynists.[1] (The figures are based on a random-sample community census.)

*Marriage, Division of Labor, and Property*

Marriage involves the transfer of cattle bridewealth, the amount of which (four to seven cattle) is relatively small when viewed in terms of the cattle/people ratio (slightly greater than 1:1). The incidence of polygyny in Nandi District as a whole is probably a bit over 25 percent.[2] Postmarital residence is normally

1. This is a smaller figure than the polygyny rate that seems to characterize Nandi as a whole (see note 2). I believe this discrepancy is due to a slightly younger average age of household heads in the research community than in most other Nandi communities. With age controlled, the difference in the incidence of polygyny between Christians and non-Christians is not statistically significant.

2. In a survey of 454 men from throughout Nandi District, I found that 30.6 percent had more than one wife. This sample was not statistically random, but I

patrilocal, and the local community is markedly endogamous.

Adults of both sexes sometimes herd cattle, but the task falls primarily to children, particularly boys. Both sexes participate in cultivation and the care of livestock (Oboler 1977, 1985). Each wife has her own plot. Husband and wife divide their maize harvest, the wife's share being allocated to subsistence whereas the husband usually sells his for cash. Nonhousehold labor is also commonly recruited for busy periods such as planting and harvesting. Households of close kin and neighbors exchange labor, planting or harvesting the fields of one household one week and another the next. Affluent households use hired contract labor. In the past, surplus labor was recruited through invitations to beer-drinking parties. Male household heads invited to such parties were obliged to provide labor from their own households for a task undertaken by the host household.

At marriage a woman is assigned certain animals from her husband's herds as house property. These animals and their offspring are augmented by others that she receives as gifts at her initiation or marriage, acquires through her own efforts, or receives as bridewealth for her daughters. Each wife in a polygynous marriage is supposed to receive from her husband the same number of house-property animals as every other wife. Cattle a man inherits should be distributed as house property. Husband and wife normatively have joint rights in such property, though in practice husbands have significantly more control over these cattle than do wives (see Oboler 1985). It is considered the prerogative of men to manage property, though wives should be consulted when their house property is concerned. A man's rights to independent control are even stronger for animals acquired by his own initiative (e.g., formerly by raiding and today by wage labor) that have not been assigned as house property.

---

believe it is representative of the population. I think that the phrasing of the question was unclear to some of the informants, who may therefore have reported consecutive rather than simultaneous marriages. Langley (1979: 84) found a 31 percent incidence of polygyny among families with children at primary school. It is possible that because of the method of examining only families with children at school, certain categories of men least likely to be polygynous—the youngest and poorest married men, for example—were undercounted. For these reasons, I regard 30 percent of married men as the maximum probable incidence of polygynists, the actual incidence probably being closer to 25 percent.

A woman's house property is inherited only by her own sons and cannot be reassigned by her husband to another wife's house. Bridewealth cattle must remain within a house. A young man pays bridewealth from the bridewealth cattle received for his full-sister, never his half-sister. A husband/father may, however, disproportionately allocate cattle acquired by his own efforts for the marriages of sons in a house that lacks daughters, and other kin such as mother's brothers may contribute to a young man's bridewealth. The property of a woman who has no heir goes to her husband's closest patrilineal descendant, though inheritance of house property by collateral lines is considered highly undesirable. There is a way in which a woman without a male heir can keep her house property from reverting to collateral lines. She may use some of her house property, including cattle gained as bridewealth for her daughters, to marry another woman in the hope that her wife will produce a male heir for the house (see Oboler 1980).

In cases of separation,[3] husbands' families have the right of custody of children. If they are very young, the mother may take them with her, but they are expected to return eventually to the father's family. Their only legitimate rights of inheritance lie with their agnatic kin. Though a separated woman has no right to take any animals with her, she always has the right to return to her husband's home and resume her rights in her house property. This can occur either while the husband is still living or after his death. I recorded several cases in which elderly women, long-since separated from their husbands, returned to take up property rights in their husbands' homes. Often the woman was sought out and persuaded to return by an adult son she had left behind with his father. The return of the mother in no way improves her son's inheritance rights; the motivation of sons in such cases would seem to be simple filial love. It must be noted, however, that in none of the cases I recorded did adult sons persuade mothers to return with younger sons begotten during the

3. Of 123 marriages of male household heads for which I have complete data, 6 ended in permanent separation. Of 168 adult women living in 115 compounds in the census, 8 were separated from their husbands on a long-term basis and living permanently with other relatives. The latter figure probably underrepresents the incidence of separation, since women who separate from their husbands also frequently migrate to large towns. In any case, these figures show that permanent or long-term separation, though it occurs, is not very common.

separation. Such sons could presumably claim a share of the mother's house property. The point is that such a woman can re-assume her own property rights as if she had never left.

## Nandi Widows

There is a high rate of widowhood in Nandi. I collected census data for 115 randomly selected households in my research community, a 40 percent random sample of the community. There were 168 adult women living in these 115 households, and of these, 43 (25.5 percent) were widows. The high rate of widowhood is probably accounted for by a large modal age difference between husbands and wives. The ages of the widows in the random sample census, according to the indigenous system of reckoning,[4] are given in Table 1. Most of the widows (86 percent) were over 49 years old. In my census data, there were no widows among the youngest age group of married women (under 19). Only two of the widows (4.7 percent) were younger than about 34, and only six (14 percent) were under about 49.

Most widows (63 percent) reside in compounds headed by their married adult sons. Informants say that customary law assigns responsibility for a widow to her youngest adult son, but in fact a widow may co-reside with any of her sons. Judging by cases known to me personally, I would speculate that there is no more than a slight tendency for widows with several sons to live more frequently in the compound of the youngest. The decision to live with one of her older sons may be made by a widow on the basis of intangible factors such as personal liking, or it may be made because it facilitates mutual aid arrangements.

Such arrangements work both ways. In one case, the widow was elderly and ailing. She lived with her older son because his children were older and required less care, and because his wife had two younger sisters living with her in the compound. This daughter-in-law was thus in a better position to care for her

4. Women are referred to as wives of their husbands' age-sets. When the age difference between spouses is great, a woman can be referred to as a wife of the age-set into which she would have been expected to marry in the normal course of events. People will say, for example, "She was married by a Maina, but she really should have been a wife of Chuma." Here, women are placed in categories according to the age-sets they would normally have married rather than those of their actual husbands. It is difficult to get a better approximation of age than this for any but young women.

TABLE 1

Nandi Widows by Age-Set: Random Sample Census

| Age-set | Age range[a] (approx.) | Number of widows | Percent of all widows |
|---|---|---|---|
| Wives of Sawe | 19-34 | 2 | 4.7% |
| Wives of Chuma | 35-48 | 4 | 9.3 |
| Wives of Maina | 49-63 | 13 | 30.2 |
| Wives of Nyongi | 64-78 | 17 | 39.5 |
| Wives of Kimnyigei | 79+ | 7 | 16.3 |
| TOTAL | | 43 | 100.0% |

[a]These ages are approximations, and though they are shown as discrete categories, in actuality there is some overlapping at the margins; that is, some wives of Sawe are older than some wives of Chuma, and so forth.

mother-in-law than the wife of the youngest son. In another case, a widow who had been living with a younger son left his compound for that of her older son when the latter's wife died. She took on the domestic chores in his compound and cared for his minor children. A widow who shares a compound with her son or another relative usually has her own house within the compound, cooks for herself, and conducts her own affairs as independently of those of other residents as she chooses. Grandchildren not infrequently spend the night with older widows, or share some of their meals, but not necessarily.

When a widow co-resides with a married adult son, it is the son, not the mother, who is held to be the head of the compound and owner of the land. (If the son is not yet married, the question of who is head of the compound may be somewhat blurred.) Most informants say that widows usually prefer to pool resources with this son and not take independent responsibility for the management of their property. They keep working as long as they are able, generally in cooperation with the wives of their sons, and are given their share of maize and milk from the general supply of the family. Widows living with sons usually have their own houses and sometimes their own granaries. They also may maintain some resources of their own—for example, chickens or a vegetable plot—from which they may gain small amounts of cash. A number of widows I knew brewed and sold beer on a more or less regular basis. In a fairly typical case, the family had one maize field, but the widowed mother weeded only in the section immediately behind her own house. She referred to this section as "my field," though the son and the daughter-in-law recognized no such distinction. At the time of the harvest the maize from this section was not kept separate. The widow's granary was filled from the general harvest. This woman also kept a few chickens and brewed occasionally.

Although older widows usually prefer to pool resources with a son, informants unanimously agree that a widow is perfectly within her rights to cultivate her own plot of maize independently. There is no limit to the size of the area she may cultivate (provided there is enough land for the daughter-in-law to cultivate her maize as well), and the produce belongs to her absolutely. It is considered the son's responsibility to provide his mother with seeds, fertilizer, and labor for plowing and clearing without any reciprocal obligation. If the widowed mother grows more maize than she needs for her own food, she may sell the surplus and use the profit for whatever she pleases. She may own any type of property whatsoever. If she can save enough money, she is free to buy a cow or even a piece of land. One widow I knew lived with her son and cultivated separately. The son was a poor property manager who had been forced to sell all his cattle, whereas his mother owned a number of cows, including two milk cows. She gave a small quantity of milk to her daughter-in-law to feed the children but sold the rest and used the money for her own purposes. This is not the most commonly chosen alternative, but stories abound of widows who took over the management of their property "as if they were men," and even became wealthy in their own right.

The residential arrangements of widows in the sample are shown in Table 2. The usual pattern is for widows to continue living in their own compounds, either with a married son as head, or with an unmarried son and other children. I have created a separate category for cases where the oldest son is mature and has begun to assume the responsibilities of a male household head. One of the cases coded as "independent household head" is a female husband who lives with her wife and child. The other four are relatively young widows with minor children. In a few cases, widows are incorporated in compounds other than those of their sons through a variety of kinship links and

TABLE 2

*Residences of Widows: Random Sample Census*

| Residential arrangement | Number of widows |
| --- | --- |
| Living with married adult son | 27 |
| Living with unmarried adult son | 4 |
| Living with other relative | 5 |
| Living with non-relative | 2 |
| Independent household head | 5 |
| TOTAL | 43 |

even ties of friendship. Cases recorded in my census include residence with a daughter and daughter's husband, with a sister's son, with parents-in-law, and even with brothers and brothers' sons. In rare instances widows reside with other relatives when they cannot get along with their own sons. Widows do not move in with lovers or levirs, but maintain their own residences and receive them as visitors. I encountered only one case of a widow residing with a lover, a widower who shared his compound with his son and daughter-in-law.

Widows, unlike wives, are not usually reserved in their public demeanor. They frequent beer halls, as men do, and often become involved in informal debate with men in this setting. Widows do not, however, take on any formal role in the political and judicial apparatus of the community; that is the preserve of men. On the domestic front, widows are frequently heard giving pointed advice or instructions to both sons and daughters-in-law, though this is also true of elderly women whose husbands are still alive. Elderly widows take advantage of their freedom from domestic responsibilities and freedom of movement. They commonly spend weeks at a time away from home visiting a wide range of relatives. Though older wives too have greater freedom of movement than younger wives, they are still somewhat bound by domestic responsibilities. Freedom of movement is much more pronounced among widows.

A widow can hold and manage property in her own right. A widow with minor sons holds her sons' share of the house property in trust for them and manages it in their names until they come of age. Such management includes the right to sell animals, if necessary, but the goal is to hold the property intact insofar as possible until the sons reach their majority. Informants, especially men, say that it is the duty of the dead man's brother, whether or not he is the widow's levir, to oversee the management of the property and make sure the wife does not "misuse" or "squander" it. Women are commonly stereotyped as wasteful and irresponsible. Thus if a widow with minor sons wishes to sell a cow, and the need to do so is not obvious, her husband's brother might successfully intervene. However, most informants agree that if the widow is administering the property capably, the dead man's brother really doesn't have the right to interfere.

The bulk of a widow's house property is inherited by her adult sons at their father's death, or by minor sons when they reach maturity. Certain categories of cattle, however, become her personal property. She also maintains full cultivation rights in the family land. Snell (1954: 53) says that "each of the deceased's widows, in order of seniority, received one or more cows, according to the number available." I was told that a widow has a right to retain as her own property one cow from the bridewealth given for each of her daughters. She also has the right to control the distribution among her sons of the offspring of cattle she received as gifts at her marriage or initiation. As one informant described her situation: "The cow is referred to as belonging to the family [using the husband's name] but everyone knows it is mine. I will divide its offspring among my sons in my old age."

Although the property of a widow without sons reverts to a collateral line upon her death, she is in control of the disposition of this property as long as she is alive. In one case, a widow with a daughter but no sons sold her farm. She gave the money to her son-in-law, who pooled it with his own and purchased a large farm in another sublocation. The widow then moved to live with her daughter and son-in-law, taking her cattle with her.

The Nandi property system, then, gives wives secure rights in a well-defined estate. During the husband's lifetime these rights are residual, in the sense that a wife is not free to make autonomous decisions regarding the use of the property. The role of widow is marked by the activation of the woman's residual right to manage her house property. Certain categories of property, particularly of cattle, are not involved in the division of property among sons following a man's death, but remain his widow's own property—and the division of this property among her sons is a woman's personal decision.

## The Levirate

Informants report that it is Nandi custom for a widow to be "taken over" (the verb used is *kindii*, which means "to inherit" in a more general sense) by a brother (or classificatory brother, for example a father's brother's son) of her deceased husband. I do not have statistical data on the incidence of the levirate; only three cases came directly to my attention during my fieldwork. However, I think that the levirate would not ordinarily be obvious to an outsider in a Nandi community unless cases were actively sought out. Of my close associates who were widows (at least fifteen women of varying ages), I know that all but one were not involved in leviratic relationships. For this reason I conclude that the practice of the levirate is uncommon.

The levir's normative role is to sire children, if the widow's family is not already considered complete; to manage the property held in trust for her minor sons; to assist her by providing labor for clearing, plowing, planting, and harvesting (either performing this labor himself or hiring someone else to do it); and to contribute to the maintenance of her household through occasional gifts of cash or small consumer items. I encountered so few cases of the levirate in practice that I cannot say whether levirs as a class actually do these things.

A widow is not required to become involved in a levirate arrangement. Indeed, it is unlikely that a widow with a grown son will enter such a relationship. With an adult male heir for her house, such a woman will not feel under pressure to continue bearing children. She will probably depend on her son to perform the male role in the sexual division of labor and to give her cash assistance that might otherwise be provided by a levir (paying for her land to be plowed, for example, buying seeds and fertilizer, or making occasional small gifts of money, tea, sugar). If such a woman has a lover, it is a man of her own choice, and generally one unrelated to her late husband. I was told that according to customary law it is tantamount to adultery for a

widow to be sexually involved with a man other than a close agnate of her late husband, but in practice such involvements do
not seem to be negatively sanctioned. Whether this discrepancy
between the stated norm and commonly accepted practice is
a recent change is impossible to say on the basis of available
information.

A young widow is expected to go on bearing children, especially if she does not already have a large family. The children
she bears will belong to her "house" and thus will be considered
descendants of her first (and only) husband, whoever their genitor may be.[5] Like an older widow, a young widow is free to form
a liaison with any man of her choosing, though many informants
told me that such a woman *should* enter a levirate relationship. I
personally knew three widows under age 40 in my research
community. Only one was in a levirate union. Another had been
the wife of a female husband. Her consort was a neighbor, unrelated to either the female husband or the family of the latter's
male husband. This relationship continued after the female husband's death. The third widow was visited from time to time by a
man she met while she was brewing and selling beer in the sublocation Centre.

Each of these widows had five children, including two sons,
at the time of her husband's death. The case of the first young
widow (the one with a levir) is described below. Informants told
me of several other leviratic relationships, but I know the details
of only two. One involved a woman in the research community
who was widowed in her early thirties. She was left with a son
and daughter. Later she had another son and daughter by her

---

5. Langley (1979: 73) says that "if the widow had heirs by her first marriage the
children of the subsequent union, *kindi*, inherited from their biological father."
My informants say that sons of a levirate marriage have inheritance rights only in
their mother's house property (the property of her dead husband), regardless of
whether they were born before or after her husband's death, and that whether or
not they are biological sons of the deceased has no bearing on their inheritance
status. If a levir chooses to assign some of his personal property (as opposed to
his wife's house property) to his sons of a levirate relationship, I was told, it is
theoretically possible for him to do so. However, I never heard of a levir who
actually did. "Personal property" refers to cattle acquired by a man through his
own efforts and not assigned as house property—for example, a cow bought
with money earned by wage-labor. A man's wife still has a strong moral claim on
such property, but he may theoretically disburse it at his own discretion.

husband's half-brother (the husband had no living full-brother). The other involved a young widow in a neighboring community who was left with daughters only. In these cases, and in all recent cases described to me where any indication of age was given, the widows practicing the levirate were young, under age 35. Among older widows, I knew only the case cited below, in which the levir was named but never came to visit. No other cases were called to my attention by informants, but this obviously doesn't mean that none exist.

I believe that a young widow is typically more likely to choose the levirate for several reasons. She is under considerable pressure to have more children as quickly as possible, particularly if she has no son. It is possible that she will form a relationship based on mutual attraction with an unrelated man after her husband's death, but if she does not do so soon as a matter of course, the levirate represents a ready-made alternative. It is frequently easier and less demanding psychologically for the widow to take this route, since it does not require her to launch herself into the process of courtship at a difficult life-crisis point. Further, a widow who is very young and inexperienced may welcome the advice of an older man in managing her property.

There is a marked discrepancy between reports of male and female informants about what usually happens when a young widow is left with minor children. Male informants generally report that the dead man's brother takes the widow in the levirate, manages the house property, and provides for the children (by giving the widow cash to buy them clothes, paying their school fees, etc.). Female informants tend to report that widows manage their own property and provide for their children themselves.

This discrepancy may arise partly from the fact that, as in the case described below, a levir may be appointed by the family but have no relationship with the widow other than that of an affinal kinsman: he is a levir in name only. Nonetheless, he may be assumed by nonintimates to be performing the levir's normative role, whether or not he is actually doing so. If he is not fulfilling the formal role expectations, he is much less likely to reveal this fact to his male associates than the widow is to reveal it to her female associates. Thus the fact that levirs often do not act as levirs would become more widely known among women than among men. In general, my observations and discussions with informants lead me to believe that a brother's voice in property management is minimal unless he is also an active levir. The extent to which the widow rather than the brother manages the property, as well as the amount of help provided to a widow by a levir, is flexible and depends on individual circumstances.

Langley (1979: 73) says that "the levirate is looked upon with distaste and is resorted to only in secret." It is not my impression that this is so, except perhaps among very active Christians. It is true that the levirate is not frequently practiced. It is also true that the practice of the levirate may not be immediately obvious to the outside observer, not because there is any particular secrecy surrounding the levirate, but rather because it is treated very casually and because widows and levirs do not co-reside. However, it is viewed by most informants as the respectable and socially correct thing for a childbearing widow and her husband's brother to do.

The following case study illustrates some of the points made above.[6] I became very closely involved with the compound of Kobot Cheptarus, a woman in her mid-forties, and her 24-year-old co-wife, Milcah. Their husband, Arap Lelei, died less than a year before I met them. Kobot Cheptarus had six daughters between the ages of 7 and 23. Milcah had one 5-year-old son. Kobot Cheptarus and Arap Lelei had been friends of Milcah's parents, and according to Kobot Cheptarus it had been their joint decision to ask for Milcah in marriage. The two women subsequently developed a close relationship.

When I first met them, Milcah lamented that it was impossible for her to leave and remarry without losing custody of her child. She had had a boyfriend whom she had hoped eventually to marry before she was married to Arap Lelei, and that man was still unmarried. However, she was resigned to the fact that she could never be his wife. For his part, the former boyfriend was not prepared to resume his relationship with her, since he was courting and planning to marry another woman. I asked Kobot Cheptarus and Milcah who managed their property. Both women

---

6. I use pseudonyms in the case study to protect the anonymity of the informants.

were adamant that they did so themselves, though they acknowledged that technically the brothers of their husband, who
lived nearby, were supposed to advise them. Did they have
levirs? Milcah said the family had decided that she should be
taken over by Arap Tuwei, her husband's younger brother, who
was her senior by thirteen years. She had not yet allowed him to
approach her sexually. Kobot Cheptarus was to be taken over by
Arap Bet, the husband's older brother, Milcah said, but Kobot
Cheptarus treated this idea as a joke.

Gradually, during the time I knew the women, Milcah became
involved in a true leviratic relationship with Arap Tuwei, who
regularly spent nights with her. Affection grew between them,
and Milcah became visibly brighter and happier. Arap Tuwei
brought Milcah gifts and advised her economically, though in
the latter capacity she always seemed to rely more on Kobot
Cheptarus. At the time I left the field, Kobot Cheptarus had not
engaged in a sexual relationship with Arap Bet, and he had no
part in her economic affairs beyond giving such mutual aid as
assistance at planting and harvest, which is common among kin
and neighbors. A few years after leaving the field, I received
news that to the amazement of the community, Kobot Cheptarus
had given birth to a son. I have not been able to learn whether
Arap Bet was the genitor.

Except that Milcah and Kobot Cheptarus had separate cultivation plots, it was impossible to distinguish the house property of
one from that of the other by observation alone. The entire family, including Arap Tuwei's wife, seemed to treat the relationship
between Tuwei and Milcah as a source of pride and boasted to
me that they were doing the correct thing. Tuwei's wife told me
that Milcah exemplified a "good woman" since she had accepted
her husband's brother as levir instead of going "outside" to find a
companion.

Thus the levirate is viewed rather positively, not with distaste.
It is nevertheless uncommon in practice. What accounts for this
seemingly contradictory situation? In the first place, as I have
noted above, only young widows are good candidates for leviratic relationships, and young widowhood is not a very common
occurrence. But why is the older, more experienced, more self-
confident woman unlikely, as a widow, to engage in the levirate?

First, marriage confers upon a woman secure rights in a definite estate, and these rights are held by her independently of any ongoing relationship with a living man. A widow does not need either remarriage (which in any case is forbidden to her) or a levir to secure her property rights. Second, Nandi rules of inheritance provide that a woman's house property is inherited by her sons regardless of the identity of their genitor.[7] A child born to a married woman in Nandi cannot be illegitimate. The identity of the child's mother and her marital status are what counts.

But it is commonly argued that the levirate is not in essence an institution designed to tie a woman and her children to her dead husband's family; rather, it is an institution designed to provide for women and children. The levir has a responsibility to take care of his dead brother's dependents, who cannot get along without male assistance. Who will plow the woman's fields? Who will pay the children's school fees? For older widows, assistance in the form of labor may be provided by adult sons. Further, because of the general level of affluence, the argument that a widow must have a levir's help to meet cash needs doesn't apply to Nandi. Surplus production, not male wage labor, is the principal source of cash. Income can be used for consumption or to hire labor so that a widow does not need cash gifts or assistance that a levir might otherwise provide. A typical Nandi widow's house property is sufficient to support her and her children. Since she does not *need* a levir, a Nandi widow is freer than widows in less affluent societies to form a liaison with a man or not to wholly on the basis of her own personal preference.

It is possible that the levirate used to be more common than it is today. Before cash was readily available, widows were presumably less able to replace the labor and other kinds of assistance that it is theoretically the levir's responsibility to provide. However, it may be that widows with adult sons could always turn to them for male labor, and it is possible that there has not been a

---

7. This does not imply that the identity of the genitor of a married woman's children is irrelevant to the Nandi. A Nandi man wants to sire his wife's children and reacts negatively to the idea that another man may have done so. However, he cannot deny the child his heritage on this account. In general, the question of biological paternity seems to be a matter of less concern and intensity of feeling for Nandi than for Euro-American husband/fathers.

significant change in the incidence of the levirate. Furthermore, if the incidence of the levirate declined, the penetration of Christianity may also have had an impact. Most of the Christian denominations active in Nandi disapprove of the levirate and teach that—despite the Nandi prohibition—widows should be free to remarry. But hardly any widows, Christian or not, remarry, and not all Christian widows abstain from the levirate. I have no data that can answer the question whether the levirate was indeed more common one or two generations ago than it is now.

## Conclusion

Though a Nandi widow's behavior is constrained in some ways, it is quite unconstrained in others. A Nandi widow is not free to remarry. She is not free to leave her husband's family and take her minor children with her. However, she *is* free to hold and manage her own property. The economic security such a woman typically enjoys gives her freedom not to form a liaison with a man, if that is her wish. She is free, if she does choose to form such a liaison, to exercise her personal preference. Because the local community is not agnatically structured, a widow's lover is unlikely to be an agnate of her late husband; lovers are not levirs.

I would suggest that it is precisely because of the constraints imposed upon women's marital choices that they are able, as widows, to enjoy the freedoms cited above. The Nandi widow's freedom of choice and action has its basis in a secure and indissoluble relation to property. The house-property system as practiced in Nandi, conferring a permanent estate on a wife, goes hand in hand with indissoluble marriage. The severe constraints on Nandi widows in exercising certain options, and the unusual autonomy they enjoy in other spheres, are best viewed as two sides of the same coin.

# Some East African Widows

### CHRISTINE OBBO

WIDOWS IN EAST AFRICA experience a number of difficulties in dealing with in-laws' attempts to acquire control over their property and their persons, in managing grief, and in coping with mistreatment. Although societal ideologies—particularly as reflected in family and marriage laws, resource distribution, and public stereotypes—usually constrain the latitude of an individual's decision making and actions, widows from groups with differing social systems often encounter similar problems. How widows adjust to the husbandless status may be as much a function of their personalities as of differences in societal ideologies.

The position taken in this paper is that widows are actors who calculate the risks and benefits involved in the options they choose or create within their own societies (Barth 1966). Rules of marriage that regulate the affiliation and inheritance of children and the marital status of widows are property relations. Women who take control over resources are also able to make decisions about their own persons, but the options of resourceless women are limited.

### "Wives of the Grave" and Survivors of Dead Men

In the Nilotic world, a woman is in theory usually married to the men of a lineage in perpetuity, so that the union continues

The material on which this paper is based was collected in 1974, 1977, 1979, and 1980, and covers the lives of rural, urban, and elite women. My earlier work (1971-73) among low-income urban migrants in Kampala, Uganda, included four widows in a sample of 200. However, there were 11 widows in a sample drawn from the rural end of the migration process in the Buganda Province of Uganda, and the Machakos and East Kano districts of Kenya. In this paper one widow is reported on from the urban samples, and four widows from the rural samples.

after her original partner is in the grave. She may be his widow, but she is still "a wife of the grave" (*chi liel*)[1] and a wife of her dead husband's agnates, who may cohabit with her and continue to beget his children. In the Bantu world, by contrast, widows are not wives of the grave but survivors of dead men in a different sense: the children they bear to those men who cohabit with them belong to those genitors and not to the deceased.

In all African systems, the social networks continue in some form after the death of a spouse. But it is usually the widow, not the widower, who visits the sick and attends weddings and burials at the home of the in-laws. This is particularly so in patrilineal societies, where descent and access to the principal societal resources are reckoned through men. Expectations about the nature of the widow's involvement with in-laws differ in kind and degree, depending on whether the physical father (genitor) or the social father (pater) is regarded as paramount. In other words, the ideological elaborations concerning the filiation of children do constrain the rights and choices of widows when it comes to questions of remarriage.

My data suggest that where the importance of the genitor is stressed, the widow seems free to remain a widow or to remarry a man from any social grouping; when the pater or jural father is emphasized, the widow is expected to be inherited by a levir, i.e. a brother or close male relative of the deceased. The distinction between these differing expectations is explained by the fol-

1. There is no counterpart in the form of "husband of the grave." The Luo, Akamba, and Nuer systems would have coped, without too much fuss, with the paternity problem recently raised by a 23-year-old French woman, Corinne Parpalaix. According to newswire reports (see *Newsweek*, July 16, 1984), Alain Parpalaix, fearing that chemotherapy for testicular cancer might make him sterile, deposited his semen with the Center for the Study and Conservation of Sperm (CECOS) before undergoing the treatment. He died two days after marrying Corinne, who a few months later brought a lawsuit that involved CECOS and the Ministry of Health and precipitated a national debate. The CECOS lawyer insisted at the trial that "if cadavers cannot be inherited, sperm shouldn't be inherited either." But Corinne's lawyer retorted, "Just because the father is not seen does not mean that he is absent." The Appeals Court overruled the lower court, avoided the inheritance and legal issues, and allowed Corinne to inherit the sperm. "I will be able to realize my most cherished dream to have my husband's baby" ("MacNeil-Lehrer Report," Aug. 1, 1984). She failed to conceive after several inseminations.

lowing emic theories regarding children. Theories emphasizing genitorial rights argue that "It is bad to exile a man's blood; and supernatural consequences befall women who refuse to acknowledge the genitor of their children." The case for social fatherhood, on the other hand, is linked with bridewealth, which gives a man rights to a woman's sexual and childbearing capacities. Upon his death these rights are passed on to his "brother," which ensures first that the bridewealth is protected, second that the widow and children are secure under a male guardian, and third that their identity as a household unit is protected.

These theories are found in both agriculturalist and pastoralist societies. Whether the theories are contradicted in practice depends both on the widow's personal characteristics, such as age, hard work, and shrewdness—which can be used to defy societal rules or create nonthreatening options—and on the extent of penetration by the capitalist economy. For instance, women can use their labor to earn income. Women in cash-cropping areas fare better in this respect than those who depend on the sale of food surpluses. The money so obtained can be used to acquire land or to attract dependents.

Apart from Kirwen's study (1979), which treated widows as a central theme,[2] widows have received little attention in African scholarship. There are scattered references to them, but much of the literature focuses on norms, and little mention is made of actual practice. The following review of the literature dealing with widows suggests the background against which this paper should be viewed.

In a classic study based on research on the Nilotic-speaking Nuer of the Sudan in the late 1930's, E. E. Evans-Pritchard (1945) described not only the types of marriage but the choices available to widows. Relevant to this paper is the leviratic marriage. If a man died the union was not regarded as broken; the wife was inherited by "one of her husbands," i.e. husband's near kinsmen, and continued to bear children for the dead man (ibid.: 13). Apparently her production and reproduction were exchanged for bridewealth. In fact, Nuer never referred to the leviratic

2. In the study the perspectives of widows are not elaborated, but men restated the societal ideologies pertaining to widows.

union as a remarriage, but as a continuation of a marriage. Evans-Pritchard treated the union as a marriage because the levir had legal rights by virtue of the bridewealth to which the brothers had contributed, at least in theory and occasionally in practice. He could divorce her, or sue any man who had relations with her while she lived with him (ibid.). Leviratic unions gave marriage stability and durability according to Nuer theories. A widow, particularly a young one of childbearing age, was expected on threat of divorce to bow to tradition and cohabit with her husband's brother or one of his sons by another wife.

The leviratic theory implied that fathers, brothers, or guardians and husbands had great control over women, but this was contradicted by practice. Brothers apparently had little control over widows, and many widows in fact did not live with kinsmen of their dead husband (ibid.: 16). If a dead man had no brothers, a young widow could take a lover from an unrelated or distantly related lineage (ibid.: 15). Among the Eastern Nuer, at her husband's mortuary ceremony a widow could declare her unwillingness to live with one of the kinsmen. In that case, she was persuaded to accept the leviratic arrangement but not threatened with the sanction of divorce for failing to do so. If she decided to become a (widow) concubine, she was said to "give birth in the bush," but the children belonged to the dead husband.

Eventually, as they grew old, some widows apparently returned to live with their husbands' people (ibid.: 16). Among the Nilotic-speaking Luo of western Kenya, a widow who decided to marry a man who was not agnatically related to her husband was and still is frowned upon. Although it was possible to sue for a return of bridewealth, legal recourse was not often taken, according to John Ndisi (1973: 82) because it was hoped that the widow would eventually return and marry a close relative of the dead husband. Among the Western Nuer, a woman who had only one child or no children would be pressured by the dead man's kinsmen to live with them. If she refused, they might reclaim their bridewealth, i.e. divorce her. If she had one child, six head of cattle were left with her parents to ensure the affiliation of the child with the patrilineage. But if she had two or more children before her husband died, his people could not demand the return of their bridewealth cattle even if she refused to live with one of his brothers (Evans-Pritchard, 1945: 16). This suggests that the options available to Nuer women often contradicted the ideology.

Writing about the Bantu-speaking Akamba of central Kenya, Joseph Muthiani (1977: 34-35) argued that the levirate as an institution protected the bridewealth exchanged between clans, ensured the retention of friendly social relations between the man's and the woman's families, and was a good assurance for the security of the children and the widow. Muthiani asserted that the social status of a wife did not change when she was widowed, for a woman's status derived from motherhood (ibid.: 36). Muthiani was more interested in the institutional expectations than the widow's concerns, but apparently the leviratic practice was one cause of polygyny. Young men married to old widows could always take a younger girl as a second wife or as the wife (ibid.). One suspects that the life of a widow married to a young man was precarious. During my fieldwork I came across cases of Akamba women who had established themselves as independent householders. These women could achieve social fatherhood by marrying wives to bear them children, whether or not they themselves already had children (ibid.: 37).[3] It seemed that the widows in these situations had opted not to become involved in leviratic unions.

The rationalization of the leviratic institution among the Nuer, the Akamba, and the Luo rested upon the premise that death does not dissolve a marriage (Ocholla-Ayayo 1976: 144; Ndisi 1973: 82). A wife remained the legal wife of the dead man, and a caretaker in the person of a real or classificatory brother ensured that his name lived on by looking after the children and begetting more (Ocholla-Ayayo 1976: 144).

The only work that systematically treats widows as a central theme and not merely under headings such as death or marriage is that of Michael Kirwen (1979). He studied the position of the Catholic church on the issue of widows in four adjacent societies in Tanzania that had different rules regarding widows. He found

3. See also Oboler (this volume) for comparable data from Nandi, where widows and other childless women also become female husbands.

that the Bantu-speaking matrilineal Kwaya, who reckoned descent through women, allowed widows the choice of remarrying, remaining single, or living under a leviratic union (1974: 49). The Bantu-speaking patrilineal Sukuma respondents told Kirwen that the widow is free to marry, but the patrilineal Nilotic-speaking Luo and patrilineal Bantu-speaking Kuria stressed that widows could not remarry because "a wife of bridewealth is a wife of a lineage and is cared for by her brother-in-law. Further, those who remarry are like prostitutes" (ibid.). In 1974 I found that among the Luo the stereotyping as "prostitutes" of widows who remarried meant labeling them bad mothers who would abandon their young children without sustenance and jeopardize their grown-up children's inheritance. Consequently, some informants stressed, most widows "stayed married because of their children." Others attributed widows' behavior to the effectiveness of the sanctions against divorce or remarriage outside the dead husband's lineage.

Besides being regarded as a disloyal wife and a bad mother by her husband's people, a divorced widow, like other divorced women, suffered loss of esteem in her natal family. She was forced to keep a low profile as a disgraced daughter and sister responsible for the loss of bridewealth—which had to be returned to her husband's people. Her brothers and father were likely to be more tolerant if it could be ascertained that the bridewealth had been cancelled by the number of children the widow had born for the lineage. Most women did not have the stamina to endure such an onus in the community, so they stayed married.[4] In theory the ideology of inheritance ensured that sons received property, particularly land, through the house property complex, i.e., through mothers who constituted the subunits of the polygynous household. However, women's fears that competition from co-wives or half brothers might jeopardize that in-

4. Potash (1978), in her analysis of marital stability in another Luo community, found that few women, including widows, actually leave once they have had children; 79.7 percent of all marriages remained intact. The factors affecting marital stability—ties to children, the lack of residential alternatives, the reluctance of a woman's kin to have her return, and her reputation—are similar to those reported here. Potash also discussed some of the complexities and uncertainties regarding the return of bridewealth, which she found less important as an incentive to maintaining a marriage.

heritance seemed to be an effective deterrent to divorce. Both male and female informants stress that except in the cases of very stupid women, "ultimately no mother wants to dispossess her children."

Among the Nuer, the Akamba, and the Luo, wives and mothers acquired usufructuary rights in land, which enabled them to grow food and feed their families. This gave women an important role not only as food producers but as managers of food consumption. Fearn (1961) has suggested that one of the reasons cotton failed to become a successful cash crop in Nyanza at the beginning of the century was that women did not consider it beneficial. Instead, some Luo women became successful traders in East African urban centers, where they specialized in food produce. Even those who stayed permanently in the rural areas acquired incomes by selling peanuts, ghee, and eggs. Thus, if Luo women could not own land in their own right, they could nonetheless obtain maximum benefit by exploiting fully their ascribed access guaranteeing their usufructuary rights.

The Bantu-speaking, patrilineal, cattle-herding Hima of western Uganda, however, had a system that excluded women from economically productive labor and thus deprived them of resources and surplus. The women did not even have usufructuary rights to cattle (Elam 1973: 16-21, 47-52). Herding, milking and watering cattle, collecting firewood, drawing water, and sweeping the dung from the yard were men's work. The division of labor between the sexes strictly confined married women— wives and daughters-in-law—to those activities related to food processing, housekeeping, and feeding calves. The father retained legal power over all his herd throughout his lifetime, and sons had to accept his authority, since he could disinherit any who deserted his home or otherwise disobeyed or mistreated him. Even after marriage a son depended on the father, who had to authorize the use of milk to feed his son's wife and children. The only apparent control a man whose father was still living enjoyed was that over his wife's sexual and reproductive rights.[5] But even these rights were acquired for him by the father who had given the bridewealth cattle to the wife's father or guardian.

5. According to Elam, the brothers and age-mates had access to the sexual favors of each other's wives. This practice was sanctioned by custom, but it is not clear how the women viewed it.

Hima women were completely excluded from exploiting societal resources. When they became widowed they had to depend on the charity of their sons. The Hima use a different rationalization for discouraging widows from marrying outside the husband's lineage. To the Hima, such outmarriages jeopardized the sons' inheritance, which passes through women through the house-property complex. The propertyless widow was free to leave or to depend on her grown-up children. Widows with small children presumably continued to depend on the father-in-law, or on brothers-in-law if he were dead.

Among the Bantu-speaking Ganda, by contrast, I found that widows could inherit property from their husbands and thus had some control over resources. They usually continued to participate in the important ceremonies and life crisis rituals of their deceased husband's clan, but this was voluntary. Widows were free to remain single, to remarry, or to live with whomever they pleased. The children belonged to the genitor, on whom they depended for their patrimony.

Thus there are considerable differences in systems of kinship and marriage and in patterns of economic organization in East Africa. Yet the widows in my sample, who come from a variety of societies, encountered certain similar problems. In group after group I was told that the widow must be vigilant and resourceful to protect herself against harsh treatment and to retain control over her resources. Alternative ways of mitigating the situation were rural-rural or rural-urban migration and inter-ethnic marriages. The following case studies report widows' accounts of their own problems and indicate how they view their situation. Such reports contrast with the literature described above, in which the women's point of view is muted. These case studies highlight such issues as handling grief, dealing with affines (in the Nilotic system), and coping with mistreatment generally.

## Handling Grief

The four case studies below illustrate the vulnerability of the widows as they adjust to the death of their husbands. Friends, acquaintances, relatives, or lovers may exploit a widow at this stage. Some widows may also decide to remarry (according to societal prescriptions) soon after they become bereaved because they are afraid to live alone or to be stereotyped as single women, a label that implies promiscuity and immorality.

*Case Study I: Grieving widows are vulnerable.* Gutabingi was an unschooled wife of a Ganda primary school teacher. She managed their banana and coffee farm in a rural area in the Buganda district of Uganda. In 1979 her husband was killed by thieves who raided their house. She, having barely escaped, was full of remorse for months afterward. She kept asking, "Why didn't I die too? Why didn't I die instead of him?" She continued to prepare her husband's favorite dishes, to wash and iron his clothes, to tidy his books. Her four sisters and two daughters visited her regularly, but they had their own homes to look after. Two distant relatives and two of the relatives' friends came to stay with her. She appreciated their concern. Before long she became totally dependent upon their companionship and company.

As her neighbors and her daughters saw it, she virtually became their slave, growing food, cooking, and fetching water for them. She grumbled privately but was afraid to say anything to them. It was the daughters, not the freeloading relatives, who repaired the animal houses and cut the hedge. She kept saying, "I miss having a man around. My husband used to get things done." Gutabingi became very thin. She used to suffer from headaches even when her husband was alive, but during this period the attacks became much more frequent. It seemed as if she could not deal effectively with anything: the younger children's disobedience, the freeloading relatives, and the attitude of the men in the village, who when visiting her home would refuse to be served by her son because they wanted her to serve them on her knees. This is one example of the problems of adjustment to the initial stages of widowhood: grief, guilt, and inability to cope with all the maintenance chores of the homestead and the vulnerability of widows.

*Case Study II: Grieving widows behave in unexpected ways.* Mary was a senior Ugandan civil servant in the Ministry of Education. When her husband, John, died mysteriously during a business trip abroad, she tried to deal with her suffering by burying herself in her work. She also had three very young children to care for. Whenever she was not working or taking her children to school, she would sit in a dark room and brood. She resented socializing because seeing and watching other couples made her cry. Two years after her husband's death she married one of her colleagues. Although Mary's previous marriage had been interethnic, her friends were surprised because her new husband came from an ethnic group generally disdained by the Ganda, Mary's ethnic group. She explained her emancipation from ethnic chauvinism to her friends by declaring that love had triumphed over her ethnic biases. "I'm tired of living alone, coping alone. I need a man to help me out, and to love and guide my children." These sentiments were often exploited by some unscrupulous men.

*Case Study III: Grieving widows find themselves in liaisons with unscrupulous men.* Nancy, an Acholi woman, had been a nurse before she married Paul, a career civil servant. He had started as a clerk in the colonial government and became a department head with the coming of independence. He had read about and indeed adopted the methods termed "progressive" by colonial extension officers. As time went on, he invested in land and then in cattle and a contraption for making jaggery (crude sugar), an important component in the brew distilled into local gin. Meanwhile he had sent his unschooled wife of fifteen years, a mother of six children, back to the village, because he wanted to marry Nancy, who was already the mother of his two children. Nancy was persuaded to agree to the marriage. Then he asked her to stop working because he was capable of keeping her like a Victorian lady married to a man of means. (This imported notion was often invoked by Ugandan men who argued that they could afford to support their wives. However, the women knew that men did not want their wives to work for fear that they would become financially independent and difficult to control.)

Paul brought a distant male relative from his village to work as foreman, supervising the five laborers who maintained the estate. Nancy was chauffeured anywhere she wanted to go. Sometimes she accompanied her husband abroad and shopped in expensive stores in New York, Paris, and London. Then, in the mid-1970's, her husband disappeared and was rumored to have been killed by government agents. The foreman offered her consolation and very soon they became lovers. Her in-laws protested, but she was deaf to anything they said. Before the year was over, the laborers had quit, the cows were producing very little milk, and the jaggery machine and the cars were in disrepair. The foreman offered to buy them, but she told him to take them because they were not functioning anyway. Meanwhile the foreman had bought five acres of land nearby and was pressuring Nancy to marry him. By the time she had taken stock of herself and realized he was not interested in her, most of her wealth was gone. She did not have enough money to pay school fees for the three children, who were studying in Europe. The children were taken in by former friends of her husband, who eventually helped them obtain American scholarships to complete their education. Nancy was the laughingstock of her friends and neighbors, but she managed to pull herself together and return to her nursing profession.

*Case Study IV: Grieving widows easily decide to observe customs.* When Jane, an elite Luo woman, lost her high-powered, womanizing husband of fifteen years, she agreed to accept as a levir his brother, who already had two wives. Her elite friends, Luo and non-Luo, raised eyebrows, because in her role as guardian to her two children, as well as in her own right, she controlled houses and land as well as businesses in Nairobi. She let her brother and sister stay in her house while she moved to her new "husband's" house in the same prestigious neighborhood. The non-elite Luo, who had apparently applauded Jane for her observance of the valued tradition by allowing herself to be inherited through the levirate, were appalled when her husband "deported" his first two wives to the village because they were less sophisticated and had had little schooling.

Jane may have accepted this relationship for a complex of reasons; let us attempt a sketch. During the husband's lifetime, Jane had asserted her sexual independence to counteract her husband's philandering. When he died, however, people were willing to overlook his sexual promiscuity, but they gossiped behind her back and speculated on what she would do now that she was free. She realized that the gossip would be ruinous to her and the children. She put a stop to it by her acceptance of the leviratic institution. Although Jane could have chosen one of her unmarried admirers, she maintained that she had been in love with her brother-in-law for many years, and besides, that she was not the first educated woman to opt for a leviratic union. She pointed out that she personally knew several women, the first university-educated women, who had done the same.

One of Jane's close friends was a Luyia who initially had found it difficult to marry because she encouraged her father (who probably did not need persuading) to demand what most people regarded as the highest bridewealth in the district. Anyhow, she had married a university-trained secondary school teacher who had managed to pay the bridewealth in installments over a period of ten years. After they had been married for fourteen years her husband died and she chose to be inherited by her brother-in-law, an American-trained engineer. He was apparently "too dull in appearance and manners to attract women" and had given up searching for a wife. Family members and friends were relieved at the leviratic union that "killed three birds with one stone." A woman who would have been difficult to court was paired off with a man who had been a failure at courting, and the bridewealth plus children were protected.

After five years of marriage, Jane divorced her leviratic husband, to the relief of all her friends, who had predicted all along that she would "overcome her silliness."

Widows in East Africa react to the tragedy of losing their husbands and adjust to widowhood in different ways. They brood with anger and guilt over being the survivor. They are grateful to anyone who offers sympathy, but often they are too involved in their grief to distinguish true friendship from sycophancy. Widows miss male companionship as well as general help with the chores connected with maintaining the homestead. These findings are similar to those reported by Peter Marris in his London study (1958). He found in East London that widowhood impoverished social life (1958: 127), and that some widows were driven to suicide by loneliness (ibid: 65). Many remarried because "you can't live with the dead" (ibid: 51)—that is, the dead make poor companions.

## "Wives of the Grave" Dealing with Affines

In many ethnic groups widows have to observe mortuary etiquette and taboos such as wailing, fasting, and shaving the head or leaving hair uncombed. Sometimes there may be arguments about the heir and the deceased's estate that bring the widow and her affines into conflict. This section highlights the perennial problems relating to in-laws' demands for access to the widow's labor, her sexual and reproductive services, and other resources perceived as being part of her husband's estate within the Nilotic "wives of the grave" system. The first of the case studies below shows a widow able to defy the demands of her affines because she is not of the same ethnic group. In the second, because she was of the same ethnic group, the widow had to escape and abandon everything to a levir, but her children later dispossessed him.

*Case Study V: An urban woman copes with foreign in-laws.* Okwaro had come to Kampala, Uganda, at age 14 and stayed until he died at 49. He rarely visited his village in the Kano district of western Kenya. His Luo relatives believed he was "lost to the city," a belief that was strengthened when instead of marrying a Luo woman he wed a Hima, from the Ankole people of western Uganda. By this time he owned a shop, which he had opened with savings from his previous employment as a carpenter's apprentice and baker's assistant.

When Okwaro died, the Luo Union of Namuwongo (the low-income suburb where he had lived and worked) collected money to buy a coffin and to send his body back to his village. His widow accompanied the body and fulfilled the expected mortuary rituals, but as she was planning to depart, her in-laws suggested that she might want to leave the two girls and three boys behind. When she refused, they suggested that one of the male relatives go with her and help run the shop. She hoped to stop the discussion by saying that she would probably have to sell everything and close the shop to pay the funeral expenses. This was incomprehensible to the in-laws. They cursed her and raved that their brother should not have married a foreigner, that she deprived them not only of control of his children, but of his wealth as well. As a parting shot, some of the in-laws said they would visit her regularly to ensure that she was bringing up the children as true Luo. In fact, six years after these discussions she continued to welcome her in-laws into her home when they visited Kampala, but she made it clear that they stayed at her pleasure. Some of the in-laws wanted to assist her in operating the shop, but she soon learned that they were much more interested in stealing from her than in helping.

*Case Study VI: A widow is dispossessed and then vindicated.* Apio, an Adhola woman, was born in Mulanda, a county in the Eastern Province of Uganda. At age 18, she married a Teso man and migrated with him to the Buganda Province of Uganda. This was during the 1940's. They settled in a village in Bulemezi, a county populated by migrants from many other parts of Uganda. Almost one-third of the settlers were from Apio's home area. Several relatives joined them over the years.

Apio had four children, three boys and a girl. She and her husband were happy and prosperous. A few days before Apio's 34th birthday her husband died. Her unmarried and seemingly unassuming 25-year-old brother-in-law, who had been living with them, assured everyone at the funeral that he would look after their brother's wife. In effect, he was telling all present that he would assume the role of a levir and live with his brother's widow, as was the accepted custom. After the funeral the husband's relatives emptied the house of belongings and departed for their homes. It was socially accepted that these things belong to the dead husband, and they had a right to take them. Apio's sister had to bring chairs, utensils, and bedding so that Apio would "not sleep blanketless on the floor or have to borrow cooking pots."

Three years later the "unassuming" poor brother-in-law she had allowed to cohabit with her showed no signs of finding a place of his own. Apio knew that her husband had told all the relatives that if anything ever happened to him, she was to be the guardian of the land for their two sons. However, the cohabiting brother-in-law had other designs. He had found himself a wife and planned to bring her to stay in Apio's house. Apio felt that this was not proper. She convened a meeting of three male in-laws, who lived nearby. They agreed with her and suggested that her brother-in-law construct his own house. But the brother-in-law felt that Apio should move out of the big house into a room attached to the kitchen. The relatives told him that it would be wrong. He began drinking and beating Apio, and within six months his constant beatings became so severe that she had to be hospitalized.

Apio's sister and the sister's husband, Okello, decided to invite her to come and stay with them. She was reluctant at first because moving away would mean that her brother-in-law had succeeded in driving her away from her home and children. She agreed to come for a visit. Her relatives worked hard to make her see that her life was more valuable than property. They argued, "He is not your husband, but you cook for him. He cheats you out of coffee and cotton sales, although you grow it. Would you not like to find a job and be independent?" She agreed. "I was the wife of a dead man who could not fight back. I had no rights as long as this was my identity."

Apio stayed with her sister, but every morning she went to work as a cook for a retired Ganda teacher. His wife was busy running a shop, and their three grown children lived in the capital. Before the year was over, Apio was expecting her employer's child. Her sister thought this scandalous. Apio gave birth to a beautiful baby boy who was "the real picture of the boss." It was even more scandalous when the boss abandoned his home of many years and moved ten miles away to live with Apio on a plot of land by Lake Victoria. According to Apio's sister, they "lived happily on bananas and fish." The child was named Ochieng, which means someone born when the sun (chieng) is shining, i.e. during the day. Since her son was born at night, he should have been called Owori, but according to Apio the baby was the sun of her life. The child was also given a Ganda name, Mukasa.

When her "husband" died ten years later, Apio was left a "widow" again. But this time widowhood carried a status of respect. Her "husband" had left the lakeshore plot of land as "a gift in her name." She had occupier rights over the land and she was happy. Her sister and brother, whose marriages had failed, came to live with her. Significantly, the children by her first marriage were regular visitors. In 1980, Ochieng was twenty years old. She told her sisters and nieces that having him brought sunshine into her life and stopped her from going crazy thinking about the children she had once been forced to abandon.

As for the brother-in-law, he developed epilepsy and his wife deserted him, taking their two children with her. He was unable to claim them back because, apart from entertaining his in-laws at Apio's expense, he had never managed to accumulate sufficient bridewealth (three cows and 500 shillings) to enable him to claim social fatherhood. He sent desperate messages asking Apio to come back to him, but it was too late. Those connected with the case felt that his dead brother was punishing him for mistreating "his (widow) wife." Apio's three sons, with a little help from some paternal uncles, eventually managed to kick him off their land.

In Case Studies V and VI, custom dictated that the marriages did not end with the death of the husband. The relatives wanted to ensure that the children and property remained under clan control. Consequently, the widows were expected to live under the leviratic union with one of the dead husband's relatives. In Case Study V there were no problems. The Hima woman was non-Luo and the wealth Okwaro had accumulated in the city was not really part of the relatives' patrimony. She refused to bow to custom. But if she had married a Hima man, the same issues would have come up. Hima women in the rural areas must accept the protection of a man because they are not allowed to own the major resource, cattle. In this instance migration and settlement not only provided an opportunity for interethnic marriage, but also distanced relatives from the assets and thereby saved the widow from being propertyless.

Apio accepted the leviratic union, but she was abused. Some women, however, do seem to live happily under the system. A few women even use it to gain respectability, as Case Study IV showed. The levir is under moral obligation to maintain the homestead by helping with tilling of the land and repairing the house. But if a man has a family of his own, he may be too busy to care for the widow properly. The neglected widow, who then has to rely on children and other relatives, usually accuses the levir of irresponsibility. When neglect occurs, the women most affected are those with very small children or older women with no sons or no children. Apio got out of the predicament, first by going to stay with her sister, then by seeking wage employment, and finally by marrying a man from a group that did not practice the levirate.

Basically, the levirate as an institution stipulates that a deceased husband's relatives continue the control he exercised over his wife's production (labor) and reproduction (children). Women can reject this by stepping outside their groups, either by marrying foreigners or migrating to the urban areas. In this way, if they so wish, women can take control of their life situation, for better or worse.

## Coping with Mistreatment

The following section illustrates what happens to some widows after they have grieved, and after they have dealt with the in-laws and established effective access to or control over resources. It seems that sheer determination, hard work, and resourcefulness make a difference in a widow's life and may be important tools in coping with mistreatment by relatives and other members of one's society.

*Case Study VII: A widow needs management skills and a host of dependents.* Anyango, an Adhola woman, was in her mid-sixties and lived as an independent householder in the Bukedi District of eastern Uganda. She had been a shy bride who used to hide in order to have a puff at a cigarette. Ogola, her husband, a clerk in the colonial administration, spent the first two years of their marriage weaning her away from the habit. On one occasion he was even prepared to beat her to stop her behaving like "pagan" women. She gave up smoking, but not before he promised that he would never beat her again.

Ogola was successful at work and received rapid promotions. The household expanded as relatives came to stay with Ogola and Anyango. All in all, there were twenty relatives who helped Anyango with baby-sitting and garden work. Anyango's whole life-style changed. She no longer worked in the garden, fetched water, or collected and chopped firewood. Her energies became focused instead on bearing children, administering the household, and entertaining neighbors and friends who dropped in daily. The relatives who came to stay were unmarried young men and women who expected to be sent to school or paid off with a spouse whose future seemed promising.

Anyango became a powerful homemaker and estate manager. The local hangers-on, accustomed to her hospitality, resented her relatives who ate the food that would otherwise have gone to them. They still ate, but the increase in numbers meant that each person got a smaller amount. Her husband, who was busy "working for the government," saw her as a good wife and mother. Other women envied her because her husband left her a wide latitude in decision making, particularly when it came to the spending of money. She supervised her children's and dependents' affairs with regard to health, clothing, schooling, and of course discipline and nourishment.

When her husband died suddenly after a short illness, one of the first things Anyango did was to lock up all the valuables in one room (chairs, pictures, china, clothing, and the like). The result was some lengthy and at times acrimonious speeches at the funeral. Funeral speeches are a socially accepted means of publicly expressing disagreement and anger and of exerting pressure on others. The husband's brothers, some of whom had never been close to him, demanded to see what was in the locked room. Anyango's friends and relatives whispered that her husband had told her for many years to do what she had done; Ogola had felt it would not be right for his relatives to take everything and leave his family—his wife and twelve children—to starve.

The heated discussions continued after the funeral, when the family met to hear the will. The brothers and relatives wanted to share in the life insurance money, but Ogola had stipulated that the money be used to educate his children and to ensure that his widow lived decently and was economically independent of his relatives. Ogola's relatives blamed Anyango and considered her responsible for the will. Furthermore, they said that the older children, who held good jobs, should educate the younger children. Some even claimed that Ogola had appropriated more lineage land than was his share. In fact, Ogola had bought their so-called wastelands from neighbouring clans. The sellers had either wanted to tide themselves over financially or planned to migrate to the urban areas. None of the land had ever belonged to the relatives who were complaining. During the following months some of Ogola's cows and goats were stolen. Everyone suspected that the brothers who had made the fuss were responsible. However, when some of the brothers tried to appropriate land by extending their gardens, Anyango took them to court. By this time she enjoyed even greater respect in the community as patron of a large clientele. She won the case and the in-laws never bothered her again.

Case Study VIII: "A widow must be taught to escape harsh treatment." Nalumansi was the third wife of an important Ganda chief, and when he died she inherited about sixteen acres of land in Kyagwe county, in the Buganda Province of Uganda. She had three very young children, two girls and a boy. The husband had stipulated that at least five acres were for the women (the mother and the daughters) and the remainder were for the boy, who was the heir. Nalumansi had two sisters and no brother. "This, of course, is a tragedy. Everyone must have a brother, because people listen to men," according to Nalumansi.

Shortly after her husband died, two tenants, who occupied about three acres each, began to encroach upon land bordering the plots in which, for a yearly rental fee of ten shillings, they had rights of occupancy (bibanja). She tried to persuade them not to extend their boundaries any further, but "they thought they could browbeat me because I am a woman," she said. Over the years Nalumansi was in and out of court over the land disputes with these two tenants. When her son attained social adulthood at eighteen, he demanded to be shown his share of the land. Within five years he had sold about three-quarters of the land, using the money for drinking with his friends. He had married a local beauty who resented the fact that Nalumansi constantly reproached her husband for wasting his patrimony. Mother and daughter-in-law became enemies. When the daughter-in-law had a difficult birth that left her slightly crippled in one leg, she blamed Nalumansi, whose midwifery skills and herbal medical knowledge were unequaled by anyone in the subcounty (Gombolola).

The tenants she had taken to court were only too happy to pass on an elaborated version of how Nalumansi was a witch. Mothers warned their children not to pick any fruit from Nalumansi's garden, which was near the road and seemed to have an abundance of mangoes, lemons, oranges, guavas, pineapples, and avocados. Children were told that it was better to go home wet than to stop at Nalumansi's home when it rained. Some children ignored their parents' advice and would stop at Nalumansi's and ask her for fruit to take to school, or they would stop at her place when it rained. These children at first acted secretly, but as years went by they convinced their parents that Nalumansi was quite harmless. Nalumansi's reputation for being a witch persisted, however, and was not helped by the fact that she had a chronic cough and, when she visited the neighbors, insisted on drinking tea or beer in a mug she carried with her and eating from roasted banana leaves instead of plates.

In 1980 Nalumansi was in her mid-eighties and had been reconciled with her son, a trucker who drove between Kampala and Mombasa. The relationship with her daughter-in-law was still lukewarm, but the grandchildren thought she was marvelous. Villagers regarded her as a benign witch. Some saw her as a nuisance because of her insistence that the people who worked for her earn every cent and because she required tenants to observe the land boundaries. She was nevertheless greatly respected, because no one else was as old as she—at least when her age was measured by the three sets of grandchildren she had. She thus had several honorific titles: *Namwandu* (widow), *Nakasatwe* (great-great-great grandmother), and *Jjaja* (grandmother). This last was also a respectful alternative to addressing an elderly person by name or as an old man or woman (*omussajja* or *omukazzi omukadde*). I was told repeatedly by the people in the village that they owed her respect. After all, the distinguished midwife had helped deliver most of them.

Although Nalumansi was not as strong as she used to be, in 1980 she still made rounds to see what was happening to her land. One day she found that someone had left some sorcery medicine (*eddogo*) in her potato patch. She was frightened, but she threw the medicine in the bush. The next time she went to dig her potatoes someone attacked her from behind with a stone. On the way to the hospital she murmured his name, and a few days later the villagers hounded him out of the village. He was one of the two butchers among the four shop owners, but it did not matter. In this case respect for age took precedence over other considerations. Even people who hated Nalumansi admired her courage, resilience, and persistence. She was "tougher than any man," according to the men of the village.

These two case studies show that widows not only need resources, but also must be shrewd and not easily intimidated. The two women's principal resource was land, and it is clear that a change from a system of communal land rights to individualized rights does benefit women. Both women were bequeathed the land by their husbands.

In the case of Anyango, the arguments used by the brothers-in-law reflected a cherished but outmoded ideal and practice. Land in Padhola had become more individualized in the last 50 years as cotton cultivation became a way of getting cash. Although there is no tradition of women landowners, some widows, like Anyango, gained ownership rights to land because their husbands insist on it—either in a will or on their deathbed. Even so, the relatives gave Anyango a hard time and continued to refer to her land as belonging to their brother. Typically, a widow has no say in resource management; the brothers have a right to everything from the moment of her husband's death. Anyango, therefore, was hardly a typical widow, and her powerful position was fortified by her husband's actions. However, if a husband is not "enlightened" enough to leave a will or to have trustworthy guardians for his family, the widow does indeed suffer at the hands of her husband's people. She may, like other married women, continue to enjoy usufructuary rights over land by virtue of being a mother and wife, but she has no say in what ultimately happens to the land.

The case of Nalumansi highlights some interesting aspects of land tenure in Buganda Province and shows the constant irritations endured by landowners in general and women landowners in particular. Many widowed informants insist that "a widow cannot escape harsh treatment but has to be strong—particularly if she has property such as land." Although Nalumansi was poor, she was a representative of a class of privileged women associated with powerful men. She had benefited from the individualized land tenure system introduced in Buganda in 1900.[6]

Ganda women are obsessed with "owning land," and in both rural and urban areas land is the most common investment venture. Women acquire occupier rights[7] by paying cash or by inheriting rights from mothers, from paternal or maternal grandmothers, or as gifts from their husbands. A daughter can also

6. For details of the Uganda Agreement, see Low 1971.
7. This was legislated by the Busulu and Envujjo Law, 1927. For a detailed presentation, see Mukwaya 1953.

inherit land if a father (landlord or peasant with occupier rights) has no sons, or if the only son is mentally unstable or irresponsible, or if the father either has no brothers or does not get on with his brothers or is not particularly fond of his sisters' male children.

Nalumansi did not remarry because, in her words, "Having lived at court, I could not bring myself to accept the peasant ways (*amaalo*) of most men here." There was really no pressure for her to remarry. She had land and children. Moreover, widowhood (*obwanamwandu*) is prestigious for women who have land in their own right or who wish to emphasize their Christian leanings. The title *Namwandu* (widow) so-and-so is rivaled only by *Mukyala* (Mrs.) so-and-so. It seems to emphasize, "I was once a respected married woman and although my husband is no longer alive, I wish to remain so."

## Concluding Remarks

The systems of family, marriage, and inheritance either prohibit or encourage the choices women make, but in the final analysis it seems that what is most important is how widows adjust to the husbandless status. I was told repeatedly that "widows must be wide-eyed, resourceful, and tough." The wide-eyed widows prevented people from taking advantage of them. The resourceful widows took charge of the situation in order to control resources and production. And the tough widows were willing to fight for their rights, which often meant going to court. The decision to remarry often depended upon whether the woman was young, had children who were very small, or had difficulty obtaining and keeping labor to work the land. Older widows tended to opt for remaining single and concentrating on manipulating the resources at their disposal to cope with their social status.

Although some of my informants spoke of widows who had committed suicide immediately after their husband's death, I have no direct knowledge of such a case. Very poor widows are absent from my case studies, not because I ignore them but because they were not represented among the widows I encountered in my research. Moreover, even when it looked as if the woman would end up being impoverished, other factors intervened, such as remarriage or having the support of grown-up children. It is, however, still a man's world in terms of marriage, property, and inheritance laws; and women have to struggle to transcend social expectations. The case studies show that widows are more vulnerable than married women who have husbands to protect and help them with labor. Their vulnerability depends on the actions taken by their husbands, such as the leaving of a will to protect the widow's rights to resources. Relatives and other hangers-on can exploit a widow's vulnerability during and after the period of bereavement, depending on the psychological profile of the widow. Loneliness, too, may be a factor that creates an excessive dependence of the widow on others. A widow must indeed be strong, shrewd, and resourceful in order to protect her rights.

# Widows and Divorced Women in Swahili Society

PAMELA LANDBERG

THIS PAPER examines the status of widows and divorced women in Kigombe, a Swahili[1] community on the coast of northeastern Tanzania. This community and others like it are composed primarily of Swahili-speaking Sunni Muslims whose traditional economic orientation was toward fishing and the maritime trade of the western Indian Ocean. The Swahili coast is an area of social heterogeneity and mobility, but it is also one of cultural homogeneity and historical continuity. Its precolonial economy was dependent not only on maritime trade, but also on plantation slavery with its resulting hierarchical sociopolitical structure. Slaveholders and freemen were dominant over slaves, and men held primary authority over women. With the colonial period and the abolition of slavery, a new emphasis on a modern wage economy changed the focus on the coast from maritime trade to new pursuits. Some once-flourishing communities became backwaters, and other, once-peripheral communities took on new prominence. Kigombe is one of the latter, having achieved relatively continuous economic success since Tanzanian independence. Although many older social and political relationships have changed, those between males and females remain asymmetrical. It is in this setting that the status of unmarried women is considered.

I undertook my fieldwork in the Swahili community of Kigombe in 1968-69 with the support of a Foreign Area Predoctoral Grant and as a research associate of the Department of Sociology, University College, Dar es Salaam. I would like to thank Leif C. W. Landberg and T. O. Beidelman for reading drafts of this paper.

1. For attempts to define the label *Swahili* culturally, historically, and politically, see Arens 1975; Eastman 1971, 1976; Middleton and Campbell 1965; and Wijeyewardene 1959, 1961.

The research providing the background for this paper was conducted in Kigombe in 1968 and 1969. Although there have undoubtedly been changes with the passage of time, much remains the same. Fieldwork in other areas of the coast, both before and after this period (some of which is cited in this paper), indicates that even with the variations of place and time, the information presented here on the women of Kigombe is still relevant for understanding the status and position of coastal Swahili women.

Both widows and divorced women are discussed here because, with one exception in terms of ritual procedure, both have the same options available and are exposed to the same constraints. It should be noted, however, that in most Swahili communities, more marriages are terminated by divorce than by the death of a spouse. To understand the position of unmarried women in Kigombe, it is important to examine several factors concerning marriage. These include the circumstances surrounding first marriages, the implication for women of the high divorce rate, the legitimization of the role of unmarried women, the nature of remarriages, and the options open to women who choose not to remarry. Important factors affecting a woman's choices include her age, relative social and economic resources, residential options, and the care of children. These will be considered particularly in the context of the household, the basic social and economic unit in Swahili society.

## The Local Setting

Kigombe, a large fishing village of 900 to 1,000 inhabitants, is located on the northern coast of Tanzania. On its southern border is a large and successful sisal estate. The village itself is bisected by the main road, which leads from the estate and coastal communities of the south to Tanga, about 20 miles north of Kigombe and the second largest city in the country. Thus the village includes both rural and urban industrial sectors within its social and economic field.

The main economic activity of the male inhabitants is fishing (Landberg 1975), although many engage in other occupations and most fishermen themselves also farm or work at other jobs. Indeed, most adults, male and female, farm some crops. Most villagers farm subsistence crops, but a large minority—primarily men—also produce cash crops, particularly coconuts and cashew nuts. In addition to these two cash crops, Kigombe villagers also farm cassava, bananas, rice, maize, several varieties of beans, various fruits and some vegetables. Of these, rice is the most seasonal, yet in nearly constant demand for ritual and ceremonial occasions. The production of rice is almost entirely in the hands of the women.

Some male villagers are also involved in the selling of fish and other produce, petty trading, the provision of important local skills (carpentry, house construction, tailoring, some retail trade, to name a few), and in government work (Landberg and Weaver 1974). Some work on the sisal estate or at other wage labor. Women, however, are more restricted to the traditional sectors—subsistence agriculture, handicraft production, and some petty trading. This restrictive characteristic of women's work has important implications for an unmarried woman's options. For this reason, it is considered in some detail in a later section.

Kigombe village is the administrative center for its ward of Tanga District (Tanga Region), and the headquarters for the local branch of TANU, the national political party. The village has several governmental facilities: a primary court, an extended primary school, a medical dispensary, a veterinary center, and a Tanga District Council produce market. It also has a wholesale fish market, built by the local fishing cooperative.

Although Kigombe's political and economic alliances have traditionally been with similar Swahili communities along the coast, the village has also had economic and social ties with "tribal" groups in its immediate hinterland. The coast has long been a magnet for people from up-country, and with the development of sisal as a major cash crop, villages such as Kigombe became particularly attractive to migrants. Large numbers began arriving in Tanga Region to work on the estates in the early 1900's (Gulliver 1955: 1; Roberts and Tanner, 1959-60: 74-76). By 1940, Tanga, with its employment opportunities on the estates and at the port, was the second most popular destination for migrants from one of the prime up-country areas of labor migration (Gulliver 1955: 7). Many of these migrants eventually returned to their home areas, and others remained on the coast and settled in local communities. In recent years, a worldwide drop in sisal prices that began in 1964 led to layoffs of the work force and the closing of a number of estates (Mascarenhas 1970: 101).

Nonetheless, people are still attracted to the coast by possibilities of urban and government employment. Kigombe continues to attract a variety of outsiders. Fishermen from other coastal communities come to Kigombe because it is near good fishing grounds, yet also on a main road with ready access to urban markets. Some up-country migrants from nearby estates have retired and moved to Kigombe. Others who have particular occupational specialties such as carpentry and tinsmithing have moved there because it is relatively prosperous and expanding fairly rapidly. Thus it is a village with a relatively high degree of social diversity.

## Marriage and the Dissolution of Marriage

On the Swahili coast, the village is the basic social and political unit and an explicit distinction is made between "citizens" (wenyeji or "owners") of the village and those who are guests or strangers (wageni).[2] This difference concerns those who are born in the village and have full rights within it and those born elsewhere who have more limited rights or none at all. There are variations on this principle and in the procedures by which one can become assimilated into a village. As I explain later, divorced women and widows play an important role in the assimilation of newcomers to Kigombe, entering into marriages that have advantages for both parties.

For present purposes, it is important to know that people are members of cognatic descent groups and consequently may have rights and responsibilities toward more than one descent group. There is a tendency for first marriages, and some subsequent marriages, to be with kin, a factor that can limit descent group memberships. Throughout Swahili society, however, the divorce rate is high, with a tendency for subsequent marriages to be with non-kin. Marriages may cut across village lines, linking people and groups from different coastal villages. The end result

2. Various definitions of wenyeji and wageni and their implications for social organization and social relations are considered in more detail in Landberg 1977.

is that a person may have several options with regard to resi- ⱴ
dence as well as to political and economic affiliation.[3]

The very factor of choice, however, can lead to conflict. Caplan
(1968: 51) points out that there is a certain patrilineal bias in the
Swahili system. Residence upon marriage is virilocal, and paternal kin have primary responsibilities and rights with regard to
the burial of a kinsman. This bias is counterbalanced by the high
divorce rate. Following divorce, women often return to live with
their mothers and their mothers' kin. Children then grow up
around maternal kinsmen, and their residential and marital
choices may thereby be affected. In addition, relationships with
these kinsmen may also figure importantly in economic and political strategies.

Inherent tensions between maternal and paternal kin groups
is a recurring theme in Swahili social relations. These arise most
clearly in the context of marriage arrangements and rights of
burial, but they may also be manifested in conflicting claims concerning choice of residence. Although persons may be able to
use their various kinship ties to advantage, they are also often
caught up in conflicting loyalties to paternal and maternal kinsmen. Even so, the fact that children sometimes grow up in the
care of their maternal kinsmen may have a more important effect
on the social and economic choices they make than the biases
toward paternal kin mentioned above.

Before discussing the choices open for a woman upon the dissolution of her marriage, I will treat the institution of marriage
in Kigombe in more general terms. Briefly I describe first marriages, which are the most important ones from the standpoint
of a descent group. Then I consider divorce procedures and their
implications. Since one of the options open to a woman may be
to remarry, I also discuss the nature of subsequent marriages.

*First marriages.* In terms of both the status of women and descent group ritual events, first marriages of females are more important than subsequent ones. First marriage is the main ritual
occasion marking the female's transition from young girl (*mwari*

3. The effect such options have for individuals in Swahili society is the central
topic of Caplan's study of a similar Swahili community on Mafia Island (1968,
1969, 1975).

or virgin) to adult woman (*mtu mzima* or adult). Prior to her marriage, a young girl is excluded from almost all the main activities
undertaken by women. With her change in status, however, she
can participate fully in the rituals of her cognatic descent
groups, primarily funerals and weddings, and she can belong to
a women's dance group. Previously she may have given her
mother minimal assistance in the fields (mainly chasing birds
away from grain crops) or around the house (carrying out minor
chores and watching smaller children). After marriage she may
begin farming her own field if she so desires. The only step remaining before her complete acceptance as an adult woman is
the birth of a child.

Marriage does not have quite the same importance in demar-
cating status for young men, since their adulthood begins with
the acquisition of skills and the acceptance of a fully adult occupation. Most men do marry at least once and first marriages
are also important events for young men and their kinsmen. Yet
young unmarried men who want to begin farming are free to
open up and cultivate fields. Moreover, some men in the village
are middle-aged or elderly but have never married. This would
rarely be true of a woman, since it is marriage that establishes
her status as an adult. Only those who have certain rare handi-
caps are considered unmarriageable under Islamic law.

First marriages tend to be arranged marriages, although the
couple often have a part in the arrangement themselves and have
agreed to the union. Many such marriages (61 percent for males
and 62 percent for females in my sample) are with kinsmen
(Table 1).[4] Preferred marriages are primarily with classificatory
cousins as well as with real first cousins, so kin marriages include a broad range of people and allow for a degree of choice
for those involved. One's cognatic relatives may be dispersed in
other villages also, but many first marriages take place between
persons within the same village. Such marriages, which emphasize preferential cousin marriages and/or intravillage unions,

4. Data presented here derive from a census of Kigombe Village and its related community of Sinawe undertaken by myself and Leif C. W. Landberg in the
course of fieldwork (see Landberg 1977). All information on marriages in Kigombe
derives from this census. The tendency for first marriages to be with kin is cited
for other areas of the coast as well (Bujra 1968; Caplan 1968, 1975; Prins 1967: 87).

TABLE 1

*Marriages of Kigombe Men and Women*

(N = 440)

| Form of marriage | Males | Females | Total |
|---|---|---|---|
| First marriages: | | | |
| With relative | 70 (61%) | 55 (62%) | |
| With nonrelative | 45 (39%) | 34 (38%) | |
| TOTAL | 115 | 89 | 204 |
| Subsequent marriages: | | | |
| With relative | 52 (42%) | 31 (28%) | |
| With nonrelative | 73 (58%) | 80 (72%) | |
| TOTAL | 125 | 111 | 236 |
| GRAND TOTAL | 240 | 200 | 440 |

stress the solidarity of descent groups and/or the unity of the village. It might be thought that such intravillage kin marriages would alleviate the difficulties inherent with virilocal residence, but the data on marital careers indicate otherwise. Subsequent marriages tend more to cut across village lines and to be with non-kin (58 percent for males and 72 percent for females), thus reinforcing the network of relationships between coastal communities (Table 1). Such marriages potentially expand the range of those reckoned as kin.

*Divorce.* It was difficult to get accurate data on divorce since women were reluctant to say whether a marriage had ended in divorce or had been terminated by a spouse's death. It appeared, however, that more marriages had been terminated by divorce than by death. The data on the number of marriages per person suggest a fairly high rate of divorce. Thus Kigombe men were found to have an average of 2.94 marriages during their marital careers and women to have an average of 2.86.[5]

The only study of a coastal community where divorce is reported to be infrequent, with most marriages ending with death

5. A high rate of divorce is noted by various authors for communities throughout the Swahili coastal area. See, for example, Lienhardt 1968: 33; Prins 1967: 87; Roberts and Tanner 1959-60: 66, 75; Strobel 1979: 88; Swartz 1982: 34; and Trimingham 1964: 138. Caplan gives marriage and divorce figures for Mafia similar to those for Kigombe, citing an average of 2.75 wives for men and about 2 husbands for women during the course of their marital careers (1975: 31).

of spouse, is Tanner's (1964) account of Afro-Arabs in Mombasa. However, Strobel, in her historical and sociological study of non-Asian Muslim women in Mombasa (1979: 88), found the same high rate of divorce that is seen throughout the coast. She points out that Tanner himself admits that his study was biased toward "elite families," which, she argues, are more closely bound by religious strictures (1979: 92, n. 136).

Whereas divorce and remarriage are frequent occurrences, serial polygamy is the norm for both sexes in most Swahili communities (Prins 1967: 87; Caplan 1968: 51; 1975: 27). Under Islamic law, marriage is viewed as a contract, easily broken if one or both members are dissatisfied (Cohen 1971: 175; Wijeyewardene 1959). The right to dissolve that contract is not, however, shared equally. Under Islamic law, a man may easily effect a divorce (talaka) by a simple pronouncement to his wife (Hemedi 1959: 14; Tanner 1962: 71; Wijeyewardene 1959). It is more difficult for a woman, since with few exceptions she has little recourse under Islamic law for obtaining a divorce if her husband does not want it. In such a situation, a Swahili wife who is really unhappy with her marriage must bring informal pressure to bear on her husband. She may make life miserable for him until he agrees to give her a divorce or else she may make an agreed-upon payment (hului) to him in exchange for a divorce (Hemedi 1959: 9-13; Wijeyewardene 1959).

Legally it is permissible for a man to have as many as four wives at a time, provided he is able to maintain them properly, preferably in separate households; however, few men choose to do so. Of the males interviewed in Kigombe, only nine (6.5 percent of the total sample of currently married men) had more than one wife, and none had more than two.[6] In short, polygy-

6. Caplan (1975: 48) gives a slightly higher figure of 10 percent for polygynous marriages in Mafia. She also says that the various co-wives were all placed in separate households. Roberts and Tanner (1959-60: 64) comment that on the coast (the Pangani area) there is little polygyny; but they also argue that the relatively high number of unmarried women is a recent phenomenon. In the past, they argue, "surplus women" were taken up by polygynous marriages and by a form of leviratic marriage (1959-60: 75; see also Tanner 1962: 75). The only other author for the coast who mentions a "pseudo-levirate" is Wijeyewardene (1959). Even if a form of levirate did exist on the coast, the authors mentioned all agree that, at the time of their writing, it did not exist. There is little evidence that polygyny was more widespread in the past, although modern changes on the coast

nous marriages represent only a small portion of total marriages contracted. Those men who have more than one wife usually have sufficient wealth to enable them to support several households. Even so, a husband's taking another wife was often cited by Kigombe women as reason for pressing for a divorce.

*The unmarried state: widows and divorced women.* So far the discussion has centered on the dissolution of marriage through divorce. However, it should be noted that from the standpoint of Swahili women, the statuses of a divorced woman and a widow are much the same, with similar constraints on the woman involved and similar options for her. Thus, unless indicated otherwise, this paper treats widows and divorced women as sociologically similar.

Even so, one important difference between widowhood and divorce relates to prescribed procedures for establishing legal paternity of children born after death or divorce. Traditionally there is a specified waiting period before a widow or divorced woman can remarry. Among the Swahili this time is called the *eda* (Arabic *'idda*). Theoretically it is required of both widows and divorcées, but there are some important differences. According to Shafi'i law, a widow must go into seclusion for a period of four months and ten days (Anderson 1970: 363; Hemedi 1959: 29). Her behavior is closely regulated during this period. A divorced woman is forbidden to remarry for either a period of three months or "three periods of purity," the latter being the intervals between menstrual periods (Hemedi 1959: 27). The time requirements vary if a woman is past childbearing or if she is pregnant at the time of divorce.

At the time of my fieldwork, women who had recently been widowed adhered strictly to the required period of seclusion and the strictures surrounding it. Most spent their *edas* in their mothers' homes, where they could be cared for while they were cut off from all normal discourse. On the other hand, although divorced women might not remarry within this period, they did not otherwise seem unduly restricted in their movements or behavior, either by their ex-husbands or by their kin. Indeed, some

---

probably increased a woman's opportunities for mobility, affecting her marital choices.

young Kigombe women did not hesitate to take lovers soon after separating from their husbands. Despite Islamic regulations concerning legal paternity, most husbands of divorced women show little interest in claiming children born after divorce, whether or not they are their own biological offspring.

In summary, except for the differences concerning the *eda*, indicated above, the problems faced by widows and divorced women in Swahili society are the same. Sometimes they remarry, either after a short time or after a longer waiting period. Sometimes, for reasons to be considered, women either are unable to remarry or choose not to do so. In any case, there are institutionalized ways for legitimating their role as unmarried women while they are in this state and for providing for the socialization of their children outside the nuclear family structure (see also Cohen 1971: 176-77).

## The Dissolution of Marriage and Women's Options

With the dissolution of a marriage—whether through death or divorce—a woman's options and choices are affected by a number of factors: her age, the ages of her children, her economic and social resources, and the availability of housing (which can affect her choice of residence). With few exceptions, a woman has scant resources to support herself independently. A number of women cite this as a reason for remarriage, but many are able to live independently of a husband—albeit with the support of friends and relatives. As I make clear later, it is often a household or households of kin, particularly female kin, that enables a woman to maintain herself and support her children. First, however, I would like to discuss the economic factors affecting women. The care of children and the importance of the Swahili household in providing a support system for unmarried women and children will be discussed afterward.

*Economic factors.* When a couple is remarried, the husband is supposed to bear the main financial responsibilities for maintaining his wife and children and for providing food and shelter. His failure to provide adequately constitutes grounds for divorce, and indeed it is often cited as a frequent cause of divorce (Caplan 1975: 31; Roberts and Tanner 1959-60: 77; Strobel 1979: 57, 92-93; Tanner 1962: 71; Wijeyewardene 1959). The wife herself may have some agricultural holdings or financial resources of her own. Theoretically, a husband has no control over his wife's property. She, for her part, is not required to contribute her money or crops to the household, although she usually does so. She may contribute food from her fields to the household to which she belongs, and she may also share it with households of other relatives.

Upon divorce, whatever is the woman's property, including certain household belongings purchased for her from marital payments made by the husband and his kin, goes with the wife. Women in Kigombe said that men are also obligated to help with the upbringing of their children, but many men do not substantially assist the children of their divorced wives, nor do they otherwise contribute to their ex-wives' households. This does not mean that men cut off all relations with their children by former wives. Contact may be maintained if the ex-spouses live in the same village or nearby. Sometimes children may be sent to live with some of the father's kin following a divorce. Many fathers take a particular interest in their sons when they are old enough to begin learning an occupation. Often it is the fathers or other paternal kinsmen who teach young men the occupations they then pursue (Landberg 1975). But many divorced women receive no financial assistance from their children's fathers.

Economically, Swahili women are disadvantaged in yet another way. The men on the coast have become much more integrated into a wage labor economy than the women, whose activities still tend to be in the traditional sectors. Women also cultivate, but only a very few who have developed some holdings in trees are involved in the relatively lucrative area of cash cropping. Even then, their participation is on a minor scale, and women usually have to depend upon male relatives to market and sell the crops on their behalf.

Women mostly cultivate subsistence crops, particularly cassava, rice, and maize, as well as some fruits and vegetables in kitchen gardens. Cassava, a highly drought-resistant crop, is grown by most adults, but more often by older single women than by the younger ones, who tend to put their efforts into rice. Men leave rice cultivation to women because it does not confer permanent land use rights. Moreover, despite its ritual importance, rice has little cash value because relatively small marketable surpluses can be produced. Most of the crops grown by women are strictly for household consumption. Occasionally they sell some excess produce, but sales rarely contribute much to their income.

Women can obtain rights in land, permanent tree crops, and other property through inheritance from their fathers, mothers, or husbands. A woman is eligible for a share in her parents' estates, but in accordance with Islamic law, that share is equal to only half that of a male heir. Her legal portion of a husband's estate is one-eighth of his property, but he can receive one-fourth of hers (Caplan 1975: 41; Strobel 1979: 58).

Of the property that can be inherited, considerable value is placed on permanent trees, which rank highly not only because of the income they generate, but also because ownership of such trees confers long-term rights to use land.[7] For several reasons, most women have only small holdings of trees, if that. Besides having a smaller share in inherited property, women are often bought out of the property by their brothers, who are in a better position to develop and expand it. Even when women keep the property, it is often managed by male kin, who may eventually appropriate some or all of it as part of their own. Even so, some women manage to accrue a few holdings, usually through inheritance, and augment them occasionally by buying trees and planting seedlings.

When a house is part of an estate, however, there is often a trade-off: the house may be left to a woman in lieu of trees or be given to a sister by a brother in exchange for trees. Ownership of a house also gives a person long-term rights over the land on which it stands. If a woman goes to another village to reside with her husband, she may allow her relatives to live in the house or may sometimes even rent it out. If she should marry within the village, her husband may live with her in her own house, especially if the house is a substantial one or if the marriage is polygynous. If the husband is an outsider but chooses to live in his wife's village, he will usually live in her house. Between marriages the house provides the woman with a secure base of

7. Swahili concepts and principles of land tenure are considered in some detail in Middleton 1961 and Caplan 1975. For a comparison with those for Kigombe, see Landberg 1977.

operations. In any case, unless she decides to sell it or to give it to another relative, the house remains hers.

Owning other property may present a woman with some difficulties. Whether inherited from a mother, father, or husband, that property may be located in a place other than where she is living. Or she may have permanent crops in one area and be farming subsistence crops in another. A woman usually begins farming with her closest female relatives: her mother, or a mother's sister, or an older female relative of her own generation. If a woman and her mother live in different villages, the woman may return home at frequent intervals to farm with her mother and female kin, especially during the rice-growing season, and such trips can lead to dissension between husband and wife.

It is one of the ironies of coastal Swahili society that the nature of the marriage contract and the frequency of divorce weaken ties between a husband and wife while emphasizing and strengthening those between a woman and her mother. Since a woman's security usually rests with her mother and her uterine kin, she strives to maintain those ties first and foremost. Efforts to keep up those relationships may be factors contributing to the high divorce rate (Bujra 1968; Lienhardt 1968: 34-35; Tanner 1962: 79). On occasion, a woman's desire to maintain these ties may lead her to turn over distant property to the management of male kin, or even to exchange or sell it.

In addition to living with these limitations on owning and managing property, women are economically handicapped in other ways. Selling traditional handicrafts and peddling cooked foods and produce do not bring them much income. Under British rule, Swahili men and women were both effectively excluded from one important economic sphere of activity on the coast— the retail trade, which instead was dominated by Asians. After Independence, more and more coastal men, particularly in cities and towns, became involved in retail trade, mostly in small shops and stores. The women, however, unlike their counterparts in West Africa, have not had the opportunity to become involved in the larger-scale marketing trade (Strobel 1979: 135). As a result, the divorced or widowed Swahili woman usually has comparatively few economic resources with which to support herself and her children.

*Choices with regard to remarriage.* Ideally, according to Islamic law, a woman should always be under the guardianship and protection of a man, whether father, husband, brother, or another male relative. In practice a woman who is no longer married may have considerable freedom from male control, even if she resides in the same household with a male relative. Thus the divorced or widowed woman may have considerable independence, and not readily yield it to enter into a new marriage. Although the circumstances of some divorces may cause a scandal, it is not an automatic disgrace for a man or a woman to be divorced—or widowed. In comparison with men, however, women usually have less income to live on and are more likely to have to pool their resources to form viable household units. Otherwise they must attach themselves to male kin or, through a daughter, to a male affine.

Because of their inferior economic situation, as well as for reasons of sentiment and security, most unmarried women want to be and often are remarried, but their choices concerning remarriage, are limited by their age. In Kigombe, some older women have been unable to find new husbands because many middle-aged and older men prefer to take younger wives. Men are likely to remarry, no matter what their age. It is accepted that they need wives to carry out domestic chores, although some of them depend on female relatives instead. But whereas considerable age differences between older husbands and younger wives are acceptable, the reverse situation is not. This does not mean that an older woman no longer has any chance of remarriage, but that her opportunities are reduced.

I knew of several women in their late fifties and older who were offered opportunities to be remarried, and most accepted the offer. One woman, however, in her sixties, declined an offer of marriage from her current lover. She was living fairly comfortably on her own resources and had close kin nearby. She liked receiving visits from her lover and entertaining him, but she was emphatic in saying that she did not want to be in a position where he could dictate what she could or could not do. She therefore opted for continuing their existing relationship rather than entering into marriage. Other old women like her who had been through a number of marriages echoed her sentiments.

The situation for younger women, particularly those who find themselves either divorced or widowed after just a few years of marriage, is rather different. Most remarry sooner or later, many several times. Some young women choose not to remarry, at least not right away. Instead they have lovers and raise their children by themselves. Several young women in Kigombe had made this choice. One, in her middle to late twenties, had had a succession of lovers and children, most fathered by different men. Another young woman who had been divorced from her first husband and had entertained several lovers seemed set on the same path. People spoke of these women as *wahuni* (sing. *mhuni*). The term is defined in Johnson's Dictionary (1939: 138) as "vagabond, profligate, wastrel, gadabout." There are other meanings as well, but the general sense of this definition seems close to the way the word is used in Kigombe. The term does not have the meaning of prostitute, nor should the behavior of the young women be equated with that of a woman who would be regarded in Kigombe as a prostitute.[8] Rather, young people in general, including young men and boys, whose behavior is somewhat wild and undisciplined, are termed *wahuni*.

Since the emphasis in first marriages is on the virginity of the bride, most Swahili women are married when quite young. Until then, in order to maintain both their virginity and proper female behavior, young women are raised in a more sheltered fashion than young men. Indeed, young men are encouraged to travel around and to kick up their heels a bit. Although they may be learning occupations as well, they are still allowed to enjoy themselves, attending dances, taking on lovers, traveling to Tanga and other areas. This period of traveling around and enjoying a variety of experiences is referred to as *kutembea* (lit. "to

8. Some Swahili women move to larger urban areas and do become professional prostitutes. According to Strobel (1979) and Bujra (1968, 1977: 24), Mombasa is an attraction for divorced or widowed women who go there as prostitutes to raise money to support themselves and their children. Pate Island, until recently an important coastal area, has become a somewhat marginal backwater. Many of its men have migrated to other parts of the coast looking for work, and a number of the women have done the same. The main difference between the men and women, according to Bujra (1968, 1977: 37), is that the women, many of whom work as prostitutes, have sent money home to assist their children and relatives. They have also purchased or built houses there and have otherwise invested in their home communities. Strobel (1979: 145) comments generally for the coast that "prostitution has lost some of its social stigma for many people."

walk, to travel"; see also Caplan 1975: 16). Before marriage, young women do not have these opportunities.

With the termination of a first marriage, a young woman often decides not to remarry quickly, even though marriage may be her ultimate goal. She may use this time to travel, visiting the city of Tanga and other coastal villages. If she has children, she usually leaves them with her mother or other female relatives. It is accepted that she may have lovers. In the context of Kigombe village, such informal sexual liaisons do not have the same meaning as they may have in different societies or contexts. Although marriage is important, it is not an essential state for a woman who has married once (Tanner 1962: 75). Children born out of wedlock are not ostracized but within the Swahili kinship system have rights and responsibilities in relation to their maternal kin. Although a woman's lover may provide gifts or help to maintain her, she is not considered to be a prostitute by other villagers; indeed, a lover may become her future husband.

Most women do remarry at some point. In the period between marriages, they must be able to support themselves or find some assistance for themselves and their children. Women who do not remarry, whether by choice or otherwise, have the same needs for maintenance and security.

*An alternative choice: marriage to a "stranger."* For economic reasons, some women may opt for relationships in which they are able to maintain some degree of independence from male authority while still enjoying the marital state. One arrangement that offers Kigombe women a certain degree of freedom is marriage to an *mgeni,* or "stranger," often a migrant from elsewhere on the coast or sometimes from up-country. Historically, such marriages have contributed to a social diversity in many coastal areas. I consider this factor first in terms of its implications for coastal social structure and mobility and then examine its possible advantages for women.

The Swahili coast is in an area of considerable ethnic heterogeneity, coupled, however, with a certain cultural homogeneity. It has absorbed people of diverse ethnic origins, most of them migrants arriving singly or in small groups. The process of assimilation involves the adoption of certain minimal cultural features and the acceptance of village religious and social values.

TABLE 2

*Places of Origin of Spouses of Kigombe Citizens (Wenyeji)*

(N = 433)

| Place of origin | Wife | | Husband | |
|---|---|---|---|---|
| | First marriages | Other marriages | First marriages | Other marriages |
| Coast: | | | | |
| Kigombe/Sinawe | 63 (56%) | 48 (41%) | 49 (51%) | 37 (35%) |
| Other coastal villages | 44 (39%) | 60 (51%) | 46 (47%) | 53 (51%) |
| TOTAL | 107 (95%) | 108 (92%) | 95 (98%) | 90 (86%) |
| Up-country | 6 (5%) | 10 (8%) | 2 (2%) | 15 (14%) |
| GRAND TOTAL | 113 | 118 | 97 | 105 |

Marriage is one of the most important elements in the assimilation of migrants, particularly those from up-country or distant coastal areas (Wijeyewardene 1961). Marriage establishes the legal status of children born to that marriage and sets forth the rights and duties of a child with regard to both his paternal and maternal kin. Because of the cognatic kinship system on the coast, the children of a male migrant and a Swahili woman have the rights and duties of citizens in their mother's village. Such marriages not only help assimilate migrants, but establish coastal status for the offspring.

In this context, widowhood and divorce have certain implications for Swahili social organization and ethnic composition. Although first marriages are arranged with kinsmen or fellow villagers, subsequent marriages are more a matter of individual choice and tend to be with non-kin. Also, more are contracted with men and women from other coastal communities and with men from up-country.

Table 2 gives a breakdown of marriages, first and subsequent, for Kigombe men and women. Since marital residence is virilocal, women often become very familiar with several parts of the coast during their marital careers. Marriage is thus a source of mobility for women, although much greater mobility is available to men, who may travel widely when fishing, trading, or working on estates.

For a migrant male, marriage to a local woman provides one of the most important ways to become incorporated in a community. Such men are unlikely candidates for women's first marriages. It is divorced and widowed women, free to make their own choices, who provide migrants—coastal and up-country—with entrée into local Swahili communities through marriage.

By the same token, marriage to migrant men can offer some advantages to Swahili women. Such remarriage may provide women with the relative security of marriage while allowing them a certain independence from male authority, particularly if the men involved are up-country migrants with few or no local ties. In several of these marriages, Kigombe women maintain their own households, surrounded and supported by kin. Their husbands have only marginal roles in the households and the community, whereas they themselves tend to be the heads of the households and the main decision makers. At the same time, because they are married, they can resist some of the demands made by their male relatives.

### The Unmarried Woman, the Care of Children, and the Swahili Household

The normal pattern of action for a woman, upon divorce or the death of her spouse, is to return to her own village, often that of her close maternal kin. She also might go to the village of her paternal kin or to the village where her mother resides. Her closest ties are usually with her mother and her uterine siblings, those of *tumbo moja* ("one stomach"), and it is to them that she looks for assistance when she is between marriages. Swahili children, particularly young ones, usually accompany their mother, living with her or her maternal kin.

The most important support unit for both the woman and her children is the Swahili household. This is the basic unit of production and consumption and the central locus for socialization of children. Members of several houses may cooperate as an economic and social unit (Caplan 1968: 66), but usually the occupants of single houses form such groups. Divorce or widowhood may break the relationship between husbands and wives, but households still provide care for the children. Moreover, divorced or widowed women themselves retain legitimate roles in society. Hence continuity is maintained despite the frequency of divorce on the coast. Although the Swahili ideal may be said to be the nuclear household, which most married couples prefer, given the high divorce rate and other problems encountered in maintaining viable households, this is not the prevailing or only form.[9] In Kigombe, a household consisting of a divorced or widowed woman and other female relatives often provides the central focus for economic and social relations for both the woman and her children.

The core of such a household is usually an older unmarried woman and one or more older female relatives or friends who group together to share expenses and daily chores. These older women frequently own their own houses. Younger kinswomen or their own daughters who have returned to the village during periods between marriages may take up residence with them. In such situations, older women take care of the children while the younger ones work in the fields or look for new husbands or lovers. Older women and some younger ones in such households often work as petty entrepreneurs in order to make money for household items that have to be purchased.

In a few instances, young or middle-aged men, usually divorced, live in the households of their female kin, particularly their mothers. Occasionally this is because the women are old and in ill health. Sometimes neither sons nor mothers have much money, and they can only form viable households together, but such cases are distinctly in the minority. Unmarried men tend to live alone or with other males, sharing meals with nearby kinswomen. Older women who have no independent sources of income or are no longer able to take care of themselves may look to their sons for economic support and may occasionally live in their households, but they are more likely to live with their daughters or other female kin.

An older woman who has a house of her own may attract other kinswomen, giving her a position of some power and authority. Older women are more likely than young ones to have some property of their own, houses in particular. Middle-aged and older women will often try to obtain houses—by inheri-

9. For a discussion of household types, see Caplan 1975: 48; Landberg 1977; and Wijeyewardene 1961.

tance, by purchase, or even by having them constructed. In many ways, a house is the most important item of property a Swahili woman can own. By conferring long-term use rights in the land on which it stands, it represents permanence and continuity. Strobel (1979: 91) points to the ownership of houses by freeborn Mombasa women at the turn of the century as one structural feature of coastal society that "further weakened the reality of male dominance." In writing about another area of the northern Swahili coast, Bujra (1968: 79, 1977: 30) points out that in Tundwa (Pate Island) a woman's ideal household contains her closest female kin, not her nuclear family, since her security lies with her mother or her sisters and daughters. Indeed, she says, ownership of a house by a woman is itself a symbol of that ideal.

Even so, there is at least one important difference between Kigombe and these areas of the northern Swahili coast. In Pate (Bujra 1968, 1977: 22) and Mombasa (Strobel 1979: 132), women have historically been excluded from the agricultural sector unless they can pay wage laborers to cultivate for them. Bujra (1977: 22-23) attributes this to a precolonial economy in which slaves did the cultivation and the wives and female relatives of slave owners specifically did not cultivate. In other areas of the coast, such as Malindi, some freeborn women began to cultivate after the abolition of slavery (Strobel 1979: 132), but women did not do so in either Pate Island or Mombasa (Bujra 1977: 23, 1979: 132). As a result, many women are excluded from owning this form of cash-producing property. Those who do have money—prostitutes and others—have invested in other forms of property, especially houses. Although the extent to which women in Kigombe are involved in cultivating more lucrative cash crops is limited, subsistence cropping is still an important economic activity for them. Moreover, a few women are active in cultivating cash crops. Ownership of houses is important to Kigombe women also, but less so than for Pate and Mombasa Swahili women.[10]

10. According to Bujra (1968, 1977: 29), 86.5 percent of the houses belong to women, their husbands residing there only as long as the marriages last. This is in marked contrast to Kigombe and some other areas of the coast (Caplan 1975: 46), where the virilocal pattern of marriage often takes women out of their own village or neighborhood. There are women in Kigombe who obtain houses, particularly by inheritance, but they are far fewer than Bujra indicates for Pate.

Older women may also have accumulated some money during their marital careers. In Kigombe, middle-aged and elderly women often have agricultural plots of various kinds, sometimes including the more valuable permanent tree crops. Women who are middle-aged and those beyond childbearing also have more opportunities to become involved in local political and ritual affairs in the village. Those who attain leadership roles gain prestige within the community and augment their authority over other women. Occasionally they also reap some financial benefits.

In a number of cases, young children live with their mothers, who themselves are absorbed into viable households. Other children live in households with one or another of their parents' siblings or with grandparents. Such arrangements free the younger women from constant child care so that they can pursue their own activities or seek new husbands. Even if there is no dissolution of marriage, children may be sent to reside with other relatives. This form of fostering (*ulezi*) is a common practice in Swahili society (see also Caplan 1968: 67-70, 1975: 49). In all of these cases, the members of a household where a child resides have primary responsibility for its raising and care, whether or not its parents reside in the household. Parents and other kinsmen may contribute money toward a child's support, but the primary responsibility for day-to-day care rests with the household.

Generally, however, children are incorporated in the households of their mother and their mother's kin. The ties between a woman and her mother and her uterine siblings may be maintained and demonstrated in a number of contexts, but it is when a woman is unmarried that they are of greatest importance, providing support for her and helping to socialize her children. Throughout the coast the household is the paramount institution that provides a sustaining framework for a woman and her children. For many coastal women, ownership of a house itself is important both as a base for the development of a household

---

I suggest that although the value placed by women on owning houses may be a common pattern throughout the Swahili coast, it may be stressed less in communities where women are involved in cultivation.

and as a symbol of a certain degree of independence from male authority.[11]

## Concluding Remarks

Although some Swahili marriages end with the death of a spouse, most end in divorce. Even so, widows and divorced women find themselves in similar positions. In Swahili society, there is a sharp division of labor and of spheres of activity for men and women. Authority over women, married or single, is legally and customarily vested in males—husbands, fathers, brothers, and other relatives. Historically the authority and dominance of males over females were buttressed by the Swahili interpretation of Islamic strictures. Strobel (1979: 55-56) points out that this ideology, as represented in turn-of-the-century Swahili Islamic literature, justified seclusion and veiling by stressing the "weakness" of women and the need for men to mediate between them and their environment. But she also points out that reality did not strictly conform to ideology. Although excluded from formal religious and political positions, women still played (and still do play) important roles involving kinship and ritual (ibid.: 76-78). In Kigombe, at the time of my fieldwork, women were actively involved in a number of important activities—planning and organizing weddings, funerals, the village's annual *Maulidi* celebration for the birth of the Prophet Mohammed, and spirit possession dances. The Tanzanian government tried to bring coastal women into more formal political positions, but with varying success. Those who filled these positions were middle-aged and older women already involved in more traditional female leadership roles.

The relationship between men and women in Kigombe, as elsewhere on the coast, remains for the most part an asymmetrical one in which men are dominant and women dependent. Even in a more modern economy, Swahili women tend to remain in more traditional spheres of work. In spite of the mea-

11. The word for house, as a physical structure, and for household, as a social unit, is the same—*nyumba*. *Nyumba* also has other important meanings for Swahili social relations. In Kigombe the main term for the cognatic kin group is *ukoo* (Landberg 1977), but in the village and elsewhere on the coast (Wijeyewardene 1959), *nyumba* is used as a synonym for this wider kin group. In addition, *nyumba* may refer to a woman and her children as a social unit. In this more restricted meaning, it stands for the solidarity of women and their children.

gerness of the resources available to them, their exclusion from most areas of power and authority, and the likelihood of their remaining unmarried when widowed or divorced, Kigombe women, along with other Swahili women, demonstrate considerable resourcefulness. For unmarried women—widows or divorcées—houses and households provide important bases of support that also symbolize their autonomy and the strong bonds linking them with their mothers and their uterine kin.

The divorce rate itself indicates the nature of male-female relationships on the coast. Strobel finds few data on the divorce rate before 1910, but in her studies of British administrative records for the Mombasa area between 1915 and the 1950's she found a rate of "one divorce for every two marriages," a sign of considerable "marital discord" (1979: 88). In the 1960's, Bujra found that the women of Pate were far from being "submissive or acquiescent marriage partners," in spite of their economic dependence on males; rather, they were "defiant, quick to take offense, and very ready to demand to be divorced" (1977: 31). Even so, and in spite of considerable economic and political changes on the coast, male authority and female obedience are still important elements of Swahili ideology. Depending on the circumstances, this authority may be exercised in varying degrees by men; but an adult woman's ability to control her own life and make her own decisions is most severely limited in the context of marriage.

Despite the frequency of divorce, most women spend much of their adult lives married. Some remain married to the same husbands throughout their lives, but many spend intervals between marriages relying on their own resources or looking to their kin for aid and support. Because of their meager economic resources, they usually seek security in remarriage. Some seek instead to minimize male authority and control over their daily lives either by not remarrying or by making marriages such as those with migrants. Strobel, in discussing the rigidity of upper-class sex roles historically in Mombasa, comments that "the instability of marriage actually contributed to women's autonomy" (1979: 92). Some Swahili women choose to retain this autonomy in spite of their economic disadvantages and the difficulties of maintaining themselves and their children, and they remain single for extended periods.

In her study of Tundwa (Pate Island), Bujra (1968, 1977: 3) sees a sharp division between the needs and the orientation of men toward nuclear family units where they dominate and those of women toward female-oriented households where their long-term security rests. Bujra (1968) and Swartz (1982: 27, 30), writing about the Kenya coast, describe the relationships among Swahili women as intense and supportive, and those among men as less cooperative and even reserved. Without unduly stressing these observations with regard to Kigombe men and women,[12] I note that women, who do have fewer choices regarding marriage, are more dependent upon the social relationships I have described, if only because it is much easier for men than for women to remarry. When men remarry, they establish new households in which they have overall control.

Given the brittleness of Swahili marriages, women generally maintain strong ties over time with their mothers and their uterine siblings, especially their sisters. These bonds are maintained not only out of mutual sympathy, but because they provide a woman with a source of security and assistance in a society where the chances of undergoing more than one marriage are quite good.

12. It should be pointed out that although the authority of men over women is sanctioned by law and custom throughout Swahili society, the actual extent to which a man can exercise that authority differs over time, and from place to place, as well as in terms of particular relationships. Strobel (1979: 54-55), for example, points out that adherence to male authority was more rigid in earlier periods among the "elite" class—those who considered themselves "Arab"—of Mombasa Swahili society. In Kigombe, where historically such class distinctions seem to have been lower key, men's control over women generally seems to be looser than that described by Strobel. Even so, male authority and control are perceived as onerous by some women.

# Widows in Hausa Society:
# Ritual Phase or Social Status?

ENID SCHILDKROUT

THE HAUSA of northern Nigeria, as well as the Hausa living in other parts of West Africa (see Adamu 1978), make no linguistic distinction between a divorcée and a widow: both are known as *bazawara* (pl. *zazarawa*). According to Bargery's dictionary of the Hausa language (1934: 100), the term also means "anything which has been used and is to be reused." In this sense, widowhood among the Hausa is a ritual phase and not a distinct social status. Although details of the ritual waiting period before remarriage differ for divorcées and widows, nothing in the formal status of divorcées and widows distinguishes them: both are single, previously married women eligible for remarriage. However, a more profound examination of widowhood and divorce in relation to women's age and childbearing histories reveals important differences: these pertain to women's rights of residence, their rights to inherit property, and their ability to claim support from their adult children.

This paper explores these issues by examining the marital histories of a group of Muslim Hausa women in the city of Kano. The research on which this paper is based was undertaken between 1976 and 1978 and during a six week follow-up visit in 1982. During the last trip, detailed data on widows were gathered. The data on women who were single at the time now include 34 women reported as widowed, 16 reported as di-

The research on which this paper is based has been supported by the National Science Foundation, the American Museum of Natural History, the Wenner-Gren Foundation, and the Social Science Research Council. The author thanks Carol Gelber, who did much of the 1982 field research on widows and has been involved in the ongoing analysis of the Kano data.

TABLE 1

*Marital Status and Age of Widows and Divorcées in Kano,*
*January 1982*

| | Age | | |
| Marital status | Under 40 | 40 or over | Unknown |
| --- | --- | --- | --- |
| Widowed | 5[a] | 28 | 1 |
| Divorced | 9 | 6 | 1 |
| Widowed or divorced? | 1 | 4 | 2 |
| Widowed and remarried | 4 | 1 | – |

[a]One was 39; three were widows for less than two years and are likely to remarry; and one who was widowed in 1978 may have remarried (data incomplete).

vorced, 7 reported as widowed or divorced (status uncertain), and 5 married women who had previously been widowed (Table 1).

This research focused on the economic roles of children and their relationship to women's domestic and economic roles. In the course of this study, the activities of 112 children in 69 houses were recorded. At the same time the female caretakers—mothers, grandmothers, and foster mothers—of these children were interviewed, and detailed information was collected on the women's marital histories, household budgets and schedules, and income-earning activities. Although marital histories were collected for only 82 women, several women have been included in the sample of widows who were not caretakers of children in the study, but who were members of the children's households. In some cases, therefore, we have information on the current residence and relationships of widows without having their complete marital histories.

Of the 82 women on whom we have detailed marital histories, there are only 7 widowed women and 13 women who have ever been widowed. These 82 women report a total of 123 marriages, of which 13 ended with the death of the husband, 29 with divorce, and 2 with either death or divorce. There are two biases in these figures: first, since the sample was selected to include women with young children, the average age of the women is young; second, some Hausa women fail to report previously terminated marriages. They are often reluctant to mention the name of their first and sometimes second child because of a strongly entrenched custom of first-child avoidance. They sometimes, we suspect, also omit to mention brief and terminated marriages. This is particularly true of those Hausa women who regard themselves as Fulani in origin—slightly less than half the women in our sample.

This study was conducted in two wards of urban Kano,[1] Nigeria's third largest city; estimates of its population range from one million to three million. Both wards in this study, Kurawa and Kofar Mazugal, are long-settled urban areas. In 1977 Kurawa had a population of about a thousand, and that of Kofar Mazugal was thought to be between one thousand and three thousand. Kurawa is settled primarily by people of Fulani origin. All of them speak Hausa exclusively and identify themelves as Hausa except when they distinguish themselves from the original Hausa-speaking inhabitants known as the Habe. The population of Kofar Mazugal, on the other hand, is primarily Habe.

The men in Kurawa are salaried workers and functionaries in the local government. The ward is adjacent to the Emir's palace, and formerly most people who lived there were connected to the palace in one way or another. Most of the men in Kofar Mazugal are merchants working for themselves or for others. In both wards family incomes range from very poor to quite affluent— that is, from servants and families of renters who have no income above barest subsistence to families who own several houses and several vehicles and who employ household help. Like all traditional Kano neighborhoods, Kurawa and Kofar Mazugal are not economically segregated; rather they are internally stratified, though many links of kinship and community cross-cut the strata.

Most of the women in the study were born in Kano city, many in the neighborhoods where they were married. They come from households in all of the economic strata represented in the two wards. Although these urban communities are heavily involved in the market economy, this is also true of the vast majority of

1. Throughout this paper "urban Kano" refers to the area of Kano settled by people who are ethnically and linguistically Hausa. This is the area known as *birni*, which refers to the walls surrounding the old town. More recently settled areas are very different, ethnically, linguistically, and socially, and the descriptions of "urban Kano" in this paper do not refer to these areas.

Hausa rural villages. These two wards can be viewed as "urban villages," and we feel confident in suggesting that in relation to the question of widowhood at least, women's life histories in these wards are not very different from women's life histories in rural Hausaland (see Hill 1969, 1972). In this sense this study is applicable to the Hausa in general, with the exception noted below regarding those women known as *karuwai*, or courtesans.

Virtually all of Hausaland has been involved in active mercantilism for centuries. Both men and women trade, and occupational specialization is common. In both rural and urban areas women supplement the basic support provided by their husbands—whether the men are farmers, laborers, traders, or salaried workers. The most common female occupation is the preparation and sale of cooked food (see Raynaut 1977 and Schildkrout 1983). This is the case throughout Hausa society, except that among the wealthiest families women are more likely not to work at all or to deal in less labor-intensive and less perishable commodities.

The one respect in which this study is not applicable to the majority of Hausa women is that it pertains to residential neighborhoods in which marriage is the norm. Prostitution has been described frequently in writings on Hausaland and is by no means uncommon. However, prostitutes generally live in distinct quarters away from their natal residential areas. They therefore are unrepresented in neighborhoods such as those described in this study. Although prostitutes do marry and divorce (more frequently than other women), they generally live in their own houses or in *gidan mata*, houses of women (see Pittin 1983); thus many of the issues described here, such as the choices divorced and widowed women must make about residence and support, do not apply.

## Marriage and Divorce in Hausa Society

Marriage is the most important way of defining adult status for women in Hausa society, and it is still common for girls to be married before puberty, by eleven years of age. This is true in both urban and rural areas, although the pattern is beginning to change as a consequence of increasing female attendance in western (in contrast to Islamic) schools. Schoolgirls are marrying later, but parents are still anxious that their daughters marry before there is any possibility of extramarital pregnancy. Some are still reluctant to send their daughters to schools other than Islamic neighborhood schools because of fear of that perceived risk.

When they marry, most girls leave the homes of their parents or guardians to live neolocally or virilocally with their husbands. The most traditional form of residential group is that of the compound, composed of several agnatically related households. Traditionally, in rural farming communities, this type of residential unit coincided with a unit of production, the *gandu*, which was a cooperative farming group that owned land and farmed together. In urban Kano, even where large compounds composed of agnates and their immediate families exist, they are rarely units of production. However, large residential units on the model of the traditional *gandu* still exist in urban Kano. Some compounds are composed of two or three generations of men with their spouses and children, and sometimes other relatives including widowed and divorced women who are the daughters or sisters of these men. Large compounds may include seven or eight households, whereas small compounds may be composed of a single household consisting of a nuclear family or a woman and her children.

Although female-headed households exist, male-headed households are the norm. Most compounds include only kin or individuals who are in some sense attached to the family, as clients, servants, or the descendants of these. Many compounds also include rent-paying tenants and some consist entirely of unrelated tenant households and may even have an absentee landlord. For the most part, however, in urban (Hausa) Kano kinbased households prevail.

When women move to their husbands' houses at the time of marriage, they also enter purdah or seclusion. Seclusion is strictly enforced at virtually all economic levels of Hausa society in northern Nigeria, except among the *maguzawa*—non-Islamic Hausa-speaking peasants. Married women do not leave their homes during the day except to attend ceremonies, visit relatives, or procure medical treatment. The extent to which a woman ventures out depends partly upon her husband's attitude, but there is no doubt that all married women's spatial movements are circumscribed. This means that married women are highly dependent upon children for all forms of communication outside their homes. Children shop for women, deliver messages and gossip, and assist women in their income-earning occupations by buying goods and marketing finished products such as cooked and raw food and sewn garments (see Schildkrout 1978, 1979, 1981, 1983).

Although the vast majority of Hausa women move to their husbands' homes, and husbands are responsible for wives' support, women do not lose touch with their own families. They visit frequently, exchange gifts, and sometimes exchange children in fostering relationships for long or short periods of time. They retain inheritance rights in their fathers' estates (inheriting one half the share that their brothers inherit, according to Maliki Muslim law), and they retain the right to return to their fathers' or brothers' homes at the termination of marriage, whether termination is a result of divorce or widowhood (see Table 2).

At marriage, women retain some control over their own property and their labor. They are obliged to cook for their husbands, and husbands are obliged to provide funds or ingredients for cooking. But wives are also permitted to engage in income-earning occupations and keep the proceeds for themselves. They also enter marriage with a dowry of household goods: a large collection of enamel and glass bowls and furniture for their room. Upon the termination of marriage, this property remains the woman's; at any time it can be sold to raise cash.

Husbands acquire the right to their wives' domestic and sexual services, and also the right to raise any children of the marriage, even after divorce or in the event of the woman's death. Occasionally a husband allows a divorced wife to keep one daughter with her, but most of the time, as soon as a child has been weaned, it joins the husband or is entrusted by him to one of his relatives. Although Maliki law stipulates that the wife should keep the child for seven or eight years, among the Hausa the general practice is for the child to be taken by the husband or his family as soon as it is weaned. Although some divorced women resume contact with their children once the children are grown, during their entire childhood contact may be completely severed. This depends upon how acrimonious the divorce was, but in any case divorced women do not have the *right* to spend

TABLE 2

*Living Arrangements of Kano Widows and Divorcées*

| Living arrangement or companion | Marital status | | |
|---|---|---|---|
| | Widowed | Divorced | Widowed or divorced |
| Nonrelative | 1 | 3 | 1 |
| Late husband's home | 15 | – | – |
| Son | 6 | – | – |
| Sister or sister's husband | 1 | 1 | 1 |
| Brother | 1 | 4 | 1 |
| Own home (inherited from father) | 2 | 1 | – |
| Father or mother | 4 | 2 | 1 |
| New husband | 4 | – | – |
| Daughter | 1 | – | – |
| Alone | 1 | – | 1 |
| Other | 2[a] | 4[b] | – |
| Unknown | 1 | 1 | 2 |

[a] One with mother's father's brother's daughter; one with father's sister.
[b] Two with brother's sons; one with father's brother; one with a relative, but relationship unknown.

time with their children; rather they must rely on the good will of their ex-husbands. Considerable modification of this practice occurs in the case of widows; this will be discussed in more detail below.

Hausa society is usually referred to as a "high divorce" society (Pittin 1979), similar in many ways to the Kanuri as described by Cohen (1971). The likelihood of some underreporting in our data has been noted, but 29 divorces among 82 women does not, in itself, suggest a very high divorce rate. However, the rate of divorce varies according to age and according to other socio-economic factors that are not evident in a sample as small as ours. It may be that since this sample was drawn from two quite stable residential neighborhoods, those women who divorce most frequently—and are the ones who raise total figures in some studies—were omitted from our sample. Such women tend to move away from their families, and therefore would not appear in a sample such as this one.[2]

Our Kano data suggest very strongly that most divorces occur

2. M. G. Smith (1955: 62) reports that exactly half of the 280 married women studied in one village were currently in their second or later marriages.

in the early years of marriage, mainly among younger women, especially those who have not yet had children. Women who have been divorced and have consequently had to give up their children are often reluctant to mention this. Yet the observational data we gathered in two years of fieldwork suggest that older women try harder to avoid divorce than younger (especially childless) women. For one thing, younger women have more chance of remarrying after divorce and they can more easily perceive divorce as a means of upward mobility.

In examining terminated first marriages whose duration we know, we see that of fourteen marriages only one lasted ten years, two lasted four years, and all the rest lasted under three years. Of these fourteen, twelve were childless and two produced one child each. Although these data are limited, they suggest that women with children less often get divorced. Women are aware that not only do they lose the companionship and assistance of their young children, but they also risk losing the support of their children in old age. Strictly speaking, these claims still exist whether or not a woman has been divorced, but they are much more difficult to realize if there has been little contact over many years and if the children, when grown, remain in their father's house. Once a woman has children, she is generally in a better position as a widow than as a divorcée, for it is only by remaining married that she can fully exercise her claim, as a mother, to support from her children.

A related factor discouraging women from divorcing in later life is the cultural expectation that women will be supported by men: their fathers, husbands, and sons consecutively. Women who divorce and do not remarry usually have to fend for themselves, and the occupations open to single women in traditional Hausa society are limited. Divorced women who do not remarry after some time enter a kind of liminal status. The term *bazawara* applies only to women who return to their families, do not go out, and keep away from men—publicly at least—until they remarry.

Upon divorce a woman is expected to return to the house of her father or brother, and these male relatives have the obligation to accept her. However, she is expected to remain there only until she remarries, and it is not uncommon for a woman's father and brothers to pressure her into remarrying. During this period the divorcée is referred to as *bazawara*. If after some time the woman does not remarry, however, and it appears that she will not remarry, she is no longer referred to as *bazawara*. Since older women less often remarry—because men choose to marry younger women, or because the women choose not to remarry— many older women who do not have children with whom they can live, live with brothers or live alone. This applies both to divorcées and to widows.

Younger women who live alone may become *karuwai*, cour- tesans (see Pittin 1979 for a detailed study of the lives of *karuwai* in Katsina). *Karuwai* typically leave their natal homes to exercise their independence. "*Karuwai*," our research assistant said, "cannot live in their own [family] houses because *karuwanci* is supposed to be a profession. *Karuwai* do not have the protection of their houses—their brothers, sons and daughters, for they are despised even by their own families." Single women who do not become courtesans or prostitutes engage in a variety of occupa- tions, including maidservant or trader. But there is no Hausa term to describe this category of women. As western education for women becomes more prevalent, divorcées, like widows, who do not remarry can expect to have more occupational op- tions.

One example of a previously married woman who is neither a *bazawara* or a *karuwa* was 'Yar Tanko. According to our research assistant:

She stays outside selling meat until one A.M. This is a questionable, not quite decent practice, but it is not so bad as *karuwanci*. She is living on her own, although she is in her family's house. Since she has an occupa- tion she doesn't depend on anybody. She has even been to Mecca and paid for herself. The strange thing about her is that she is young enough to get married. She has been in this position for over twelve years. She could have been married, so this is her choice. She also had a beautiful sister [now deceased] who stayed unmarried. They sold meat together [they are from a family of butchers]. They were probably married once or twice years ago, but now it's not likely that 'Yar Tanko will marry. It is always difficult for a middle-aged woman to get a husband if she has a good occupation. This works both ways: the woman shuns the restric- tions of marriage and men fear her independence.

As Table 1 shows, a slight majority of the presently divorced women in our study were under age 40 (9 out of 16); and of the divorced women (Table 2), none was able to exercise the option, theoretically available to all, of living with grown children. The divorcées were living with non-relatives, on their own, or with siblings and more distant relatives. Two were living with their parents. The small number of divorced women in the 69 compounds suggests that many divorced women either remarry or leave their familial neighborhoods if they take up unacceptable occupations. We learned of very few such women, although Pittin's data suggest that they may be more common in the overall population than our sample indicates.

### Widowhood

I have suggested that the significance of widowhood varies with age among the Hausa, and that for young women, divorce and widowhood have similar implications: both divorcées and widows usually attempt to remarry, both return by right to their natal families in the interim between marriage and widowhood or divorce, and both lose many of their rights vis-à-vis their own children. The divorcée loses the right to bring up her own children, and the widow risks losing her children in a de facto sense by remarrying. Therefore, although divorcées have nothing further to lose by remarrying, widows who have children may have reasons not to remarry. If they do not remarry, they retain the right to live in their late husband's houses and raise their children there. As Table 3 shows, this was the choice of most of the widows in our study.

Many women are divorced or widowed early in life and subsequently do remarry—particularly, in the case of widows, if they have no children. Many women are first married to men much older than themselves. Subsequent marriages are usually to men closer in age, which decreases the likelihood of widowhood in middle age. The length of the ritual waiting period following the termination of marriage, the *idda*, differs slightly for widows and divorcées. The *idda* is prescribed by Islamic law and is intended to ensure that the woman is not pregnant before she remarries. For divorcées the *idda* lasts for three months and for widows it lasts for four months and ten days if the woman is of childbear-

TABLE 3

*Living Arrangements of Kano Widows With and Without Children*

| Living arrangement or companion | Widows with sons | Widows with sons and daughters | No children from deceased husband | Unknown |
|---|---|---|---|---|
| | | Family unit | | |
| Lives with sons | 4 | 2 | – | – |
| Late husband's house | 4 | 7 | – | – |
| Daughter | – | – | – | – |
| Sister or sister's husband | – | 1 | – | – |
| Brother | – | 1 | – | – |
| Late father's house | 1 | 1 | – | – |
| Parents | 1 | – | 2 | 1 |
| Distant relative | – | – | 1 | – |
| New husband | – | 3 | 1 | – |
| Father's sister | – | 1 | – | – |
| Nonrelative | – | – | – | – |
| Alone | – | – | – | – |
| Unknown | 1 | – | – | – |

ing age, and for three months if she is past menopause. Divorcées generally return to their fathers' or brothers' houses for the *idda*, during which time the husband provides some support.

The *idda* of widows is also distinguished from that of divorcées in that it is, in addition, a period of mourning, known as *takaba*. During *takaba* most widows stay in their late husbands' houses, in their own rooms. During *takaba*, the widow packs up the main material symbol of her married status, the collection of enamel and glass bowls (*kayan daki*) that she brought to the marriage. These are regarded as "decoration" (*ado*) and must be put out of sight during *takaba*. The cupboard in which the *kayan daki* are stored is turned to the wall until the completion of mourning. After *takaba* a widow never entirely redecorates her room; rather, she leaves her dowry packed up, sells it, or distributes it to her children, friends, and relatives.

During *takaba* the widow does not adorn her body; she does not use perfumed soap, only a traditional black Nupe soap (*sabulun salo*), which is also used to wash a newborn infant. The hair is not plaited and is washed with potash, *kanwa*. No makeup is worn. The head is kept covered with a light *maiyafi*, or shawl. The traditional dress of a widow is a strong, old, unadorned wrapper, which is not changed until the end of mourning. It can be washed after seven days, on Fridays, and alternated with a second, similar wrapper. Before starting *takaba* the widow takes a ritual bath, on a Friday, and she repeats this every Friday, reciting certain Koranic verses as she bathes. The bath has a certain *niyya* (ritual intention), like baths for ablution before prayer and the ritual bath taken after sexual intercourse.

The ritual of mourning does not seem to have changed very much in the past 30 years at least; the description given by Baba of Karo (M. Smith 1954: 212) is similar to that we elicited from our informants. Baba told Mary Smith:

When you are in mourning you boil water every Friday morning, you make it very hot, and you go behind your hut and wash your body; you come in and massage your body with oil. Every day you do your ordinary ablutions before you say your prayers, you wash your face, your feet, your underneath, and your hands. The cloth and blouse and kerchief that you wore at the beginning of your mourning are not changed until the end of it. There is no Friday when you don't wash all over, but on the other days of the week you only do your ablutions. You wash your head thoroughly but you cannot cut your hair. You may go out in the daytime, quietly, to greet someone or to do some work. You don't have your hair dressed; every Friday you wash it and leave it as it is. You cannot go to feasts or naming-feasts or any ceremonies. You cannot rub tobacco-flowers on your teeth, but you eat kola nuts—they are food, they aren't forbidden. You may put on antimony and you may shave round the edge of your hair to tidy it. When your husband dies, you must wail. If you loved him, then you are sad at heart also; he isn't there. If you didn't particularly like him, you wail because of compassion, and you had got used to him and now he isn't here.

## Residence

When a man dies, his wives have to make decisions about their place of residence. A number of factors are involved, not the least important of which is the availability of alternative sources of male support. Although many women have independent incomes, these are often insufficient for self-support. The norm in Hausa society is still that men—fathers, husbands, brothers, and sons—are responsible for providing food and

TABLE 4

*Living Arrangements of Kano Widows, by Age*

| Place of residence | Under 40 | 40 or over | Age unknown |
|---|---|---|---|
| House of late husband or of child | 21 | 1 | – |
| With own kin | 3 | 3 | 2 |
| Alone or with nonrelatives or with new husband | 3 | 5 | – |
| Unknown | – | 1 | – |

shelter for their female relatives. With the exception of widows in very wealthy families, most women cannot rely on their inheritance from their husbands to assure them of a continuing income or of ownership rights in their husbands' houses. Widows are entitled to one-quarter of their husband's estate, but if there are children or grandchildren the widows' portion is reduced to one-eighth. That share is divided among all the widows—of whom there may be up to four, according to Islamic (Sharia) law. This means that in practice few women inherit entire houses. They do, however, retain certain residence rights in their husband's houses.

In deciding where she will live after her husband's death, a widow has a number of options, depending upon her age, her prospects of remarrying, the number, sex, and ages of her children, and her financial position. Women who have not reached menopause usually attempt to remarry, particularly if they do not have young children. This probably accounts for the fact that 28 of the 34 then widowed women in our study were over 40 years of age (Table 1). In examining the residential choices of these women, differentiated by age (Table 4), we can see that 21 out of 28 women over 40 were living either in their late husbands' houses or with their children, whereas only one out of ten women under 40 (and she was 39) resided in her late husband's house. All of the younger women had moved back with their own relatives, had remarried, or were living on their own.

Widows are still able to claim support from their children in later years if they have remarried. One old woman we knew had been married and had several children including a pair of twins—

a boy and a girl. When her husband died, the twins were raised by the late husband's patron and his wives. The widow remarried and traveled to a village with her second husband. Many years later she returned to Kano, having been either widowed again or divorced, and she located her children after not having seen them for many years. By then her daughter was married and her daughter's husband, though not wealthy, had a second house in which he gave his mother-in-law a room. When this man died, the woman moved into her widowed daughter's house, where her grandchild was by this time the oldest male. She would not live in the house before her son-in-law's death, because of a strong pattern of mother-in-law avoidance, but the son-in-law did help support her until his death, at which time her daughter and grandson took over.

Older widows very often continue to live in their late husbands' houses, for they recognize that they have virtually no prospect of remarrying. Hausa men are not interested in marrying women who are past childbearing age, and in any case older Hausa women who can support themselves are likely to choose to be independent and not to remarry. Few women in Hausa society look to their husbands for close companionship. This they seek from their children and from other women. Also, once a woman is past menopause, she does not risk being accused of *karuwanci* if she does not remarry.

If the husband did not own a house, the widow, regardless of her age, usually loses her residence and has to move back to her own relatives or fend for herself. Of 38 widows in our study, 15 were living in their late husbands' houses (usually with their children), 7 were living with children (6 with sons) in the children's houses, and 8 were living with their own relatives (siblings or parents) or in houses they inherited from their fathers (see Table 2). None of the widows was living with relatives of her late husband, although children are often sent to these relatives. In contrast, none of the divorced women were living with their children; 12 out of 17 were living with their consanguineal relatives.

Whether or not a widow has children is a factor that strongly influences her place of residence. As shown on Table 3, 17 of 27 (almost two-thirds) of the widows who had children were living in their late husbands' houses and/or with their children. Six widows with children were living with their consanguineal relatives, three were living with new husbands, and one woman was living with a nonrelative. In our sample, there was no childless woman who remained in her late husband's house, although this is said to be possible. One middle-aged widow moved back to her parents' house, and the explanation given by a neighbor was that she could not stay in her late husband's house because she had no children. Only three widows in our sample who had children with the deceased husband had remarried. This is due to age and perhaps also to a fear of losing their de facto claims on their children if they remarry, as they surely would if they were divorced.

The usual Hausa practice in this regard is even more severe, from the women's point of view, than that stipulated in Sharia law, the version of Islamic law nominally followed in northern Nigeria, as in many other parts of the Islamic world. According to the Sharia, women can keep their children after the termination of marriage by death or divorce, until the children reach puberty. However, among the Hausa the male in-laws—or the husband, in the case of divorce—generally claim the children at the time of weaning. Most often a deceased man's brothers accept responsibility for the deceased's children as soon as they have been weaned. Divorcées inevitably lose access to their children, but in practice many circumstances intervene to modify this "rule" in the case of widows, such as the late husband's assets or the availability of caretakers. One of the three widows with children who remarried kept her two youngest children with her, and the two oldest daughters, aged ten and twelve, went to the deceased's brother. It is likely that when the younger children reach six or seven, they will return to the late husband's family.

All of the preceding examples have presumed that the marriages followed the virilocal norm. Occasionally, however, uxorilocal marriage takes place among the Hausa. This obviously leaves the woman in an advantageous position upon widowhood since she is already in her own house. In our study there was only one clear case of this type of marriage. A widow whose youngest unmarried children were boys aged fifteen and eleven remarried, and her new husband came to live with her. He had another wife in a house he owned, and he visited the widow regularly in the house of her late husband. This type of marriage, know as *auren daukisandanka*, "marriage of take up your staff," occurs more commonly among older women or widows. According to M. G. Smith (1955: 52):

A woman may stipulate the type of marriage which she wishes to observe, during the period of courtship, and sometimes where a widow has young children by her former marriage who still need her care, or sometimes, . . . where an old woman without children dependent on her prefers to live alone, she may refuse to accept any form of marriage but that which leaves her in her own home, with a high degree of independence. The husband then visits her in her home for varying periods.

Smith also reported that in the 1950's this form of marriage was becoming more common in Zaria among economically successful women. Pittin, whose work focused on women earning income primarily from prostitution, has reported a similar phenomenon. In Kano, in our sample, although several women owned houses, they either lived in them as widows or continued to live in their husband's houses while renting their own. The phenomenon reported by Smith and Pittin may be more common among prostitutes than among other Hausa women.

Our data suggest that age is a primary consideration in whether a woman remains in her late husband's house to take care of young children or leaves them behind and remarries. Occasionally, the paucity of male relatives of the deceased may influence her to stay—that is, if she feels there is no one to look after her children. In one relatively affluent household, the husband had four wives and more than twenty children. He died in 1978, and by 1982 the youngest two wives had remarried. The youngest, who was about 20 years old and pregnant, left almost immediately. She moved back to her father's house and then sent the child permanently back to her late husband's father's house at the time of weaning. She had already left her first-born child, who was about two years old, with the deceased's father. By 1982 she was remarried and had had a child with her new husband.

The next youngest wife, who was 23 in 1978, remained in her late husband's house until late in 1981, when she went first to her brother's house in Kano and then to relatives in Lagos. She subsequently remarried in Lagos. She had had three children with her late husband (in 1978 their ages were eight, five, and three), and finally left them behind in the care of the two senior wives. Neighbors described her decision to remain in the deceased's house for three years in terms of her reluctance to leave her young children behind. (In many cases, a woman's family—her father and brothers—pressure her into remarrying.) The two senior wives in this family (aged 39 and 42 in 1978) were still living in their late husband's house in 1982, caring for their own children and for the children left behind by their co-wives. Both of these women, however, would have been considered old for remarriage, although it was not impossible.

Another widow, aged 42, told us that she was unlikely to remarry because she was "old" (she said she had started menopause at age 40, just after her husband's death), and also because she had four young children still at home. Her youngest (of eight children) was seven years old; she also had full responsibility for a four-year-old grandchild. In this family there were few other relatives who could be expected to take care of the children, and the widow said it would be virtually impossible to find a prospective husband who would assume such a burden. As mentioned above, only one widow in our study brought young children into the house of a subsequent husband.

*Occupational activities*

Unless a woman's husband was wealthy, her income is no longer a supplement to male support, but is often her only source of support. However, because widows are not in purdah, they are frequently able to earn more than secluded married women; they are able to take advantage of economic opportunities that married women must often ignore. This too, however, varies with age. From our limited data, it appears that older widows are financially more successful than married women of the same age cohort, who remain in purdah even though they are past menopause. Younger widows, the *zazarawa*, who live with their families and expect to remarry, do not go outside much more than married women, lest they appear to be "too free." Like wives, they still live as dependents on other relatives, usually brothers and fathers.

The widows who remain in their husbands' houses or who live with their grown children carry on income-producing activities but generally have a greater financial responsibility for supporting themselves and their children than they did as wives. A man's agnates do have some obligation to support his "orphaned" children, and often the children will go to live with the deceased's kin. In this case these relatives assume much of the obligation to provide day-to-day support for the children. More often than not, the widow does not join her children (there was no such example in our sample), and there seems to be little, if any, obligation on the part of a man's agnates to support the widow herself.

We have income data on eight widows over 40 years of age. There were wide variations in their incomes and in the amount of male support these women could count on; their estimated earned incomes ranged from 2.50 naira (N) a month from spinning to N105.00 a month from trading. The average income was N32.62 a month, compared with an average of N9.62 for secluded married women. When these secluded women are categorized according to age, however, the average monthly income of those over 40 was N19.35. The samples here are small—there were only ten secluded women over 40 in our entire sample—but the difference is obviously considerable.

Seven of the married women were selling cooked food with the help of child hawkers (see Schildkrout 1979, 1981). Of the eight widows over 40, only one was selling cooked food. Five others were trading in various commodities, such as cooking ingredients, thread, cloth, and medicines; one was spinning, and one was a water carrier. The widows, in other words, do not have to depend as much on the assistance of children; they are free to go out and exploit many economic activities themselves. Secluded women change their occupations frequently, depending upon their access to child helpers; nonsecluded women do not have such constraints on their activities.

Selling cooked food is the most remunerative occupation for secluded women, particularly when they have the assistance of children, but it is not necessarily the preferred occupation of widows who have more mobility. One widow who had been making a relatively high income of N66.00 a month before she was widowed expressed a desire to give up the sale of cooked rice after her husband died. She had young daughters to help her, but once her husband had died, she said that she wanted to put the girls in school (he had opposed this). She would then have no assistance in selling her rice, and she said she would like to get a salaried job. Her sister, who had a job in a biscuit factory, made ₦100.00 a month. She also knew a woman who was a matron in a school. Her adult son, who was then living in the same house with his mother and wife, was opposed to his mother's wish to work outside, but as a son he had no right to prevent her. When we left she had not yet made the change, but it is interesting that she contemplated it, particularly considering that she lived in a ward of Kano where very few of the young girls were then enrolled in school (Schildkrout 1979, 1982).

This example points to what is perhaps the most significant factor of change in the position of women, including widows, in northern Nigeria. As western education for females increases, women are likely to seek nontraditional occupations and to reject certain of the confinements of purdah. Widows, who are not subject to the limitations of seclusion in any case, are sometimes already interested in nontraditional salaried jobs. Regrettably, the woman referred to above died of cancer shortly after our last visit; her sentiments, however, can be seen as a reflection of the forces of change now impinging on Hausa Muslim women in northern Nigeria.

*Inheritance*

In Islamic law, women have limited rights to inherit property from either their parents or their husbands. It is important to examine both, since property inherited from a parent, like the money a woman earns herself, can be relevant in determining her economic status and her options as a widow. Nevertheless, although women in Hausaland earn independent incomes and inherit property from parents and husbands, few are able to accumulate enough assets to be totally independent in their later years.

In theory, women inherit from their parents half the share inherited by their brothers. As we have seen, widows are entitled to one-quarter of the deceased husband's estate, but if there are children or grandchildren, the widow's portion is reduced to one-eighth. When there are several wives, as there inevitably are if the man was wealthy enough to have a substantial estate, this eighth is shared among them (Nwogugu 1974: 315ff). Given this division of property, unless a man is wealthy, the inheritance his widow receives is often very small and rarely includes real estate.

Because most marriages are virilocal, when women do inherit real estate they have more difficulty than men in realizing immediate benefit from the inheritance, unless the woman inherits an entire house. Women who inherit real estate are often interested in selling their shares to relatives, or they may attempt to convince the co-owners to turn the entire property into cash. Women who have inherited parts of houses can realize financial gain from their assets only if other relatives in the house agree to accept tenants in their midst. Although this does sometimes happen, in Kano women often have difficulty asserting their rights to real estate except by actually residing in it.

Even though Sharia law stipulates that women can inherit real estate, for many years this was not the case in Kano, following an edict proclaimed by the Emir Abdullahi, who reigned from 1927 to 1953. Abdullahi maintained that if women inherited property they would not be induced to remarry. Moreover, he is said to have thought that female house owners could too easily turn their houses into brothels. It was not until his successor, Emir Sanusi, who ruled from 1953 to 1963, cancelled the edict that women were once again able to inherit real estate. This is an important change in the status of Hausa widows. Owing to the size of our sample, however, the significance of the change is not demonstrated in our data. In the sample of currently divorced and widowed women, two widows and one divorcée were living in houses they had inherited from their fathers. Four widows, all the former wives of one wealthy husband, had inherited houses from their late husband, which they now rented out and from which they realized income. Although many widows in our sample were living with their children in their late husbands' houses, the widow typically does not really own her own room, i.e., she can not sell or rent it; rather she maintains a right to live in her late husband's house as long as some of her children are living there as well.

*Conclusion*

The Hausa stress that biological and social paternity must co-incide; hence the absence of the levirate and the emphasis on marital fidelity as exemplified in purdah. Therefore, although marriage is an extremely important institution in defining adult status for women in Hausa society, the rights transferred to the husband and his kin at marriage do not bind the wife to continue the marriage after death. This is related to the fact that although Hausa kinship relationships have a strong patrilineal bias, bi-lateral ties remain important during and after marriage. The principle of patrilineality is recognized in the deceased husband's agnates' rights to claim the deceased husband's children. How-ever, they are unable to claim rights to the widow herself, to her services, or to her continued reproductive capacity. Having maintained her ties to her own kin throughout marriage, upon widowhood a woman can claim support from her kin as her ties to her agnates weaken.

If we refer to the comparative scheme for classifying widows proposed by Lopata (1972), the Hausa fall in the middle of a scale that classifies "solutions" to widowhood according to how much change occurs in the widows' lifestyle upon the husband's death. Among the Hausa, marriage is not a permanent institution, as it would be if the levirate were practiced; nor is widowhood a life-long social status. Given the possibility of remarriage, as well as the economic opportunities open to Hausa women, widowhood is, for most Hausa women, a phase in their lives. It is a point at which many women have the largest number of options—more than during marriage, for example, or before marriage when they are still adolescents. The number of options may depend on the age at which a woman is widowed. We have attempted to show some of the factors that influence women's choices at differ-ent phases in their lives.

In a sense women even have some control over when they are widowed—assuming that their husbands live to a "normal" old age. Women tend to be widowed either early in their first mar-riage, which is often to an older man, or later in life, if they are closer in age to their husbands. The pattern is the same as with divorce. Insofar as one can be said to "plan" for the exigencies of old age, women do so by marrying men who are closer to their own age for their second or subsequent marriages. For the same reason, women resist or at least refrain from instigating divorce when they are middle-aged and have children.

As we have seen, divorce and widowhood have somewhat different implications in terms of the support women can obtain from their children in old age. Most women look forward to help from their children, and therefore can be said to opt for widowhood rather than divorce as the preferred way of facing the termination of marriage in old age. Whereas younger women will often instigate divorce, often covertly, older women are more likely to reconcile themselves to a less than satisfactory marital arrangement. Divorce can jeopardize a woman's right to support from her children, but widowhood need not, particularly if the woman is older and not likely to remarry. Even if a husband's property is insufficient for a widow to claim a house or a room as her own, she does not lose the right to live in her late husband's house with her children.

The status of the Hausa widow depends upon her age more than on any other single factor, for her age shapes the choices open to her. In a society that defines marriage as existing to produce children, the options open to women depend very much upon their continued childbearing capacity. Since younger women often do choose to remarry, for them widowhood is usually little more than a ritual phase. Although the Hausa do not distinguish widows—either linguistically or ritually—from other older women who are living without husbands, those widows who have children and remain in their husbands' houses have something of a special status: they retain some of the rights of wives, but they are released from the constrictions of purdah. Consequently, even though they are no longer assured of male support, they may be in a better position than are many married women to improve their economic position.

# Will She or Won't She?
# Choice and Dukawa Widows

FRANK A. SALAMONE

EMPIRICALLY OBSERVING how individuals solve the problems they perceive in everyday life, rather than speculating on what they probably do or ought to do, increases our understanding of the meaning of womanhood and of basic male-female relationships. Recent anthropological literature is still afflicted by ethnocentric views, despite the correctives that have been presented by such feminists as Paulme (1960), Sacks (1981), Leacock (1981), Etienne (1979a), Poewe (1980), and Mathieu (1977).

The ethnocentric perspectives, stemming largely from Lévi-Strauss's (1969) theory of "exogamous" marriage systems—whether properly understood by others or not—neglect female contributions to a social system of alliance and exchange. Prominent among the offending works are those of Harris (1977), Divale and Harris (1976), Fox (1972), Beidelman (1971), Goldschmidt (1959), Hammond and Jablow (1973), and Schneider (1962). Even so sympathetic a theoretician as Meillasoux is burdened by a view of the world as divided between active male dominators and passive females who are the victims of domination. Indeed, he writes (1981: 75, quoted in Etienne 1979b: 242): "Women, despite their crucial role in reproduction, never appear as vectors of the social organization. They are hidden behind men, behind fathers, brothers and/or husbands."

An earlier version of this paper appeared in *Afrika und Übersee*, 64: 129-36, 1981. This paper is dedicated to the linchpins of my life and symbols of all that I find worthwhile—Virginia, Frank Charles, and Catherine Ann-Frances, my wife and children. Thanks are due the Dukawa (Hune), especially Matthew Bello, who proved generous and patient in explaining their culture and society to me. Their friendship was an unexpected bonus freely given to an admirer. I also wish to dedicate this paper to the memory of a decent man, murdered without cause—Macdonald Ibrahim Kure.

In opposition to the above presumed universals of biology or psychology, the feminist challenge suggests that observers confound dominance with activity and acceptance of domination with passivity. In reality, the feminist view claims, women are not perceived by themselves or by the men within their system in many societies, at least, as passive objects that can be exchanged at whim.[1] Perhaps Leacock states the position most succinctly (1981: 1, 4-5):

Universal male dominance is a myth and not a fact. . . . And time and again, careful reexamination of the data and of the circumstances under which they were collected have proved me right: indications of male dominance turn out to be due to either (1) the effects of colonialism and/ or involvement in market relations in a previously egalitarian society;[2] (2) the concomitant of developing inequality in a society, commonly referred to in anthropological writing as "ranking," when trade is encouraging specialization of labor, and production for exchange is accompanying production for use, thereby undercutting the collective economy on which egalitarian relations are based; (3) problems arising from interpretations of data in terms of Western concepts and assumptions.

In studying widowhood among the Dukawa of Nigeria, I contend that women do "not disappear behind their men," but only appear to do so when their men expect them to become invisible. One might argue that the dispute about male-female relations cross-culturally is addressed to the question of which hypothesis about dominance is the more problematic. The view I have characterized as ethnocentric is flawed not only because it √ fails empirical tests but because it is universalistic. Refuting such a universalistic statement about the domination of women everywhere requires only that examples of societies in which women are active be offered, not that their activity in every society be

1. Cohen's aptly titled *Dominance and Defiance* (1971) is an example of women's being active in a society traditionally stressing male dominance. The reality deviates widely from the norm. Similarly, my "Arrow and the Bird" (1976) and "Afusare Male/Female Conflict" (1981) emphasize the manner in which women use cultural forms in order to compete successfully with men in "traditionally male-dominated societies."

2. This, incidentally, is the opposite of Meillasoux's assertion. Meillasoux maintains that women's main economic functions, in terms of exercising power, occur when market opportunities expand for them.

analyzed. Indeed, I shall argue in the conclusion that examples of female passivity are more problematic than is absence.

It is not unusual to find societies in which women exert pressure and wield influence. Certainly, egalitarian societies offer example after example of women's participation in active decision making. Leacock's case, the Montagnais-Naskapi of Canada, provides an illustration of a system that, according to "accepted principles," should never have existed, namely, hunter-gatherers with a matrilocal system. Her work established that colonial influences had led to the "traditional" picture of a patrilocal band (Leacock 1981: 4).

Similarly, my work depicts an egalitarian horticultural society in which men form the primary work team. Contrary to some accepted wisdom, however, and in spite of the value placed on patrilocality, most residence is neolocal because of women's pressure to structure situations so that they can better control them.

It is not unusual, then, to find places where women exercise very real power. This fact should not be any more of a challenge than the fact that men do. What should be at issue in both cases is the manner in which each gender does so, the sources of power, constraints on it, indeed all the ingredients of the social construction of reality.

In the following analysis of the Dukawa, I endeavor to present attitudes toward widows in the people's own terms. Women can and do use force to reassert their independence when cultural pressures are brought to bear. The key to understanding both female alliances and independence in this society is the institution of bride service (*gormu*). Widows are like unmarried women in that they have a variety of choices about their future. A number of factors influence widows' choices, and a minimax model helps analyze that matrix. Finally, much of the manipulative power of women comes from their linchpin function, and the symbolic elaboration of that function, resulting from their role in the alliance system, one far more active than envisioned in standard Lévi-Straussian thought. (See Lévi-Strauss 1969 and Rossi 1974.)

## Setting

The Dukawa, self-name Hune, live mainly in Rijau District, Kontagora Division, Niger State; and Shanga District, Yauri Division, Sokoto State, Nigeria. About 30,000 of the 34,000 Dukawa live in Rijau District; the remainder live in Shanga District.

The Dukawa are a fiercely independent and egalitarian people who came to northwestern Nigeria from "the east" in order to maintain their independence from slave raiders. They continued their tradition of resistance to outside domination in struggles against the Fulani, the Hausa, and the British, earning a reputation as "truculent" troublemakers.[3]

As defense against nineteenth-century slave raids, the Dukawa at first strengthened their two towns, Duku and Iri. Later they began to disperse, under pressure from the attacks of Ngwanache and his son, Ibrahim, two Fulani raiders from nearby Kontagora.

The Pax Britannica brought further dispersal, and abandonment of the towns of Duku and Iri. The names remain only as terms for the two sections of Dukawa. Today the Dukawa live in neighborhoods, albeit neighborhoods grouped into villages and towns by the ruling Hausa. Generally, each family composes a household, which cooperates with other nearby households. Average households consist of parents, unmarried children, and married sons and their children—about 25 people. Upon a father's death, however, the compound tends to fission. Each son moves in order to begin his own compound, impelled largely by pressure from his spouse, who sees greater advantage in independent action than in fraternal sharing.

Two factors facilitate such a move. First, women generally do not work on farms, except to help bring in the harvest. They have their own crops from locust and shea nut trees. They have the right to keep any money they make from those crops and from their control of brewing and selling guinea-corn beer (*giya*) or millet beer (*barukatu*). In order to maximize their profits, Dukawa women prefer to work in compatible surroundings. Generally, that does not mean compounds where their husbands' brothers and their wives are competing for scarce resources.

3. Greenberg (1966: 174) provides the linguistic evidence for their eastern origin. Their language belongs to the Plateau division of the Benue-Congo branch of the Niger-Congo family. Mahdi (1968: 33) relates their origin myth to Persia as descendants of Dakkayanusu, a follower of Kisra, the Prophet's most determined opponent. The "truculent" tag is from a British report (NANK: K6099). The British thoroughly despised the Dukawa, and vice versa.

The other factor that encourages fissioning upon an elder's death is the composition of the male work team. That team uses relatives, if available, but is more dependent on age-mates who are ritually bound to a man through performance of bride service (*gormu*) with him for his spouse. Thus, although fraternal solidarity is a cultural ideal, it is honored mainly in the breach. Those with readily available *gormu*-mates have little need to maintain a joint compound with their brothers and can readily find reasons for arguing with them and leaving. Once separate compounds are established, reconciliations can be effected and usually are.

Although all adult Dukawa are expected to marry, some post-menopausal widows do not. They fit into the work system rather easily. They can perform the same work as other women and are generally welcomed by them as models. They have a number of options regarding residence, which are discussed in the following section. They will have little difficulty if any in obtaining accommodations or employment.

The struggle for survival takes place in a tropical savannah climate with essentially three seasons: rainy (June to October), harmattan (November to February), and *bazara* (March to May). The latter two are lumped together as the "dry season." The major climatological difference, however, is that the harmattan wind, a desiccating one, makes life extremely uncomfortable. The average diurnal temperature fluctuates about 40 degrees, from a mean maximum of 97 degrees Fahrenheit to a mean minimum of 58. The *bazara*, or hot season, sees little temperature variation; average maximum temperatures are over 100 degrees and minimum temperatures are not much lower.

The contrast between the dry and wet seasons, however, is more sociological than climatological. In the rainy season, most of the vital cultural activities occur, including marriage and bride service. Festivals, religious rituals, wrestling, hunting, farming—all the self-defining activities—occur then.

The Dukawa live in a setting of great ethnic heterogeneity. They came to northwestern Nigeria in order to escape slavery, and their stay there has been one of constant struggle to resist encroachments on their freedom. They have refused conversion to Islam, perceiving it as a surrender of their ethnic identity, and they have refused to allow *any* intermarriage, perceiving that also as a threat to ethnic independence. They are the only group in Niger and Sokoto states to refrain from marrying members of any other ethnic group. All their interethnic interactions have one underlying theme: maintenance of ethnic identity and independence. Marriage is an indispensable element in the attainment of that goal.

### Marriage and Ethnic Boundary Maintenance

In general, Dukawa use marriage as an ethnic boundary marker, one that reaffirms their own cultural values. (See Salamone 1972, 1974, 1976, 1978a, 1978b, 1979a, 1979b; Salamone and Swanson 1979; and Prazan 1977.) As such, the marriage complex, including widowhood, imposes equal responsibilities on males and females for such maintenance. Thus marital fidelity is incumbent equally on men and women. Marriage outside Dukawa society is prohibited to males and females. No distinction is made between male and female commitment to marital success. Both are culturally enjoined to work toward its success.

Dukawa perceive the need for an ethnic boundary marker. They point to their historical situation, one of seeking refuge and of defending themselves from oppressors who sought to convert or enslave them, as ample justification for that need. Their maintenance system has, in fact, succeeded in enabling them to resist Hausaization better than any other group in the region. A major factor in such resistance, connected with their marriage system, is their acephalous organization: the Dukawa do not have chiefs. Each patrilocal household, and its offshoots, is essentially independent from all others, cooperating with those with whom it perceives common interests and ties.

Their acephalous structure aided Dukawa resistance to Hausa-Fulani and British attempts at pacification. Extended families live near gardens. Ideally, each household is composed of a patrilaterally extended family. That family should continue to remain together after the death of the elder, who is usually the father of all the brothers. The eldest brother usually inherits leadership from his father. It is, of course, possible for leadership to pass from older to younger brother, if families stay together as they "should." In actuality, they typically fission upon the death of the elder, who alone commands enough respect to keep a group together. Like the Nuer (see Evans-Pritchard 1940), the Dukawa cannot be compelled to do anything against their will. Commanding one to do something ensures that it will not be done, unless the one commanding has earned great respect.

When families—or, more accurately, households—fission, they can go anywhere. They tend, however, to remain in the same neighborhood, and eventually, usually at a funeral, reconciliation will take place. Although such reconciliation rarely leads to re-fusing of the household segments, it does allow the sharing of responsibility for caring for gardens.

It is noteworthy that patterns of cooperation are usually not along matrilateral lines. Specifically, brothers of the same father and mother do not join forces against their half-brothers who have a different mother, because the Dukawa are in practice and general inclination basically a monogamous people. Therefore, such cleavages as may occur whenever there are half-brothers and sisters tend to be treated idiosyncratically rather than culturally.

Patterns of cooperation tend to be conjugal rather than matrilateral. Marriage ties therefore assume great importance in forging connections among societal segments. Since the Dukawa live in neighborhoods in which compounds are but a few hundred yards from other compounds, in-laws tend to live within easy walking distance of one another. Among the Dukawa, the only general marital restriction is that one must marry a Dukawa from one's own segment, either Duku or Iri. Within that segment no relatives from either side can marry. The Dukawa state the rule thus, "No one with a common grandparent can marry."

Although brothers tend to reside contiguously even when no longer sharing a common compound, they are not more than a few hundred yards from other Dukawa. Moreover, no Dukawa ever farms alone unless ostracized for a grievous offense. Among those who farm with them are their wives' male relatives. Affinal ties are vital in counteracting atomistic tendencies of Dukawa society. Friendly and trustworthy in-laws are essential if economic affairs are to progress smoothly.

Dukawa individuality, evident in members' readiness to take offense at any perceived slight, contributes to the tendency of a compound to segment at the slightest difficulty. In order to counteract the splitting of units into ever smaller ones, Dukawa look to ties forged by marriage to bind themselves into larger groups than nuclear families. A dynamic is set up in which patrilateral groups split and reform as extended conjugal ones in which brothers-in-law cooperate as brothers. Often these conjugal families unite to form one household and live in a single compound. At other times they may remain residentially separate but be within one or two hundred yards of one another.

Since marriage is such an integral part of Dukawa life, it is necessary to examine its meaning to Dukawa themselves. Although there are many types of marriage (bride service, leviratic, free widow, bride price, and various combinations of these), all must be understood in the light of *gormu*, or bride service. *Gormu* marriage belongs to the wider category of "progressive marriage" (Salamone 1972), in which both spouses gain increasing rights in each other. *Gormu* service begins, typically, when both partners are about eight years old, and it lasts seven years. Even in the earliest stages, both partners have the right, for whatever reason, to break off their relationship. That relationship is one of husband and wife. The Dukawa say that they have a spouse but are not yet married until the completion of all requirements of *gormu*.

About midway through the service, a man sends one of his *gormu*-mates to his wife's compound with a gift of tobacco for her father.[4] People engaged in the relationship have a progression of rights in each other, including sexual ones. (See L. Bohannan 1949 for an elaboration of the concept.) Upon appropriate signals from his wife, a man reciprocates, entrusting his intermediary with the symbolic gift. His future father-in-law's acceptance of tobacco signifies that he will not hinder the marriage's progress; specifically, it means that the young man may spend the night with his daughter, provided that he leave before dawn. The Dukawa have the institution of in-law avoidance, and for the rest

---

4. Macbride's (1935) account differs on a number of points from mine. He reports a six-year *gormu* service, sexual shyness among Dukawa, prohibition of pregnancy before completion of *gormu*, and other differences. His general view of the Dukawa, however, is governed by his concurrence with the official view of them as "truculent." In translation from colonial jargon, that means that they dared resist the imposition of the Pax Britannica. Dorward (1974) notes that the British also termed the Tiv "truculent" for daring to oppose their rule.

of his life a man must avoid his wife's parents and a woman her husband's. Dawn is chosen as a discreet time for a man to leave, for at that time the working day starts, and if a man tarries he cannot but meet his father-in-law, a serious breach of modesty. When circumstances make it unavoidable for a man, or woman, to be present with a spouse's parents, then modesty dictates shyness, quiet demeanor, and avoidance of eye contact.

Dukawa state that one of the purposes of sexual intercourse at this stage of the relationship is to find out whether the couple is sexually compatible. If not, either party can end the relationship, for the Dukawa have a rather realistic attitude regarding sex. They believe that both men and women must enjoy it. Moreover, since divorce after the completion of *gormu* is discouraged and difficult and since men and women must cooperate in many spheres, they are more likely to stay together and succeed if they enjoy each other.

It is not unusual, moreover, for either party to terminate *gormu* before its completion. Women, who end most *gormu* arrangements, typically cite lack of sexual prowess. The case of a teenage girl who rejected three husbands because, in her view, they were "but boys" is not unusual. Dukawa women are not sexually prudish and demand and expect their husbands to satisfy them. In turn, they are willing to remain totally faithful to their husbands until death, indeed, do them part.

Men, however, seek other qualities in women, specifically, fertility. Therefore, they are likely to terminate *gormu* if a woman has not borne a child. This interpretation conflicts with that of MacBride (1935), who says that Dukawa do not permit pregnancy during *gormu*. However, I discovered unanimous agreement that a woman must bear a child before the completion of *gormu* in order to be assured of marital success. No shame, certainly, was attached to such births as MacBride asserts. Since some of his informants were still alive at the time of my fieldwork (1970, 1972, 1976, 1977-78), I surmise that he simply erred, or that the Dukawa, who never got on with the British, simply fed him false information.

Men also look to their wives for advice, economic aid, and support—in sum, for stability. No flighty girl is likely to survive the surveillance integral to the *gormu* process. Good humor, a strong back, wits—those are the qualities that ensure good marital relationships in men's eyes. Sex, which can be good with almost any woman, plays less of a determining role in a man's choice of a life partner than in a woman's.

Sex, of course, is not the only determinant for a woman. She wants a good worker, a person who stands up for his rights without undue temper, one who loves children, and a person who can hold his alcohol and not be a womanizer. Again, each partner looks for qualities that ensure stability and independence.

A full description of *gormu* is impossible here (see Salamone 1978b), but its importance to the Dukawa merits attention. Although parents influence their children's decisions, they do not control them. The principle of Dukawa independence is displayed by both males and females. Either party can end the relationship at any time before the actual marriage.

It is possible, moreover, for a girl to play off one man against another by having both perform *gormu* for her. *Gormu* service is always performed communally. Young men form work teams based on their age groups and go from farm to farm working for their spouses' parents. Thus a young woman may play off members of the same work team against each other. Each rival feels compelled to perform at a higher level in order to save face and, if possible, put his competitor at a disadvantage. Such rivalry among companions who work on communal tasks is a common theme of Dukawa culture. It provides a dynamic for much Dukawa activity by furnishing an internal contradiction: unity through opposition. Even the *gormu* songs sung by the participants underscore this notion, for they must reflect traditional themes but may never be used by anyone else again after their owner's death. A man's *gormu* song belongs to him and is sung at every important event of his life, including his funeral. (See Salamone 1978b.)

*Gormu*, then, forges ties among all participants. A *gormu* wife becomes a symbol to a man of ties to his age-mates who shared in his labor to obtain her. He can call on those men in any emergency, even when he would hesitate to call on his own brothers. It is logical for the primary non-kinship unit in Dukawa society to be a unit that performs bride service and ties non-kin together in its performance. The aims of the age group are consonant with those of the wider society and complementary to them. The period of bride service serves as a rite of passage for the Dukawa, since it marks a transition from youth to adulthood. The friends, therefore, who perform bride service with a man remain his closest friends throughout life, and they must support him in all disputes—those with kin and non-kin, Dukawa and strangers.

Similarly, women whose husbands have been *gormu*-mates retain lifelong close ties with one another, ties transcending their husbands' deaths. They have, in a sense, "come out" together, for their husbands have worked in communal service together for each of them. For women, as well as men, the *gormu* complex is a means of passing to adulthood. Just as their husbands support one another in disputes, so, too, do the women band together to protect their common interests.

Generational solidarity is an overriding principle of Dukawa culture. *Gormu* service, by fostering cooperation among men and women involved in it, promotes such solidarity. The period of bride service is one of testing the potential marriage by providing spouses with opportunities to discover whether they are sexually, temperamentally, and emotionally compatible. In turn, by working together from farm to farm for six or seven years, *gormu*-mates learn quite a bit about one another. They learn their moods, tastes, and reliability. They form an identity within Dukawa society and assume responsibilities for each other's actions.

After marriage, divorce is both difficult and distasteful. Spouses are therefore encouraged to learn as much about each other as possible before the final completion of *gormu*. On the other hand, children born during the *gormu* period are especially welcome, for they bode well for its successful completion. Since no husband wants his child to be lost to his lineage, the birth of a child almost compels him to complete his service, for if he fails to do so, or if his wife rejects him, then the child belongs to her patrilineage.

## Widows

It is clear, then, that in the light of the meaning of *gormu* women have a linchpin role in Dukawa culture. They are the repositories, or at least co-repositories, of key values; they are the juncture points of major alliances. By key values, I mean fidelity, stability, independence while cooperating, love, and chastity. The importance of completing *gormu*, moreover, in the sealing of an alliance is manifest where *gormu* has not been completed but children have been conceived.

When death ends *gormu*—the time when Dukawa say they have a spouse but are not yet married—and the woman has conceived or borne the child of a man who died during *gormu*, then the man's younger brother will seek to marry the widow. Any children born before the completion of *gormu* belong to the woman's patrilineage unless she agrees to marry a man, preferably her husband's younger brother, from her husband's family. Such a marriage is a leviratic one. (See Salamone 1972 for a fuller discussion.)

Moreover, even if *gormu* has been completed, a widow with an unweaned child may take that child with her to her father's home. Although such a child is affiliated legally with the father's patrilineage, Dukawa fear that the child may never return once she or he accompanies the mother to her village. Therefore, widows with children find that their dead husbands' families urge them to remain and remarry into their group.

Especially sought-after are widows who were married by virtue of performing *gormu*. To the Dukawa such women have special meaning, for it is the *form* of Dukawa marriage that is particularly prized, requiring so much cooperative effort and symbolizing core values. In fact, even when an elderly man wishes to marry he will convert bride price marriage into *gormu* by hiring surrogates to perform a symbolic one-year *gormu* for him. (See P. Bohannan 1959 for comparable Tiv beliefs.)

The pressure of the junior levirate among the Dukawa by no means ensures that the widow will stay within her husband's family. The junior levirate, as found among the Dukawa, requires a man's younger brother to offer to marry his widow and raise up children for his name. He may, of course, also marry his own *gormu*-wife or any other wife he can afford.[5] It does not,

5. The tragedy that African converts may experience when indigenous practices conflict with Christian prohibitions against polygyny is outlined in the case of the leviratic practices of the Dukawa in Prazan 1977 and Salamone 1972. Prazan is a Catholic missionary who worked among the Dukawa. In brief, al-

however, require the woman to accept the man's offer. Such a marriage would really be a continuation of the woman's former marriage. If *gormu* has not been completed, the arrangement conforms to what Evans-Pritchard terms "ghost marriage" among the Nuer. (See Evans-Pritchard 1951. In addition, D. K. Fiawoo, personal communication, points out the similarity of Dukawa and Nuer practices, as well as those in many other societies in West Africa with which he is personally familiar.)

A widow has the option of refusing the advances of her dead husband's younger brother, or, if there is no younger brother, his equivalent: a younger male cousin, for example. She can, and usually does, bargain for additional favors, for she is fully aware of her value. Such favors might include bridewealth to induce her to stay. That the bridewealth goes to her father does not deter her, for she gains prestige through its presentation. In addition, she will probably receive clothes for her child and herself. Anything that serves to highlight her value to her husband's family is welcome, for she is a person who has her proven worth.

Whether any further bride service or, most commonly, bridewealth is required depends upon a widow's bargaining power. Traditionally, such a marriage presented few problems if any for a man. Although monogamy is common, polygyny is not forbidden, and a leviratic union is not considered by Dukawa to constitute polygyny. A widow has the option of refusing any form of remarriage, leviratic or free-choice. No one will blame her for any choice she may make. Indeed, only a man's younger brother has no real choice, for he must seek to continue his brother's marriage and raise up children for his dead brother.

Dukawa do not have a "double standard" of morality. Extramarital affairs are equally condemned for men as well as women. Therefore, widows are not easy prey for men interested in comforting them during their period of mourning. Nor is the widow

---

though the Catholic missionaries do not oppose *gormu*, and even admire it, they cannot tolerate polygyny in any form. Therefore, one of their converts was faced with the modern dilemma of choosing between his brother's widow and his *gormu* wife. Pressure to maintain the alliance forced him to marry his brother's widow and abandon his *gormu* wife. Consequently, he has left the bush and become modernized. Today he is a primary school teacher and still rather bitter about the choice his Catholicism forced upon him.

a rival to married women, pursuing their husbands' affections. No extramarital affairs are condoned by Dukawa. This does not mean that no adultery occurs. It does, and women as well as men initiate it. But the definitions vary. For a woman it consists of any extramarital liaison; for a man it consists of any liaison with a married woman. It should be noted that a man cannot simply dally with any free woman. His object must be marriage.

The only crime more grave than adultery is incest. Indeed, adultery is a more serious crime than murder, for it strikes at the cornerstone of Dukawa social structure and cultural identity, the family. In the case of a married woman, for example, the husband could kill an adulterer whom he caught in the act. He and his brothers could also attack the adulterer's home, destroying property and demanding compensation. No one will come to the adulterer's aid. There is more leeway in the treatment of the woman. Normally a wife would not be killed, but she might have her ear cut off, for "if she will act like a bitch," the husband will mark her for all to know her shame. Wives who admit their guilt and promise to reform may go unpunished; those who deny the act may be required to take an oath and undergo a poison ordeal at the home of the chief priest of *kurom njir*.

Neither do women sit by passively while their husbands engage in adultery. There have been cases of wives committing what Dukawa define as justifiable homicide against philandering husbands or the women with whom they are involved. (Salamone 1983 includes a discussion of Dukawa marriage law.)

Since celibacy among premenopausal woman is not a virtue, and is rare among postmenopausal ones, it is unlikely that a Dukawa widow will long remain unmarried. Therefore, it is pertinent to examine factors that will influence her choices regarding future actions. If a widow is happy with her husband's family, then she is likely to agree to a leviratic arrangement and remain with them. As noted above, a Dukawa compound ideally consists of a man and wife, their unmarried children of both sexes, and their married sons and the sons' wives and unmarried children. Upon the father's death, the eldest son should inherit his power. Centrifugal tendencies in Dukawa society, also noted above, tend to promote deviations from the ideal so that many Dukawa compounds are composed of men who have performed *gormu* service together—perhaps joined by some brothers, and by brothers-in-law. Variations occur and some compounds are composed of extended conjugal families.

For any given widow, happiness of course depends on subjective as well as more objective characteristics, but some common cultural traits do enter into her considerations. She will give serious thought to whether her prospective leviratic husband has treated her well before marriage. Their relationship has been one of privileged familiarity, so she will have had ample opportunity to know his moods. She will reflect on whether she has found the women in his compound compatible in their mutual performance of farming and harvesting of women's crops—shea nuts, locust nuts, and so forth. Moreover, she will put great store in whether her share of her husband's property was given her ungrudgingly. She is entitled to furniture, a share of any money, depending on how many children are alive, sufficient food for her subsistence, and adequate woman's farm land and trees to care for her needs.

She will also consider the sex and age of her children. If she has adult males, she is assured of honor and protection among her dead husband's group. If, however, she has only young daughters, or no children at all, she is in a weaker bargaining position. Young children can accompany her to her father's home if they are unweaned. Their return to their father's compound is uncertain at best. Children therefore give a widow some bargaining power. If a woman finds that she and her children get along with her dead husband's brothers, and if she discovers that her prospective levir appeals to her sexually, then there is good reason indeed to marry him.

Similarly, if her in-laws have found the widow to be an asset, to be a link to a powerful and respectable family, to be pleasant, sharing, and a hard worker—in sum, all that a Dukawa woman should be—then they will not easily let her get away. They will appeal to her family to put pressure on her to choose a spouse from among them. They will pay a good bride price, even for a leviratic union, to ease her decision and increase her family's pressure on her. Women of her dead husband's family will visit the widow and as friends entice her to remain. If she has children past weaning, then they will appeal to her to remain for the sake of her loved ones. Children belong to their father's patri-lineage, and a widow must leave weaned children behind. She can of course visit them, but upon their father's death their uncle has the responsibility for raising them.

Rarely will a widow's in-laws not be eager to keep any woman still in her childbearing years. A man's younger brother is obli-gated to raise up children for his name, echoing both the Bible and Evans-Pritchard (1951). Among traditional Dukawa, the fa-ther (*pater*) of any children resulting from a leviratic relationship was the woman's first husband. Whoever the biological father (*genitor*) may be, in fact, the children belong to the *pater's* patri-lineage. The *genitor*, ideally the dead man's younger brother, is responsible for the upkeep of the children. Among Christian and Muslim Dukawa, however, the children do not follow the leviratic rule but take their biological father's name. He then be-comes, of course, their social father (*pater*) as well.

A widow may, to reiterate, choose to marry outside her hus-band's family. If she has produced children, particularly males, she is highly desired. If she is still young, she may find men will-ing to perform at least a symbolic version of *gormu* for her on her father's lands. Such service, performed while she resides in her father's compound, gives the suitor rights to her future children (rights *in genetricium*) as well as sexual rights (rights *in uxorum*). These rights supplant those of her dead husband, and no com-pensation is due his family, a further aid to her bargaining position.

A flattering offer to perform *gormu*—consisting, in the case of widows, of a year or so of service plus a bride price—under-scores her social value. Old men often make such an offer be-cause of the large property the widow controls and the cultural need to redistribute it lest she be accused of witchcraft. These old men further redistribute money by paying young men to stand in for them during any *gormu* service.

A woman may choose her husband's death as the occasion to marry an illicit lover. Because of the intimacy of Dukawa social life, it is unlikely that such a lover would be from her husband's compound or one close to it. She must be discreet enough to hide her affair in order to avoid any homicide or witchcraft charges. Dukawa women are not sexually shy, and although extramarital affairs are forbidden, they do occur with sufficient frequency as to be not unusual.

A woman's choices regarding remarriage could be summed up in a minimax manner: she chooses the best possibility given the alternatives. Among the factors taken into account are the following. First, compatibility with her in-laws. If a woman cannot get on with her father-in-law or, more importantly, with her mother-in-law, she has little incentive to remain in their compound. Her husband's brothers are also key figures in her decision. If she cannot work well with their wives, then her life is unbearable. Second, the sexual appeal of her dead husband's younger brother. Dukawa women make no attempt to hide their enjoyment of sex, and male sexual prowess is perceived as a key factor in marital happiness and stability. Third, the equitability of the inheritance and its distribution. As noted above, there is a subjective element involved. How much, after all, is sufficient? The spirit in which her husband's family doled out her share is important. Specifically, generosity of spirit—a cheerfulness in giving—is highly prized.

But other factors are important too. The presence of children and their age and sex, as noted above, play a key role in a woman's decision. Furthermore, quite simply, a woman may find that she is not marketable. If she has no other offers, or possibilities of any, then her choices are limited. Her own age and the length of time she was married are also important considerations. If she has spent many years in her husband's compound, she will be reluctant to leave. Indeed, she and her husband may be the grandparents of the compound. If she is quite young, however, her ties to the compound may be loose and her opportunities elsewhere may be great.

The alliances created by the marriage may be relevant too. If the alliance has worked out well, then her own family will exert its influence to have her remarry within the allied group. If it has proved worthless, then there will be no such urging. If a woman is young, family pressure may be hard to resist. I have, however, known even young women to resist parental pressure rather in the manner of modern romantic heroines. Indeed, such examples coupled with other data provide a strong case for the existence of true romantic love in a setting where modern sociologists tell us it cannot exist (e.g., Persell 1983). Perhaps they have forgotten that personal, idiosyncratic factors enter into a woman's decision, including the presence of a lover, personality, attachment to parents or brothers—in fact, anything, including the mood of the moment.

If a widow decides to remain unmarried, as is her right, she will normally return to her father's compound unless she is postmenopausal or has an adult son in her husband's compound. In the latter case, she has achieved great status in that compound and has more to gain by remaining. An unmarried widow will normally remain unmarried for a considerable time only if she is nursing a child, pregnant, or postmenopausal. If she returns to her father's compound, both she and her unweaned children have rights there. She is subject to him as head of the compound, and her father will gladly treat her children as members of his family, although technically they belong to their father's lineage. The children, upon weaning, should return to their father's compound.

If her *gormu* was not completed, then a woman will keep her children with her as members of her father's compound. It is quite difficult for her in-laws to take away children who would belong to them technically by virtue of the completion of *gormu*. They therefore endeavor to keep the widow in the family. If children are weaned before their father's death, then there is no difficulty. Problems occur when an unweaned child is taken by its mother to her father's compound. For the most part, only force can effect its return. The unweaned children will be considered members of their father's compound and will inherit through that lineage, male or female, but they normally reside with their mother's father. They may choose to return to their father's family, and do so if they have any grievances against their maternal relatives. In practice, any children a woman takes with her to her father's compound in her widowhood stay there and are treated as having full rights.

Postmenopausal women are not expected to remarry. They are quite outspoken, notable even among the far from reticent Dukawa for their opinions on every topic. Their sense of humor salted with scurrilous remarks is also one of their distinguishing characteristics. They are consulted in any important decisions of the compound and have full and equal rights with any other member.

No one has to care for a healthy widow who chooses to return to her father's compound. In fact, no one has to take care of any adult Dukawa woman. Dukawa women are perfectly capable of supporting themselves, or at least of contributing their share to family economic units. Women make alcoholic beverages, shea nut butter, and other products, which they sell in the open market and to their husbands. They raise their own crops, generally those introduced by colonialism, such as rice or wheat. They tend to household tasks, and when necessary work beside men in the fields. Generally they help men during the harvest time or in clearing fields.

Married women get land from their husbands. Widows obtain it from adult sons or fathers, or from the husband's group as a reward for years of service. Although Dukawa women, like others in Africa, are capable of working horticultural land on their own, they generally work only "kitchen" fields and economic trees in that manner. They work with the iron-tipped hoe when necessary, but in general they rely on men to work the fields. A widow will turn to a son, a brother, or another male, depending on where she has located. She will market any surplus for that man just as she has done for her husband. In sum, there is a clear division of labor. There are male and female crops just as there are male and female jobs. The Dukawa recognize the complementariness of the division and the need, at times, for distinctions to be forgotten.

In a leviratic relationship, the widow moves in with the levir. She has her own hut for herself and her children. Her children belong to her first husband but her new husband has full responsibility for her care and that of her children. For all practical purposes she is "his" wife, but her children are his brother's. Whether she is a junior or senior wife depends on her relationship with her new husband's previous wife, if any. Since the junior levirate prevails among the Dukawa, in most cases she is senior to her new husband and to any other wives he may have.

Most Dukawa women, it is clear, are able to take care of themselves and base their choices accordingly. But widows who are ill do need care. In that case, it helps to have sons who will provide.

Dukawa say that no matter how much a daughter loves her mother, a daughter is mobile and a son is not. In other words, a woman's daughter has obligations that take her away to her own husband and children. A woman's son, however, has ties that draw him back to his own mother and her to him wherever he may be. In time of need she is most likely to turn to an adult son who is the guarantor of her rights in any situation of dispute.

If a woman has no surviving son and is in poor health, then once again *gormu* ties enter the picture. A widow may turn to her husband's *gormu*-mates for aid, and they are honor-bound to comply. If that is not adequate, then she must rely on her brothers, paternal uncles, affines, and so forth. No one in need will go unaided, provided there are sufficient resources. However, having to seek aid that a son would normally provide does cause embarrassment and a certain loss of prestige.

## Conclusion

Dukawa perceive the family as the institution that best defines themselves and protects their cultural identity. Any attack on the family is a danger to Dukawa culture itself, for the Dukawa see themselves as a group of brothers and sisters whose strength lies in maintaining family ties.

The cultural position of widows underscores the point, for widows are treated as part of the family, not as cultural anomalies. They participate in decision making. Far from being liminal, they are quite tangible and active and make concrete choices regarding their marriage and subsequent residential considerations.

Of course, widows do not construct their social reality from whole cloth. Cultural considerations play a role in their decision making. Since land is readily available and currently plays no significant role, other cultural factors take on increasing importance. Those considerations become concrete when applied to a widow's phenomenological situation.

Significantly, an investigation of a widow's universe of choices reveals the manner in which the essentials of Dukawa culture refract in specific cultural situations, suggesting the profitability of investigating a set of values in various cultural scenes. Dukawa widows display individuality, independence, awareness of alliances, care for children, industriousness, and related cultural virtues. They form and represent alliances—past, present, and potential. In the widow's position is found the warp and woof of Dukawa culture: namely, independence and alliance, centripetal and centrifugal tendencies bound in a dynamic tension, for women link groups. Those groups represent forces of independence and alliance and a woman's choices can destroy delicately balanced principles.

Finally, it is necessary to be explicit about the nonpassivity of Dukawa women. Contrary to the prevailing wisdom of Lévi-Strauss (1969), Harris (1977), Divale and Harris (1976), Meillasoux (1975), Hammond and Jablow (1972), and numerous others cited above, women are active shapers of their own destinies within the structural and cultural confines of their own situation. They are active members of a family unit, the basic unit of Dukawa society. They consciously make choices regarding the family with which they will affiliate. Those choices are based on a rational consideration of a number of factors, reducing to a minimax assessment. Widows form a continuum with other women, simply applying basic principles to their particular situation. Those principles serve to protect the cultural identity of the Dukawa and its members in the face of outside threats. It is interesting that the only Dukawa convert to Islam in Shanga District is a man who has openly violated Dukawa marriage sanctions on numerous occasions.

A study of Dukawa widows indicates that many facile statements regarding typical families need revision. Widows, for example, form up to 30 percent of the total adult female population. Dukawa have defined widows' positions in conformity with Dukawa principles and in a manner to incorporate them within Dukawa family life. Many Dukawa families, perhaps one-third, include widows. Studies of the relationships of various types of widows—those who have chosen the levirate, those who have remained unmarried and formed a unit with their children, those who have remarried on principles other than leviratic—are required to discover specific consequences of such arrangements. Preliminary ethnographic impressions suggest, however, that no cultural distinctions result and few microlevel ones of any consequences are noted.

Such consequences, I argue, have more implications for the epistemology of anthropology than for the study of families. It provides yet another example of anthropology rushing to apply universal principles before empirical foundations are appropriately laid or of wrongly applying valid theories because of unconscious ethnocentricism regarding the institution being studied.

# Where to Live? Widows' Choices Among the Rukuba

## JEAN-CLAUDE MULLER

THE PURPOSE of this paper is to illustrate, with reference to the particular case of the Rukuba, how systems of polygynous and polyandrous union in the Nigerian Plateau provide more options for widows than other systems. The systems common in central Nigeria (Chalifoux 1979, 1980; Meek 1931; Muller 1976, 1980, 1981; Sangree 1969; Sangree and Levine 1980; Smith 1953) and northern Cameroon (Collard 1979; Juillerat 1971; Richard 1977) are characterized by plural simultaneous marriages for both men and women. Residence is patrivirilocal and men can have several wives in residence. Women may and are often compelled to have more than one husband, but they cohabit with only one at a time, moving from husband to husband or acquiring new ones according to rules that vary for each society. Marriage is permanent and a wife retains the right to go back to any of her husbands when she pleases.

This unusual system has an important influence on a woman when she becomes widowed. Obviously the situation of a woman who becomes the widow of a man with whom she is residing is different from that of the woman who has not seen her deceased husband for years. Usually the widest options open to widows occur when a woman becomes the widow of the husband she resides with. But even these options are constrained by several factors, in particular the age of the widow, the age of her children, and the availability of help in farming. We shall examine all these factors and see from the actual behavior of widows the factors

My fieldwork among the Rukuba was conducted between 1964 and 1967, when I was stationed in Jos, working for UNESCO. Subsequent stays, from May to September 1968 and from November 1971 to February 1972, were funded by the University of Rochester, N.Y., and the Canada Council respectively.

that influence their choices among the different formal options the marriage system provides. Finally, we shall compare the fate of widows with that of widowers in order to account for their similarities and differences.

The Rukuba live 25 miles southwest of Jos, the capital of Plateau Province, Nigeria. They number about 12,000 and live in 24 villages, each headed by a chief. They are agriculturalists and grow a variety of crops, the most important being fonio (*digitaria exilis*), sorghum, and late millet. Tubers come next in importance, with yams, cocoyams, and sweet potatoes. In addition, the Rukuba keep many goats, fowl, and dogs, and some sheep. Horses used to be more numerous than they are today. The unit of production is the household, comprising a man, his wife or wives, his unmarried children, and one married son; the other sons establish their own households nearby soon after marriage. Each household is thus self-sufficient as far as food is concerned but dependent on others for tool making, tool repairs, and pottery, which are carried out by a few part-time Rukuba specialists.

## The Marriage System

Rukuba social structure can only be understood in relation to the marriage system. The tribe is divided into two exogamous moieties. A moiety is further divided into wife-taking units, which ideally coincide with a village. But usually a village harbors a demographically dominant wife-taking unit of one or the other moiety, which constitutes the agnatic core of the village, and one or two agnatically based minority groups of the opposite moiety. The latter also form wife-taking units, which are politically subordinate to the main agnatic core of the dominant moiety within the village. Each wife-taking unit is composed of several clans, which are further divided into agnatically based subclans of about 30 members, all bound by the incest taboo. Premarital sex, a prominent feature of the life of Rukuba youths, occurs within the wife-taking unit but outside of the subclan. Such relations are based on mutual agreement of the partners. The boy pays a goat or a hoe to the girl's father to initiate the union. The relationship has to last a minimum of six months but may extend much longer, sometimes for years. It must end when the girl marries into the other moiety or when she takes another lover. A girl may have only one lover at a time, but she may have several in succession before she marries. The lover visits his girlfriend at her house and spends the night.

Both partners—who call each other *izini*, "lover"—have several rights and duties to perform for each other. The boy must build a bedroom for his girlfriend in her natal compound and he must help her on several occasions during the year's agricultural cycle. She too helps him in farmwork, especially at the time of transplanting millet. On this occasion she goes to her lover's or lover's father's farm to help his family in transplanting (Muller 1976: 71-74). There are also symbolic rights and duties that make this premarital relationship a quasi-marriage (Muller 1981: 108-10). The boy must help his girlfriend collect firewood, a task performed by a husband for his wife but not by a suitor courting the girl he is going to marry. When members of the lover's house brew beer, the lover gives some grain to his girlfriend to brew for him—another wifely duty a suitor cannot ask from his betrothed. At harvest time, the lover also gives his girlfriend some grain to pound; she keeps half and returns the rest to her lover, just as a husband does with his wife.

However, these premarital relationships are not true marriage since the girl is not allowed to bear children. Abortions are performed to get rid of unwanted pregnancies, and if abortion fails, infanticide is resorted to (Muller 1976: 74-77). These aspects of the premarital relationship, a nonmarital union, should be borne in mind. In some ways they resemble (but with significant differences) an option open to widows if they choose to remain in their deceased husband's compound. This option will be examined later.

This pattern of premarital relations has a bearing on the marriage system in the next generation.[1] An eldest daughter is preferentially affianced to the son of her mother's last lover. Younger daughters are preferentially betrothed to other members of the mother's natal wife-taking unit—but not into the mother's natal subclan. The betrothal ceremony is held when the girl is about

1. A few years before my fieldwork started, the preferential marriage had been abolished by the administrative chief, who considered this custom a backward one. However, most of the women had been married in this way when I started my inquiries and I therefore use the present tense.

nine years old. Later on, while having premarital relationships within her own moiety, the girl is also courted by young men of the opposite moiety who also wish to marry her. These young men belong to wife-taking units other than that of the preferential groom. The girl finally chooses the suitor she likes best from among these young men to become her free-choice groom. Most girls have such a suitor in addition to the preferential groom; only 10 percent of the girls choose to have only a preferential groom. When they come of age they marry. Girls marry for the first time between the ages of 18 and 22; boys on the average are three to five years older. Thus the difference in age is not pronounced. Those girls who have two suitors marry their free-choice groom first and spend a month with him. After this month of cohabitation the woman is ceremonially escorted to her preferential groom, with whom she has to spend at least a month. After this one-month trial period the wife has the choice of remaining with her preferential mate or rejoining her first husband. Only 5 percent remain with the preferential husband; the rest return to their free-choice husband.

After the first year of marriage the woman can either remain with the husband with whom she is presently residing or return to the other man. Furthermore, she can also choose to contract an additional marriage with a man from another wife-taking unit, a marriage that will be as valid as the others. The woman is free to choose between these options, her husband and her parents having no say in such matters. The decision is entirely hers and the deserted husband must show no dismay. If he exhibits anger the wife will never go back to him, but if he behaves well there is always a chance that she may return to his house again. A man never sends a wife away; this is something unheard of among the Rukuba. There is no divorce in Rukuba society and each marriage remains intact. Since women perform agricultural work along with their husbands, they move from one husband to another or marry a new one at the start of the rainy season. However, women rarely have more than three free-choice marriages, because a woman with too many marriages is considered loose and unreliable by both men and women.

For the purpose of the following discussion, it will be sufficient to say that all marriages, the preferential, the first free-choice marriage, and all subsequent free-choice marriages, carry the same set of rights and duties between husband and wife as far as domestic management is concerned. There are no differences in the ways wives are treated by their various husbands except that the preferential wife of a village chief has some ritual duties to perform; in other matters she is treated exactly the same way as any other wife.

Children belong to the husband who begets them. When a woman leaves one husband for another at the time of conception and paternity is contested, the mother has the final say in designating the father. What happens to small children whose mother changes husbands will be examined later in connection with widows who have small children.

### Widowhood and Mourning Rites

Such matrimonial freedom, which would probably be envied by women of several African societies, has a direct bearing on the status of the woman as a widow. There are two contrasted cases here: a woman can lose a husband with whom she is not residing or one with whom she presently resides. In the case of a husband with whom she no longer resides, the widow pays a short mourning visit to the deceased's compound and continues to cohabit with the husband with whom she is residing. It is considered normal for the cohabiting husband to escort her to the late husband's compound, and although not mandatory it is considered a gracious gesture for the cohabiting husband to bring a goatskin with which to wrap the deceased if the latter was a man of importance, such as a blacksmith, a village chief, a clan head, or a "rich" man. Their mourning usually lasts only a few hours before they return home.

The same behavior is required of a man who becomes the widower of a wife who dies while she is residing with another husband. In that case, the man goes to mourn at the other man's compound. Again, mourning lasts only a few hours. All the co-widowers of the deceased greet one another with the standard formula *Ikpi immot iku?* ("Is our thing [wife] dead?") If a co-husband arrives quickly enough—the Rukuba bury their dead almost immediately—he may accompany the corpse to the grave, for women are buried in the cemetery of the village in which they have died. The husband with whom she was residing has his head shaved as a sign of mourning, as do all the people of his compound, including resident co-wives. A nonresidential husband does not usually shave his head.

A widow, on the death of a husband with whom she was residing, usually spends some time mourning in his compound. She will shave her head—which is not generally done by nonresident widows. The mourning period varies, depending upon individual feelings. The standard Rukuba answer when asked about the duration of mourning is that it lasts for *kiekus*, "a year" or more precisely "the rainy season," which runs from May to October. When examining actual cases, Rukuba point out that much depends on the sentiments of the woman concerned. She can "let her sorrow run" as long as she pleases. However, it is generally understood that a resident woman has to remain in her late husband's compound for a few months.

Should the widow decide to stay at the deceased's compound after the mourning period, a ritual is sometimes performed to signal the termination of mourning. This happens when the deceased is a "rich" man whose widow or widows are past childbearing age and too old to find a new husband. Of course, such widows could always go back to any of the other houses in which they had been married. The rite is held some months after the death: a goat is killed by the deceased's agnates in order to "wash" the widow, as the Rukuba put it, and to signal an end to the mourning. The ceremony is known to a great many Rukuba but they all agree that it is rarely held. Indeed, in more than four years of fieldwork I encountered it only once, after the death of the administrative chief.[2]

*Formal Options Available to Widows*

After the mourning period, a widow has three options open to her: she can remain in her husband's compound, she can rejoin a previously deserted husband, or she can remarry. If the

2. The ritual not only "washes" the widow but it shows the wealth of the deceased's house. The heirs are not always prepared to perform it, preferring to keep the riches for themselves rather than dissipate them in a rite considered to be minor. This reluctance as well as the scarcity of "rich" men may explain why the ritual is performed so rarely.

woman remains, she simply takes over from her husband and administers the land, farms, gardens, and goats. After marriage, a woman is allotted some fields from her husband's holding and she cultivates them as long as she remains with him. After her husband's death, the woman decides whether to continue using these fields or to use other plots the husband had reserved for his own use.[3]

The division of labor between the sexes in farming is more marked in theory than in practice. On their own fields, which are nearer the house than bush fields, women cultivate ground nuts, Bambara nuts, and sweet potatoes (cultigens grown exclusively by women). In addition, women are given home gardens situated around the compound where they plant various pulse and sesame (again, crops grown exclusively by women). The main staples, fonio, sorghum, and late millet, are grown primarily by men with the help of women but women may also have such fields. The proportion of each crop to be planted by each spouse will be determined jointly. After the husband's death, a widow keeps the fields she thinks best suited to her needs. There is no land shortage in Rukuba, but everyone tries to have his fields as close as possible to the compound. Moreover, there must be a delicate balance between nearby fields and distant bush farms. A widow tries to maintain this equilibrium.

Should a widow have young sons, all her husband's fields are entrusted to her on behalf of her sons and she will ensure that her late husband's agnates do not encroach upon their rights. Should a nonresident widow decide to return to her late husband's compound, fields will be reallocated to her in agreement with the co-wife or co-wives still residing in the late husband's compound—or, in the absence of co-wives, in agreement with the late husband's agnates, who will see to it that she has enough land to cultivate. Similarly, a son who is living with his mother in

3. When a man has several wives in residence with him, each of the wives manages her own affairs independently of the others as far as farming is concerned. Each of them is allotted her own fields and her own granary, and they all help their common husband in his bush farm. Each wife cooks daily for her husband, herself, and her children, using her own supplies until they are exhausted; at that time the husband's granary is opened and he distributes his grains to his wives. When a husband dies, his wife or wives are almost never suspected—and even less often accused—of having killed him by witchcraft.

the compound of another husband at the time of his father's death may decide to go back to his father's compound, or the father's agnates may press for his return. In either case, he is entitled to some land from his father's estate, and the apportionment will be made by all concerned: his mother, who retains the right to see to it that her son is well treated; the resident co-wife or co-wives; and the late husband's agnates.

If the widow has no children but is still of childbearing age, she can lend some of her fields to her late husband's agnates on the understanding that these fields will automatically revert to any son or sons she might bear while living in her late husband's compound. She will supervise the marriages of her sons and daughters, usually with the help of her late husband's agnates.

The deceased may have had several wives in residence at the time of his death, but this is not very common since the rate of residential polygyny among the Rukuba is only 28 percent. A census was taken including only men with one or more wives in residence. Men who were temporarily without wives owing to death or desertion were omitted. Of those men who had a wife in residence, 72 percent had only one wife living with them, 19 percent had two wives, and 9 percent had three or more wives. The cases in which a man had several wives in residence at the time of his death are the minority, but where there are several resident widows, the widows are left to apportion the land of the deceased as they please. Each manages her own affairs at her own convenience and decides independently whether to stay or to leave.

So long as a woman remains in her late husband's compound, she can entertain a lover: *uni kiso*, "the one who just sits." The choice is with the woman, who selects one or more lovers from those who approach her. However, such lovers must come from the deceased's moiety. A deceased's close agnate may become a widow's lover if she wishes, and the Rukuba point out this possibility by saying that any younger or older brother can sleep with the woman after his brother's death, but never before. Some add that even a son of the deceased can sleep with one of his mother's co-wives but not, of course, with his own mother.

My observations reveal, however, that lovers usually come from other compounds of the same moiety within the village and are not close agnates of the deceased. Many come from other villages, and thus from different subclans and different wife-taking units. The woman may marry such a lover, as we shall see below. The widow has the right to have several liaisons of this kind simultaneously, but in practice widows tend to stick to one man at a time. The expression depicting the lover, "the one who just sits," indicates the nature of the relationship. He has no rights over the woman and she can dismiss him at will. The widow is also called *uwa kiso*, "the wife who just sits," because she is just sitting in her house without a proper husband in residence. A widow can have lovers in her deceased husband's house even if she has living husbands elsewhere. It is her decision to remain in her deceased husband's compound that permits this kind of relationship.

A lover comes in the evening to spend the night and the widow can cook for him if she wishes, but this is not an obligation. A lover may help the widow in her agricultural tasks or in house repairs, but here again there are no obligations. These tasks are normally the responsibility of the dead husband's agnates: first the sons of the widow or, if she has no sons, the sons of her co-wives; then her late husband's brothers and their sons.

The informal relationship a man has with a widow can be very close. A woman who has a long-lasting union with a lover can be associated with his house in many ways. If his resident wife or wives view the relationship favorably, the association between a woman and her lover's compound can be so close that the lover's children by his wives refer to the widow as "mother," a term usually reserved for their mother's legal co-wives. The widow may help in her lover's house or she may prepare some beer with the grain he gives her when his compound has a marriage or a farming bee. All of this is informal and depends on an agreement between both partners in which the lover also helps the widow perform what are regarded as male tasks in the widow's compound. It also depends on the physical distance between the two houses. If a lover is from another village, and this occurs frequently, he will involve the widow less in the affairs of his house and be less involved in those of hers.

However close the relationship might be, a lover is never expected to live permanently with a widow. Most Rukuba say that this is unknown in their society, and that it is the most shameful thing a man could do. Rukuba ideology puts great emphasis on patrilocality. Men are expected to reside in the compound where they were born or to build a new compound not far away. If people move their compounds away from their natal location, it is always to their bush farms. Even though an increasing number of people move nowadays, those who remain in the old village site look down on them and proudly say, pointing to their compound, "We have been here since the beginning" (i.e., since the Rukuba arrived at their present location). Although the Rukuba deny the possibility of a man's living in a widow's compound, I did find two such cases. But I doubt that there are many others. The first dates back to about 1938 when a man of Egbak village wanted to marry a young widow of the right moiety from Imbop village. She already had children and refused to move, inviting the man to come and live with her instead. He moved to the widow's house and resided there until he died shortly after. He was derided by everyone. I discovered the second case at Kakkek while I was in the field. The chief of what remained of Uniu village, a widower, lived in one widow's compound and was also ridiculed by everyone around him.

Men liken this kind of consort relationship with a widow to the premarital relationship youths have within their own wife-taking unit. Elderly men laughingly refer to the widow they visit as their girlfriend, *izini*, this being the proper term for a premarital lover. However, a relationship with a widow carries fewer rights and obligations than a premarital relationship. As we have shown, premarital relationships demand codified work prestations between the boy's and the girl's compounds; nothing of this sort applies to a relationship with a widow. A widow can also have several lovers whereas a girl can have only one at a time. Finally, a woman's consort is always a man from her opposite moiety whereas premarital relationships are always with men of the woman's natal moiety. Thus a widow-consort relationship is informal, whereas a premarital lover-girlfriend relationship is highly formalized. More importantly, premarital relationships must not produce children. As we have noted, infanticide and abortion are resorted to in a premarital pregnancy, whereas children can be born in a widow-lover relation.

Any children born of the union of widow and lover belong to the late husband, who becomes their posthumous father. This applies to any lover, even one who comes from another wife-taking unit. The underlying idea is that any child sired in a late husband's compound belongs to him. The children bear their posthumous father's name and they inherit from him. They have all the premarital and matrimonial prohibitions given by their jural father. In addition, if the lover-genitor is known because he has had a long-term relationship with the mother, he passes on to his biological son all his premarital and matrimonial prohibitions as if the child were his jural descendant. Thus such a son is not able to have premarital relationships in his jural father's sub-clan—this being the Rukuba limit of the incest taboo—and if the biological father comes from another subclan, the son is also de-barred from such relationships in his genitor's subclan. As for marriage, he is not able to marry into his mother's subclan, his deceased father's mother's lineage, or his biological father's mother's lineage. Legally speaking, nothing else is supposed to come from his mother's lover. These are the formal rules, accord-ing to the Rukuba, and reality often corresponds to these rules.

When a widow remains in her late husband's compound and has children by both her late husband and a lover, there may be tensions between half-brothers. Biological sons of the deceased may try to appropriate the best land at the expense of half-brothers begotten by a lover. This is likely to happen when there is a great difference in age between the half-brothers. But such quarreling over land usually occurs after the mother's death. During her lifetime she makes sure that none of her sons is robbed of his rights.

Other complications sometimes arise, as the following case in-dicates. A boy was sired by a lover belonging to the same clan as the deceased. The lover had no legal son and left his fields to his biological son, who legally was the son of the deceased husband of his mother. This son, lacking adequate garden land, also claimed some of his *pater*'s gardens. But his half-brother refused to give him such land, claiming that the boy had already received enough land from his genitor and was therefore not entitled to a share of his jural father's estate. The matter went for arbitration to the clan head, who decided in consultation with the village chief that the boy was fully entitled to a part of his jural father's estate since he bore his name. The land he had received from his biological father was not a customary inheritance and did not deprive him of his rights to his *pater*'s estate.

The second formal option open to a widow is to simply go back to one of her previously deserted husbands. She will leave the deceased's compound and rejoin her other husband, exactly as she might have done during the lifetime of the deceased. However, she keeps the permanent right, as we have noted, to go back to the deceased's compound as if he were still alive. The Rukuba express this by saying that a woman retains the right to return to any compound she has married into, whether the husband is alive or dead.

Sons are a very important variable directing the choice of residence of a widow, and we will now consider the fate of children in this matrimonial system. Even though children belong to their father, a woman who changes husbands takes her small children with her to the new husband's compound. The Rukuba say that a boy or girl still needs the mother's presence until the age of six or eight. The father lets his children go, but he will reclaim them when they reach the age of eight. Then they remain permanently with him. Thus a woman who has had several husbands may have sons living with at least one previously deserted husband. When she ages, there is a tendency for her to rejoin her son and become incorporated in his household, because the support of a son is better than the care she could expect from her husband's agnates. This is also true of sons of co-wives. This tendency to join a son is even more accentuated when the woman is a widow residing without a son in her deceased husband's compound. The importance of having sons in old age is understandable since the Rukuba hold that a woman can never return to her natal compound. In a survey undertaken in the most populous village, Kakkek (with population of about 1,900), I found only two exceptions. Both were widows whose late husbands left no living agnates. These widows had returned to their natal compound at the express request of their own agnates because they lived alone. This situation was regarded as anomalous and exceptional. The importance of having a son is also reinforced by

the fact that a widow cannot live with a married daughter. When
I suggested such a possibility the Rukuba found it ridiculous
and even shocking.[4]

The third option open to a widow is to contract a new marriage. As in any free-choice marriage, the woman chooses from
among her suitors the one she likes the best. A suitor must come
from the same moiety as the deceased and must pay bridewealth
to the woman's father or father surrogate in order to be allowed to
bring the woman to his compound. Such a marriage usually occurs with a young widow, up to the age of 30 or 35. In the case of
a new marriage, the widow can marry one of her lovers provided
he comes from a different wife-taking unit than her husband.
The choice is hers. She may find certain advantages in marrying
a lover. For instance, he may be without a wife in residence because he was deserted by his wife or wives. The widow will then
have an opportunity to run a household with the full help of a
husband. This arrangement is better than asking the deceased's
relatives for help, as we shall see below. If she marries a lover
and has previously had a child with him, that child belongs to
the deceased husband, but any new child born to the new marriage will belong to the former lover, now husband.

An ambiguous situation may arise if the lover comes from the
same wife-taking unit as the widow's deceased husband and
tries to entice the woman to live with him. He then becomes a
sort of de facto but not de jure husband. The Rukuba insist that
a woman cannot have more than one husband, alive or dead, in
one wife-taking unit. Moving to a lover's house of the same wife-
taking unit is therefore regarded as anomalous, because the
woman is expected to stay in her late husband's compound, and
it occurs rarely. When it does happen, it tends to involve postmenopausal widows. In such a situation the deceased's agnates
leave the woman to do as she pleases, but they and everyone else
keep in mind her irregular status.

4. A widow can go to any son she chooses. If the son is also the deceased's
son, the mother may remain with him. But if she finds it more congenial to live
with a son of one of her deserted husbands, she may return there, even if she
does not like the husband. In that case the woman will say that she lives with
her son rather than with the husband. The husband has no say in such an
arrangement.

*Actual Behavior of Widows*

A sample was taken of 30 widows to distinguish actual behavior from what the system permits. All of the sampled widows were residing with their late husband at the time of his death. Only women who had been widowed for several years were included in order to obtain a "diachronic" view of widowhood. Nineteen of these 30 widows chose to remain in their late husband's compound. Eleven either remarried or returned to another husband. Of those who remained, 10 had taken only one lover by the time of the sampling and 9 had been involved in two or three unions lasting one year or more. Those who had the most unions were the oldest—ranging in age, as far as I could estimate, from about 40 to 60. In addition to having unions lasting one year or more, widows can at the same time have temporary unions with other men. Such temporary liaisons usually occur at festivities where beer flows abundantly and men of the right moiety try to entice the woman to spend the night with them. These relationships were not included in the data reported above.

The widows most likely to remain in their late husband's compound either had adult sons or were past menopause. After reaching the age of 40, women usually do not contract new marriages; this is equally true of widows who, like other women past this age, are not so much sought after for marriage. The age of the widow and the age of her sons are both critical factors that dictate her options.

The widows in our sample who chose to remarry or who returned to another husband were mainly under 40. Several of them had small children. Their decision to remarry may seem surprising at first. We have said that a widow is autonomous. She can choose several sexual partners and she can freely plan her work without interference from a husband who might ask her to work on his fields instead of her own. The Rukuba say that the husband's will prevails; he can require his wife to leave her own agricultural tasks if he needs her help. In contrast, a widow decides on her own how to manage her late husband's estate. She is responsible for her son's and daughter's marriages and she becomes the head of the household—this in addition to her responsibilities as mother and housewife. In other words, she has to assume on her own both the male and the female tasks pertaining to a household. Some strong-willed and energetic widows can meet this challenge, and I encountered a few such formidable women during my fieldwork. Usually, however, the tasks of food production plus housekeeping are difficult for a solitary woman to perform adequately. The heaviest part of hoeing and clearing the fields is done by men, who also make house repairs and periodically rethatch the roof. They also fell trees for firewood. Another important factor is that the seasonal distribution of agricultural activities is uneven. Transplanting millet is a very hard task that husband and wife perform jointly, but it must be done within a limited period when the rains are at their peak or else the millet sprouts will die. A widow alone cannot do as much. These difficulties are aggravated when she has small children and no one is available to take care of them while she is busy working on her farms.

The Rukuba say that a widow who cannot cope can ask her late husband's agnates for help. Such help must be given and is given, but the amount of assistance is determined by the providers. Moreover, help is given only after the agnates have carried out their own agricultural tasks for their own households. The coordinated activities of husband and wife working together produce greater returns than a widow can manage on her own or with the assistance of her late husband's agnates. For many widows, having a husband is preferable to having the freedom of working alone.

*Comparison with Widowers*

It seems fitting to end this account by contrasting the fate of widows with that of widowers. If a widower has several wives in residence, he will mourn for a month or two with the other co-wives, but little changes in his domestic arrangements. However, the case of a widower whose only resident wife dies is different. He is wifeless for the moment and is in exactly the same position as a husband who has been temporarily or permanently deserted by his only resident wife. If he has married sons, their wives will cook for him. If he has unmarried daughters, they will do likewise. But if he is alone he will fend for himself, doing his own cooking and household chores. Sometimes he can arrange to have these done by a close agnate's wife or daughter, but usually he will stay on his own. Normally men do no cooking except for ritual meals, but they know how to cook and many have to do so temporarily if their wives desert them.

Many men are likely to be deserted in marriage, and if they have no mother, daughter, or daughter-in-law, they do their own household tasks while waiting for a wife to come back or before arranging a new marriage. No stigma attaches. I have known one or two men without a resident wife who could have gone to live in a married son's compound but preferred to remain in their own house and be entirely on their own. In each case the sons had established independent households on their bush farms—a new trend we have already noted—but the fathers refused to follow.

As for the possibility of a new marriage, it depends on the age of the widower. In preferential and in their first free-choice marriage, men marry women who are of their own age or slightly younger. A few men will continue through their early 30's to marry women of marriageable age, between 20 and 22, but these are relatively rare cases. A young widower under 30 may then be in a position to marry a wife in her first free-choice marriage. After he reaches the age of 30 to 35, the only way he can find a new wife is to resort to a secondary marriage with an already married woman. Difference in age can be greater in a secondary marriage than in primary marriage, and the men who can benefit most from this are those who remain young-looking and are known as hard workers and wise house managers. Mature men up to their late 40's and early 50's can still marry women in secondary marriage, but beyond this age they no longer marry. Those still interested in sex will try to find a widow. Several old men told me privately that they were "doing *kiso*," i.e., having a relationship with a widow, because their "thing was still rising up."

As with widows, a crucial factor for widowers in obtaining assistance is the presence or the absence of a son. A widower with a son is, like a widow, incorporated in his son's household until he dies; a widower without a son is left on his own until he cannot cope any longer. His closest agnates then take care of him and help him on his farms, but this help is sparingly given. Such solitary men may have their share of hardship. Sometimes a widower without sons lives apart from the other compounds of his patriline, which are usually clustered together. In that case, he generally does not go to his own agnates but stays put. If he is too old to contemplate remarrying, he farms alone. As he grows older he is helped by the young men of the neighborhood, who hoe some of his fields. He will shift residence and join his closest agnates only when he is sick and completely unable to work. At this stage the end is usually very close.

It is noteworthy that a number of old wifeless men, either widowers or men deserted by their wife or wives, form a high proportion of the oldest widows' lovers. This is quite understandable. Menopause is not a deterrent to amorous relations and, as we have seen, age difference between spouses is usually not great (approximately five years among the Rukuba). Most widows and widowers are elderly people who have no hope of finding a new spouse. Therefore, widows and widowers are on the same footing and many a *kiso* relationship is entered into between them. As the partners grow older, the relation becomes more and more a sort of quiet companionship.

### Conclusion

This paper has shown that a Rukuba widow has a great many choices. This is the consequence of a marriage system that permits a woman to have several husbands simultaneously, and of the various strategies that custom makes available. A widow can rejoin a previously deserted husband, she may marry a new one, or she may remain in her deceased husband's compound and entertain lovers. However, these formal choices are constrained by several factors. The first is the age of the widow—she is less likely to remarry after reaching 45 and will usually rejoin another husband or stay put. Widows who have sons of farming age living at the deceased's compound tend to remain there. As for younger widows up to 35, a great proportion of them do remarry since household and farm tasks are more easily performed with the help of a husband in residence than alone or with the help of the deceased's agnates.

Social change has not brought about a new situation, nor

opened new opportunities for widows. Almost all the Rukuba, and especially the women, were still farmers at the time of field-work. Islam had made no headway, and the number of Christians amounted to a mere 4 to 5 percent of the total population. Most of the Christian women of the first generation were still married, so I do not know whether, if widowed, they would choose to remarry. It was understood that the church would insist that they remarry a Christian.

# Beti Widow Inheritance and Marriage Law: A Social History

JANE I. GUYER

LIKE MANY other African peoples, the precolonial Beti required that a widow be inherited by her deceased husband's kinsman. In early kinship studies this practice was seen as an expression of a single underlying social principle, the social identification of kin with one another, and as a means of reproducing structural relations across the vicissitudes of the human life cycle. Writing of widow inheritance and the levirate, Radcliffe-Brown (1950: 64) notes that "All these customs of preferential marriage can be seen to be continuations or renewals of the existing structure of social relations. All of them are also examples of the unity of the sibling group since brother replaces brother."

The historical record lends little support to such a simple interpretation. The search for "primary functions" (Ogbu: 1978) of marital institutions places in the background precisely what ought to be in the foreground, namely the variable ways in which ideologies about social relations have been implicated in processes of change. In the early nineteenth century Beti widow inheritance may have corresponded to Radcliffe-Brown's interpretation, but by the end of the century such important political and economic assets were implicated in the transactions of mar-

The field and archival data for this paper were collected in 1975-76 and the summer of 1979, while the author was a research associate of the National Advanced School of Agriculture in Yaoundé. Research was financed by a grant from the U.S. National Institute of Mental Health, and from the Social Science Research Council. One cannot work on southern Cameroon without acknowledging more explicitly than in the text the important work of several French and Cameroonian scholars. The section on historical reconstruction benefits from the work of Laburthe-Tolra, Ngoa, and de Thé to a greater degree than references alone can convey.

riage that widow inheritance is hardly comprehensible as simply an element in positional replacement. It was a critical aspect of inheritance in general at a time when the nature and value of assets at stake were changing rapidly; it must therefore be understood in relation to accumulation and resource control by men. By the late twentieth century the relationship between widowhood and processes in the economic and political field had shifted again, bringing to the fore those elements of widow inheritance that define women's access to the most basic of resources for making a living. All of these "functions" have been attached to and detached from the institution of widow inheritance over the course of this history.

In part this paper is a simple exploration of the changing meaning and context of Beti widow inheritance. But it is also informed by a concern with the difficult theoretical problems involved in the study of "continuity and change," or, in more recent literature, "reproduction and transformation." The incorporation of the nonindustrialized world into the structures of the industrial political economy is the most complex of historical processes and the least predictable. The designation of certain elements as "structural" is itself problematic for a period of history characterized by shifting interrelationships and feedback effects. Suffice it to say here that the paper is organized around both structural and historical approaches. It is structural in the traditional anthropological sense, in that it considers a particular named status, that of a widow, '*nkus*,' in relation to resource control under two different sets of conditions—in the late nineteenth century and the late twentieth. It is also structural in the more modern sense, in that it sees each of these conditions not as a static model, but as characterized by a particular and systematic interrelationship of certain variables of social life. It is historical in that it focuses on the processes of transition, when the relationship between aspects of the marriage system and the accumulation of power became dissociated, not only through the impersonal penetration of new forms of accumulation but through explicit conflicts at all levels of the social hierarchy. The conclusion expands on some of the problems and interpretations that are implicit and explicit in the ethnographic and historical sections.

As background one needs a brief outline of Beti history.[1] The term *Beti* defines a population of about three-quarters of a million people living in the central southern region of Cameroon, in an area surrounding the national capital of Yaoundé. The indigenous political system was segmentary, composed of autonomous villages linked by particularistic ties of patriclanship, affinity, and alliance across a very large area extending into Gabon. These peoples had common cultural characteristics and spoke mutually intelligible dialects of the same language. Ethnographers have cut into this radically segmentary system at various different levels to define its constituent groups. The largest linguistic-cultural unity is referred to as Pahouin or Bulu-Beti-Fang (Alexandre and Binet 1958). Beti itself strictly speaking denotes a status, from *nti* (pl. *beti*) implying nobility and translated into French as *seigneurs*. The term is now used, somewhat imprecisely, to refer to a set of large contiguous subgroups (Ewondo, Eton, Mvele, Bene, etc.) whose own unity is variously based on common dialect, claims to common ancestry, and geographical propinquity. The very difficulty of defining the Beti unambiguously reflects the range of principles available for social grouping above the level of the village.

The Beti-speaking peoples have inhabited the savannah-forest border region of central and southern Cameroon for several centuries and have no mythology to place them elsewhere. Within that region they have been constantly on the move in a series of migrations that seem to have had no single pattern until the late eighteenth century. Land was plentiful, and even if no other forces were at work, maximum returns to a rich and successful long-fallow agriculture system dictated some movement. After 1800, the attraction of increasing trade in European goods at the coast, and the pressure from Fulani invaders and Hausa ivory and slave traders from the north, combined as a powerful incentive to move more deeply into the coastal forest. By the time a German post was established at Yaoundé in 1889, certain elements of Beti social structure had been greatly elaborated in the context of both increased wealth and increased danger. In par-

1. The principal available sources on Beti history are Laburthe-Tolra 1977a, 1981, and Quinn 1970.

ticular, the power and regional alliances of village headmen had been extended through an increase in polygynous marriage.

After several insurrections, the Beti submitted to colonial authority and the regional chieftaincy hierarchy imposed on them. Although administration at this level had never existed and many of the chiefs had no claim to eminence in the indigenous system, the ideological and organizational underpinnings of late-nineteenth-century headmanship did provide one possible model for relations between chiefs and people. The term used for a chief under the colonial government, *nkukuma*, derives from *akuma*, meaning wealth, and referred in the past to the wealthy, powerful polygynous headman in a segmentary and competitive system.[2] The successive German and French governments treated the chieftaincy system with considerable ambivalence, their policies largely reflecting political expediency. Following the acute crisis of the Depression, chieftaincy was allowed to decline and the basic contours of the present local political economy began to emerge: villages of sedentary smallholder producers who are predominantly monogamous and Roman Catholic, and an urban-based elite that emerged after the expansion of education and the civil service in the postwar period.

*Political Economy and Widow Inheritance in the Late Nineteenth Century*

The nineteenth-century history of Beti marriage practice centers on the response of an independent indigenous population to new exchange outlets for local goods, particularly ivory. The accumulation of "wealth-in-people" and the intensification of inequalities within local groups appear to be general responses to the increased dangers and opportunities of expanding commerce in West Africa (Hopkins 1973). That the response took the form of an elaboration of the marriage system is more specific, and therefore implicates the structural premises of Beti kin relations. Not all segmentary systems have responded to similar situations in the same way; clients can be assimilated as "sons"

2. The extension of the term *nkukuma* is particularly expressive of the lack of congruence between Beti and European concepts. The term is used for colonial chiefs and for the kings of the Bible, as in Nkukuma David.

(see Meillassoux 1978), extra labor can be recruited through slavery, military expansion can be based on a descent ideology (Sahlins 1961), trade partnerships can take a variety of forms. Slavery among the Beti existed but was limited in importance. For example, a headman at Etoudi who had 40 wives is said to have had "many" slaves, in fact about six. This section first documents the implications of the expansion of polygyny, including the increased frequency and heightened meaning of widow inheritance, and then examines (post hoc, it must be admitted) the structural relations that enabled marriage to become the idiom of power.

The evidence for the expansion of polygyny in the nineteenth century is both direct and circumstantial. The earliest systematic ethnography suggests that an important headman on the savannah-forest border could have up to 100 wives (Tessman 1913: 262). Oral histories collected in the 1960's and 1970's mention a similar number for a headman from the forest region (Laburthe-Tolra 1977a: 573), 15 for a local notable at Saa, 40 for a village headman at Etoudi—all referring to a generation of men who reached the prime of life in the last decades of the nineteenth century. Two of the elderly people interviewed by Vincent (1976: 78, 132) at Minlaaba estimate the number of their fathers' wives as up to 60. Ethnographers reconstructing the principles of Beti social organization as it was on the eve of colonial rule conclude that "Whoever says wealth, means number of people to command. . . . All of Ewondo social and political life therefore rested on marriage, on women" (Ngoa 1968: 225). Wives "appear to compose the actual substance of wealth" (Laburthe-Tolra 1977a: 496).

The particularly important point Laburthe-Tolra makes on the subject of Beti polygyny is that the rates prevalent at the end of the nineteenth century were not a static outcome of social structural principles alone, but represented the interplay of changing historical conditions and shifting interpretations of kinship and affinity. He suggests that before 1800 Beti polygyny was much more limited in scale. Within the genealogy of a single descent group he finds the following sequence: the founder, living about 1700, had 4 legitimate wives; a successor, who died about 1800, had 10 wives; and a later successor, in the mid-nineteenth century, had 25 (1977a: 322-23). From the genealogy of Mvog Mvondo, in the area north of Yaoundé, it appears that none of the important figures in the first three generations after the early-eighteenth-century migration into the forest had more than 5 wives.

The change from 5 to 40, or 10 to 60, implies demographic changes. It is likely that the age at marriage was significantly altered, rising for men and declining into childhood and infancy for women. This increasing age gap between husband and wife necessarily implies a relatively high rate of female widowhood in the young age range. Vincent's (1976) interviews, for example, tell of childhood betrothal of girls, residence in their husband's village at about seven years old, and the possibility of widowhood even before the marriage had been consummated. On a quantitative basis alone, the issue of widow inheritance became more clearly a question of the circulation of reproductive women than a question of the care of the elderly.

Laburthe-Tolra argues plausibly that this was a result of "the pressure of economic forces emanating from the development of commerce" (1977a: 502), in particular from the need for men to ensure large enough local groups for defense and basic production while spreading the network of regional ties wide enough to allow for safe trade and exchange in articles of value. The elaboration of polygynous marriage was remarkably successful in achieving both aims. Important headmen took wives from each other's families, thereby establishing relations of affinity in what was otherwise a dangerous environment for travel. Smaller local groups gave their daughters to important headmen as wives with the expectation of protection. More flexible and voluntary than ties of descent, ties of affinity could be created in response to changing conditions. This allowed the rapid rise to prominence of men with exceptional personal characteristics. The development of affinity as the basis for regional political and economic networks is associated with leadership by achievement rather than through ascriptive rules of seniority.

Within polygynous villages, wives augmented their husband's following and his wealth in several ways. Their sons were his military and economic supporters as long as they remained with him, and their daughters were available from a very early age to create new alliances through marriage. Women did most of the farm work, providing the basic subsistence as well as surpluses for entertaining trading partners and other guests. Through their ritual activities in the female cult of *mevungu* (from *vu*: to bear or produce) they encouraged the fertility and productivity of the entire village economy. Finally, under large-scale polygyny, a wealthy headman attracted young men as clients (*mintobo*) by allowing them residence in the village and sexual and domestic access to certain of his wives.

It is said that a polygynous headman maintained a sexual monopoly over only about ten of his wives (Laburthe-Tolra 1977a: 32), but he retained rights in all the children born to unions with his wives. In fact, all wealth (*akuma*) produced by wives and clients reverted to the headman. As far as their own interests were concerned, wives aimed to establish themselves within the village, and above all, to bear sons through whose adulthood and independence their own status would be affirmed. Clients were generally young men either too poor or too powerless to marry, who hoped for favor and support from a wealthy patron. Under the conditions of competition over wives, "to get married one needed to be a rich and powerful man or a faithful and humble servant" (Ngoa 1968: 228).

It would be misleading to reduce the value of marriage and affinity in this system to a single primary dimension. Wives represented capital and labor (male and female), political alliance, military strength, and trading partnership, as well as domestic service and biological reproduction. Wives were the primary accumulable asset (Laburthe-Tolra 1977a: 496-97), and marriage became, as Ngoa puts it, "a total social phenomenon . . . a kind of sociological résumé where all orders of institutions inter-relate" (1968: 1).

The control of women by their fathers and husbands was clearly one fundamental condition of the polygynous system as it developed. In cultural terms women were conceived of as a part of a man's wealth (*akuma*), and their activities were under their guardian's more or less total control. Women belonged to (*a woge ai*) the man on whom they depended—the terminology is the same as that used for ownership of nonhuman assets, animate and inanimate. Once transferred at marriage, a woman's right to return to her natal family was strictly limited and at the complete discretion of her father. "The prohibition against looking back was to indicate the marriage was definitive" (Quinn 1980: 297). Sanctions against a wife's running away were physical, including military action against any other man who harbored her and forcible restraint on her own mobility.

One cannot know whether this set of constraining institutions developed alongside large-scale polygyny or whether it predates it. However, it seems clear that the Beti ideology of marriage does not contain the possibilities for the ambiguity of status implied by processual marriage transactions (Comaroff and Roberts 1977, Parkin 1980), the separate transaction of rights *in uxorem* and rights *in genetricem*, or the retention of rights as a daughter alongside rights as a wife (see, for example, Lloyd 1968). As Quinn puts it, and others agree, "Headmen enjoyed complete control over their autarchic *nda bot* ["family," hamlet], and among them the sense of individualism was pronounced" (1980: 303).[3] If one accepts Parkin's position (1980) that such provisions for the separate transactability of rights constitute basic cultural premises, one would expect that the Beti conception of total guardianship over daughter and wife was a precondition rather than a creation of polygyny on a grand scale.[4] The sanctions imposed, however, may have become more extreme as conditions changed.

Second, and related to this, is the contingent recourse by men to ties of common descent. This is a patrilineal ideology, but one that is situationally manipulated. Laburthe-Tolra documented cases of warfare and intermarriage between close patrikinsmen, in principle forbidden, and concluded that "either patrilineal kinship was less strong among the ancient Beti than the Fang, or the intensification of competition had already begun to dilute ties of kinship and usher in their replacement by voluntary alliances" (1977a: 347). The direct and final control a man had over unmarried sons was not elaborated into a general legitimation of seniority by common descent. As soon as a man was adult—that

3. See also Ngoa 1968: 70, "Dignity consists in total freedom of action."
4. Parkin (1980: 218) writes that it is "a fundamental rule of culture: where uxorial and childbirth rights are semantically distinguished in transactions they may also be thought of as separately negotiable and manipulable."

is, had passed the initiation rite *Sso* and had married—he was able to found his own settlement. The idiom of common descent was, in a sense, a resource for building and consolidating alliances, "yet the Beti never established a political structure corresponding to the lineage at its extended level" (Quinn 1980: 303).

Finally, and again a related facet of this structural complex, is the variability of bridewealth rates. Mary Douglas (1967) has discussed bridewealth goods as a kind of rationing system. Paul Spencer (1980) has gone further to suggest that patterns of polygyny rates within age cohorts are a function of the degree of variability, and therefore competition, in the bridewealth system. Where wives can be acquired only through the payment of special goods at a standard rate, the possibilities for differential accumulation are limited. Where, as among the Beti of the nineteenth century, bridewealth rates are at the personal discretion of the parties involved, the political element can become very important. A headman with some power was able to acquire more wives, first through the early marriage of his daughters, second through the use of locally produced agricultural surpluses as a part of bridewealth payments, and third through the gift of wives from various others associating themselves with his power. A man's right to discretion in fixing the level of bridewealth for his daughter is still insisted upon, although a range of acceptable rates can be quoted for various periods of history. A system in which access to bridewealth goods only partially regulates the distribution of wives allows power to concentrate, rather than to distribute evenly or on systematically gerontocratic lines. As a result, success bred success, and important headmen were able to continue to acquire young wives all their lives.

A history of bridewealth is difficult to construct. People claim that sister exchange was the original form of Beti marriage, and the historical ethnography documents the institution of pairing a brother and a sister so that her bridewealth provided him with a wife (Ngoa 1968: 139). Both these systems imply rationing rather than accumulation. This is weak but suggestive evidence that the nineteenth-century bridewealth, paid in a variety of forms and affected by the inequalities of power, has in fact been a historical development. The standard form of payment was in iron-rod money (*bikie*), which could also be used to acquire other goods and services. This suggests that the introduction of iron money may have something to do with the decline of strictly equivalent exchange of one woman for another. Once material bridewealth was established, political manipulations of the marriage system became possible. In addition, new goods could be integrated into marriage exchange. It is clear, for example, that ivories and guns figured in late-nineteenth-century Beti bridewealth, without, however, dominating the way in which it was valued. Bridewealth remained valued in *bikie* and does not seem to have responded to the prices of imports and exports to the coast. As Meillassoux has argued in his classic article (1978), trade by itself did not introduce a general price mechanism, even for the goods that could be exchanged against one another. But the social organizational repercussions of trade were nonetheless profound. They remained within the structural conditions of the indigenous society, but generated inequalities of new dimensions.

Under these cultural principles and external circumstances, widow inheritance came to constitute the most important transaction in the devolution of rights in resources. We have no data on which to reconstruct the rules of widow inheritance before this period. Clearly, lateral inheritance to a junior brother is the most common practice in Africa, and fits well with the demography of polygyny on a small scale. Beti inheritance rules do include provisions for the lateral inheritance of widows by their deceased husband's junior brother. This is practiced in a de facto fashion at present, but has also been quoted to me as a possibility for the early twentieth century. The ethnographies for the nineteenth century, however, emphasize that inheritance was lineal, from father to son, and became associated with succession to the headship of the local group. As in all cases of widow inheritance, as distinguished from the levirate, the heir takes over the wives as his own and acquires full rights in them, their work, bridewealth rights in their current and subsequent daughters, and the relationship of affinity with natal kin. What I argue here, largely on the basis of Laburthe-Tolra's ethnography, is that although the acquisition of wives was competitive, their inheritance favored older sons. These men then started their independent careers in a privileged position.

The procedure was as follows. After the husband's funeral, each wife with an adult son was assessed on the basis of the wealth she had brought into the village: bridewealth for daughters, alliances, agricultural production, and any other forms of wealth she had been instrumental in attracting. All of this wealth, including the junior wives acquired through her productivity, became the property of her sons, but particularly of her oldest son. The fortune was therefore divided quite unequally, with the oldest son of the first wife being clearly favored, and the wives with nonadult children being distributed as a part of the inheritance rather than receiving a share of their own (Laburthe-Tolra 1977a: 476). The inheritance of young widows could be a crucial step in a man's career. For example, a village headman who died in the influenza pandemic of 1918-19 had one wife when his own father died. He inherited three widows, and during the rest of his life he acquired 17 more wives. In spite of an aggressively egalitarian ideology (for men) and the ever-present possibility of mobility through personal excellence, by the end of the nineteenth century there was a set of powerful men with a strong interest in protecting their own and their fathers' past investment in wives. One of Vincent's informants, the oldest son of a headman with 60 wives, complains of conversion to Christianity that "it deprived me of 59 wives" (1976: 132).

From the woman's perspective, she was only a widow, *nkus*, for the period between the death of her husband and her assignment to an inheritor as a full wife. Such a marriage was known as *aluk ngab elig* (Ngoa 1968: 196), literally "marriage as a portion of inheritance," indicating the process of acquisition but not restricting in any way the status of the wife in comparison with others acquired by other processes. A widow had no right to choose the successor to her husband except under certain limited conditions. Widows past menopause, with adult and established sons, went to live with their sons; in fact, it was possible to make this move before the husband's death. Childless widows were assigned to an inheritor, but as relatively valueless people they were allowed to gravitate toward a guardian who would treat them well.

All widows, regardless of value, went through a painful period of deprivation as a ritual release from their husband's influence, during which their personal stores of food, planting material, and minor belongings were depleted. The period during which a woman was *nkus*, between her husband's death and the formal division of his property, was also marked by fear, restrictions, and ritual ordeals. It was *ndzuk*, an affliction. If the husband had been an important headman, one or more of his widows was executed on the grounds of having caused his death, and it was not clear in advance who this would be. The subsequent ordeals for the rest served to protect them from the still dangerous presence of their deceased husband, and also effectively to level the differences that had emerged among them in the context of the marriage.[5]

Transferred to a new husband's village, the widow started anew in many respects, establishing a new residence, new fields, and a new status within a polygynous system. Once inherited, she became a wife (*ngal*) and was no longer referred to as a widow (*nkus*). Access to the full rights of a wife, including house, fields, and protection, provided her with a set of claims she could activate and a set of obligations to which she submitted.

In summary, rights in women became a valuable good accumulated and transmitted in a system that contained bases for both radical competition and differential privilege. By the mid-nineteenth century the guarantee to a widow of house and fields in her inheritor's village was not only a welfare provision, but a critical condition of demonstrating her allegiance and controlling her productivity. Of particular value was the young widow still in the reproductive years.

### Marriage in the Colonial Period

In spite of the tight administrative control imposed on the Beti population by the successive German and French governments, the changes in marriage practice are best seen as the result of only partially regulated political and economic processes. The French government, in the years immediately following World

5. There are several sources for this, including, most notably, Laburthe-Tolra 1977a, 1981. There is also an extraordinary novel, *Tante Bella: Roman d'aujourd'hui et de demain* (Yaoundé: Librairie "Au Messager," 1959), by Joseph Owono, a Beti man. Written about his aunt, it is also in part a polemic against certain provisions of the current marriage law and contains a vivid account of the ordeals of widowhood.

War I, passed a series of laws on marriage, declaring child betrothal illegal, fixing bridewealth at a standard rate to be paid in
cash, and providing widows with the possibility of remarriage
by choice: "The divorced or widowed woman can contract another union, on condition of the repayment of the bridewealth
paid for her" (JOC, Dec. 26, 1922). Considerable concern was expressed about the high rates of polygynous marriage, which
were thought to be associated with low fertility (Kuczynski 1939:
450-56). To counteract accumulation of wives the Administration
imposed head taxes on childless women as well as on men.[6]

After this early activity, little legislative change was made for
several decades. The numbers of wives acquired by important
men continued to rise—in some cases to unprecedented levels.
In the census returns of 1932, the administrative chief at Saa,
north of Yaoundé, was reported to have 203 wives (Kuczynski
1939: 156), and he had 583 by the time he died in 1939 (document, Sous-Prefecture at Saa). Ngoa Evina, Chief for Mvele West
and last of the "*grands polygames*," had 142 wives when he died
in 1952. Onambele Mbazoa, a canton chief, had 67 wives; relatively less important "notables" in Saa had from 4 to 17; and a
male nurse in the colonial health service is reported to have had
46 (Kuczynski 1939: 154-56). Kuczynski's review of the demographic data suggests that in the Yaoundé area two out of five
marriages were polygynous and one third of adult men were not
married at all. The severity of the skewing, however, is difficult
to reconstruct as an overall picture.

Qualitative historical evidence suggests that administrative
measures scarcely diminished the political importance of marriage; rather, the imposition of a powerful chieftaincy system
backed by force actually consolidated affinity as a political strategy. The chiefs in the administrative hierarchy were responsible
for implementing a variety of repressive policies: head taxes,
forced labor recruitment, porterage, and work on village plantations. Protection from the brunt of these policies demanded that
the ordinary villager cultivate a patron, and one of the few ways
of doing this was to give a daughter in marriage. Affinity was

6. Polygyny rates were high in other areas of Cameroon and were therefore
considered a national rather than a regional problem. Local dynamics have been
regionally variable.

an idiom of clientship with cultural roots. The foreign soldiers who had helped to impose colonial rule on the peoples south of Yaoundé were given wives from among the conquered "to put them under protection." Even Christian and monogamous chiefs were offered wives (Laburthe-Tolra 1977b: 137), or if affinity was out of the question, they were sent young people of both sexes as servants. At the same time, it is clear that some chiefs demanded wives from among their subjects and that many of these political transactions did not involve the payment of bridewealth.

The structural conditions supporting large-scale polygyny broke down and were superseded between the mid-1930's and the mid-1950's. Levels of bridewealth offer a particularly important index of this critical shift. Payment of bridewealth in indigenous iron rods (*bikie*) declined during the early 1920's and the French government attempted to set a cash bridewealth of 400 francs in 1922. The data are limited, but such evidence as there is suggests that the cash component remained quite steady until the end of the 1930's (Vincent 1976: 94, 136; Bertaut 1935: 178). Like food prices and wages, bridewealth rates appear to have remained stable while commodity prices fluctuated (Guyer 1978). At the end of the 1930's the rate of change accelerated dramatically as a very rapid inflation took place (Owono Nkoudou 1953: 53; Binet 1956: 82; de Thé 1970: 269). Explaining the relationship between bridewealth and other prices is a task I cannot attempt here; the point to be made is that the pattern changed in the 1940's.

I have argued elsewhere that stability in domestic prices was a result of the tight administrative hold over the local economy and the important role of the chiefs in generating work and goods out of their population by force (Guyer 1978, 1981). Here I would argue that the "marriage market" was likewise controlled by political forces and that change in the post-Depression period is associated with a general liberalization as the colonial administration abandoned a policy of forced labor and support for the chiefs.

The history of legislation concerning other facets of traditional marriage, including widow inheritance, followed a similar course. Although the practice was attacked in the legislation of

1922, more definitive measures were not initiated until instructions were sent from Paris to all of West and Equatorial Africa in 1939, and reiterated in 1945, that declared "void, without . . . reclamation of any indemnity, . . . all claims on a widow or other person being part of a customary inheritance, if that person refuses to present herself to the home of the inheritor to whom she is attributed" (JOC, Nov. 13, 1945). The process by which this change was to take place involved political struggles at several levels.

After its initial foray into the territory of family law the French government made a rapid retreat by handing over the entire issue to the indigenous chiefs. Throughout the interwar years government representatives took an agnostic position. As Governor Marchand said on many occasions, "African society is evolving toward monogamy. The evolution is no doubt slow, but natural, and it would be, in my opinion, impolitic to precipitate it." (CNA APA 11954; Kuszynski 1939: 154.) Apart from some sermonizing about the past, official reports contain little comment about the morality of customary marriage. A Bulu chief with 35 wives was described in the 1923 Report to the League of Nations as "un indigène évolué" (AR 1923: 75), and Zogo Fouda Ngono, with his hundreds of wives, was once mildly described as "a little old-fashioned" but "ruling his people like a good family father" (CNA APA 11822/E).

As late as 1936, the law recognized the right of a widow's inheritor to the wealth she and her children represented, by insisting that she could not remarry without repayment of the bridewealth. It also implied that she could not even reside anywhere but in her inheritor's village (AN, carton 30, dossier 219): "The death of the husband does not *ipso facto* entail the rupture of the marriage contract. In principle, the woman is required to stay in her husband's family. . . . In no case can a widow's remarriage take place without the preceding repayment of the bridewealth to the inheritor." Bertaut remarked cynically of this system that the aim of the inheritor became "to sell her again to the highest bidder" (Bertaut 1935: 172). The most liberal clause in the law allowed widows to request a certificate of permission to reside elsewhere, to be signed by the local European administrator (JOC, Nov. 1, 1936).

The conservatism of the chiefs with respect to marriage and widow inheritance is illustrated by the positions they took in the impassioned controversies that developed between them, the administration, the Catholic church, and the women themselves. Abolition of widow inheritance would have undermined the major indigenous mechanisms for wealth accumulation, well adapted by then to the possibilities of applying female labor to plantation agriculture. Zogo Fouda used his wives as an agricultural labor force, and a report for 1934 claims that family income was determined by "the number of wives and widows" (CNA APA 11828/A). Although the chiefs were divided on many issues, on marriage they were relatively united. Superior Chief Charles Atangana, who was a practicing Christian and a supporter of the Catholic church, nevertheless took a traditional line. When asked for an opinion on a widow's freedom of residence he replied: "My colleagues and I . . . can only reply in demanding the upholding of custom, which requires the widow to be the property of the heir until her liberation, which can only take effect after the return of the bridewealth. She must remain with him as long as this return is not made" (CNA APA 11954).

Chief Onambele objected to the administration's attempting to fix bridewealth at 400 francs. At that rate, he claimed, in 1927, when cash crop prices peaked, it was too easy for women to free themselves or be freed by prospective husbands from their current situations. In fact, chiefs and administrators agreed that the return of bridewealth could be refused by the current husband if he so wished, and that any challengers to the authority of a "notable" over his wives could be punished under the *indigénat* (CNA APA 11954).

The documents relating to the division of Zogo Fouda Ngono's fortune provide an example of the chiefs' interpretation of customary inheritance law. Enormously wealthy, Zogo Fouda left such a complex fortune that two inventories were made when he died in 1939, one by the administration and one by a neighboring canton chief, Simon Etaba. Zogo Fouda left 33 adult sons, 32 boys, 37 unmarried daughters, and 583 wives. His oldest son and successor to the chieftaincy, Pierre Ongolo, was assigned 80 widows and 15 children, as well as farms, a house, and various kinds of movable wealth. Each of the other adult sons received about 15 widows. Every widow was listed in the inventory with a bridewealth value. If this had been repaid in the case of permission to remarry, the sum would have represented a vast cash fortune.[7] Widow inheritance was still a key aspect of the transmission of power. Significantly, the cocoa farms were divided up much more equally, reflecting the relatively minor political significance of land.

The most vocal opposition to widow inheritance came primarily from representatives of the Catholic church. Jealous of and protective toward their fledgling Christian communities, missionaries saw the practice of widow inheritance as a subversion because at any moment one of their converts could become polygynous in the eyes of the customary law. A man who undertook any kind of church position more formal than simple congregation membership, was required by the missionaries to renounce all inheritance rights of any kind (Tabi 1971: 19). For the others, the clergy went to battle with the administration. Monseigneur Vogt, head of the Catholic church in Cameroon, wrote to Governor Marchand to "expose the situation of widows who have no legislation which liberates them at the moment." In reply, Marchand simply reiterated his belief that "customs evolve under the pressures of economics" (Tabi 1971: 129).

The church's profound influence on the situation was achieved less by active lobbying on behalf of widows than by offering them an alternative retreat, namely, the *sixa*, a residential training school for Christian women. Women in different sorts of unacceptable marriages often went to the sixa to train for a Christian marriage, and by declaring themselves Christian they acquired a strong ally in the church. With outsiders involved, women were no longer completely restricted and the residential aspect of traditional marriage became increasingly difficult to enforce. The confusion grew severe because women were the subject of conflicting claims. As a Bulu chief put it in 1929, "There are interminable palavers: the legitimate husband wants

7. Unfortunately one cannot tell the ages of widows and children from the will. Ongolo almost certainly inherited a higher proportion of elderly widows than his junior brothers. However, the average age of Zogo Fouda's widows may have been quite low because he started his career relatively late and accumulated a very high proportion of his wives during the last seven years of his life, according to the census figures.

to take his wife back, the ousted pseudo-husbands want to get back the bridewealth deposits they have already given, 'the brother' has scoffed all the money and cannot pay back; in brief, all these people dispute with each other while the family falls apart" (AR 1929: 99). It is difficult to assess the extent to which these disputes reflect the shortage of wives for the ordinary man. It seems likely, however, that the chiefs' conservatism both promoted and repressed the underlying disorder in the marriage system.

During the 1930's this particular kind of elite system, legitimated by the ideologies and practices of precolonial headmanship and by the power of the colonial state, began to crumble. Christianity, an expanding economy, and its own contradictions undermined it from the bottom and the government trimmed its power from the top. Marriage law and practice were implicated in this process not only in a passive sense, responding to conditions at the macro level, but were an important element in the fragmentation of political control that shaped the transition to the smallholder political economy of the mid- and late twentieth century.

The political element in this process must be stressed. There is little evidence that economic efficiency alone dictated the transition to monogamy as the principal form of marriage. In fact, Binet's budget study done in 1953 shows two household sizes of equal efficiency in terms of maximum revenue per adult—the monogamous household of one man and one woman, and the complex household consisting of four men and seven women. He concludes (1956: 46): "Two societies are partially coexistent: one ancient, one modern. Each with its own economic cycle." In the former, household heads retained control of wives, widows, sons, and junior brothers, who were thereby incorporated. In the latter, some of these relations are placed outside the domestic unit; total control and total responsibility are thereby avoided. The competitive, inflationary, legally confusing situation that developed still retains a certain opportunistic atomism and lack of clear definition, as the rural population continues to adjust to the political economy of the market.

## Widow Inheritance in the Late Twentieth Century

The cocoa economy and the state bureaucracy define the context of wealth accumulation in southern Cameroon today. As elsewhere in West Africa, education and access to jobs outside the agricultural sector are a focus of people's economic strategies, although women have few realistic opportunities for employment in the formal sector. Within the rural economy primary accumulation is through the parastatals that control cocoa marketing. Small-scale cocoa producers, almost all of them male, earn cash incomes from cocoa and depend on their wives' fields for food.

Polygyny is now relatively infrequent and rarely involves more than three women married to the same man. In two Eton villages with a total population of 233 males more than sixteen years old, 152 (65 percent) of the men were married, 16 of them (7 percent) polygynously but none with more than two wives. Concomitant changes have taken place in the general demography of marriage; the age of marriage for women has risen into adulthood; for men it has declined into the 20's. Table 1 summarizes the adult female population in the two villages by age and marital status.

As the figures suggest, most widows are past menopause although there is about a 10 percent incidence of widowhood in the childbearing years. The customary inheritance of widows is now against the national law. The most recent legislation on marriage states: "In case of the husband's death his heirs can claim no right in the person, the freedom or the goods of the widow who . . . can remarry freely without anyone exercising any material claim" (JOC, Law of July 7, 1966, Art. 16). Women past menopause tend not to remarry at all, though they may develop personal or sexual relationships on an informal basis. As a result the proportion of the adult female population classified as widows is high, over 20 percent according to all censuses (RFC 1970: 36, de Thé 1965: 133).

The contrast with the late nineteenth century and its universal marriage for women of all ages is striking. Almost half the female population is currently unmarried, large-scale polygyny

TABLE 1

*Female Population of Two Eton Villages, by Age and Marital Status*

| Age group | Marital status | | | | Total | Percent |
|---|---|---|---|---|---|---|
| | Single[a] | Married | Separated | Widow | | |
| 16-30 | 52 | 66 | 2 | — | 120 | 39% |
| 31-45 | 9 | 66 | 7 | 8 | 90 | 29 |
| 46-60 | 1 | 27 | 4 | 19 | 51 | 16 |
| 60+ | — | 8 | 2 | 40 | 50 | 16 |
| TOTAL | 62 | 167 | 15 | 67 | 311 | |
| PERCENT | 20% | 54% | 5% | 21% | | 100% |

[a] Five of the women classified as single and one widow are *ebon*, "lovers," living with men with whom they have no legal or customary relationship. The others are daughters and sisters of men of the village.

has disappeared completely, and women are no longer transacted as a primary valuable good. However, many aspects of kinship ideology and customary practice have been retained, reworked, and validated by local courts as the basis for family law in general and inheritance rights in particular. The payment of bridewealth still legitimizes a union in custom, though no longer in law. Residence is still virilocal, and a woman's cultivation rights are still defined by her relationship with a man. A widow is still assigned to a guardian, although in only 57 percent of the cases enumerated was this person a son or a co-wife's son, i.e. a lineal heir. Thirty-two percent "depended on" other patrikinsmen of their husband, 10 percent returned to their own kin, and 1 percent had an independent situation. When a widow stays with her husband's group she no longer has to move house; she continues to live in her old home, which, because of changes in kinship practice, is now more likely than in the past to be very close to the house of his collateral kin on whom she "depends."

The most striking change in kinship organization has been a reemphasis on relations of common patrilineal descent, particularly with respect to land. This has occurred because of two preconditions. First, the forced sedentarization of the population under colonial rule, followed by the establishment of cocoa farms, has led to an unprecedented localization of men of common descent. The inheritance of immovable property from father to son has different implications for ongoing residence patterns than the inheritance of movable wealth. Consequently, the male populations of most villages can be placed on one or two patrilineal genealogies. In some cases the entire male population of the oldest living generation consists of sons of the same polygynous headman. Co-residence and access to a living are now mediated by the ideology of common descent. Although certainly invoked in the past for the organization of military and ritual activities and the definition of incestuous relations, this ideology now applies to a quite different field of activities. Sedentarization therefore goes part way to explaining the renewed importance of collateral ties.

The second precondition is the decline in polygyny. Because of infertility, mortality, skewed sex ratios, and other uncertainties of the nuclear family, the reversionary rights of collateral kin are now far more likely to be realizable than they were under the large-scale polygyny of the past. Formerly it was virtually impossible for a man of property to die without an heir. Now if a man dies with no son, his land and cocoa farms pass to his full brother, and failing that, to a half-brother. If he dies during the minority of his sons, a brother is appointed as guardian of the property. The interest of collaterals in each others' land is therefore—especially in areas of relatively high population density—a striking feature of their relationship. Collaterals oppose the registration of land in freehold tenure since it leaves open the possibility of the owner's selling or willing it outside the family. In the meantime, men try to establish themselves with an heir to make sure that land does not pass to collateral lines. Such polygyny as exists is generally a response to the problem of producing an heir. Alternatively a man with several daughters may expect one of them to bear a son to be his heir before she leaves in marriage. In the event of guardianship of farms by a brother, the temptation is very great for him to make a personal profit by shifting the boundary.

A third factor, difficult to assess but nevertheless a corrective to an unduly facile acceptance of "continuities" in indigenous ideology, is the influence of Western cultural concepts. Inheritance in the patriline is a concept for which Western culture and law incorporate a particularly large repertoire of provisions. It has profound resonances for the representatives of the state and the church. In this context it is difficult, if not impossible, to separate indigenous from received wisdom. People learn the concepts of a segmentary and patrilineal social organization, expressed in Beti terminology, from the courts and from the Bible in translation, as well as from the elders.

As a result of all these influences, the relationship between close male collateral kin is more significant in resource distribution today than in the past and also more highly charged. It should be noted, however, that the renewed importance of collateral relationships does not apply to sisters and daughters, who still activate their strongest land rights in the context of marriage. Applied to land as a form of wealth, descent takes on the primacy that marriage had in the past. The relative contingency of nineteenth-century relations of common descent now apply to marriage.

In this situation the position of the widow has become ambiguous and manipulable according to circumstances. When she was a wife, her work on the food farms supported the family in subsistence goods, reaffirmed her husband's land rights against any possible claims from collateral kin, and, in case her husband had children by another wife, defined her own children's share of his property. As a widow she stands between potentially competing claims to land that she herself needs simply in order to make a living. The greatest conflict is generated by the woman who had the greatest value in the past, the young widow with children. To understand this case one needs to turn briefly to the others: the elderly widow with adult sons, and the widow with no sons.

The simplest case is the elderly woman, widowed after menopause, who has adult sons to inherit her husband's land. She continues to farm as always and is a resource to her sons in a variety of practical and strategic ways. In particular she is the only member of the senior generation who is unambiguously on their side in case of disputes and can therefore quote precedents in their favor. Being the mother of an adult and established man has always been a position of some security and respect; it is the situation for which a woman hopes and plans—to pass her fields on to a daughter-in-law and to see her sons established. All women continue to work in old age and provide their own subsistence until it becomes absolutely impossible for them to get to the fields. Declining strength may make it difficult to earn cash for clothes, meat, and other necessities, but a widow living with her adult son rarely wants for any of these. Many such women are extremely vigorous and take an active part in the whole round of domestic life.

For widows without sons it is much harder to make a living. An elderly and childless widow is fortunate if she can live with the adult son of a co-wife. Of the widows without sons in the two Eton villages, 26 percent lived with the son of a co-wife. The cocoa farms devolve on the son and the widow claims only her basic rights of housing and land for a food farm. The widow of a monogamous husband who dies without sons, however, is in a potentially antagonistic relationship with the collateral heir. It is possible for such a widow to claim rights to the income from her husband's cocoa farm on grounds that are recognized in custom and in law, i.e., that she was instrumental in their establishment. In fact, cocoa seedlings are planted between the women's food crops and are tended by the women. This kind of claim, however, stands in the way of the heir's reaping the benefits from his inheritance, and since the widow has no children, outsiders will rarely intervene to settle the matter in her favor.

It sometimes happens in such cases that the heir evicts the widow altogether. All the same, about half of the widows without sons remained with their husband's collateral kin. The final 25 percent had returned home to their own natal kin, where their situations varied greatly; one woman's close kin had all died and she was cared for by unrelated neighbors. Another was a vigorous woman who contributed very significantly, in cash and kind, to feeding, clothing, and educating her brother's nine children. In other cases, a kinsman may send a child to be brought up by an elderly widow, to the benefit of both. Relatively few widows seem truly isolated, but those who do find themselves in this situation are vulnerable to depression and neglect. The variability in the position of widows without sons reflects their lack of importance in the structure.

The young widows with children, who make up about 10 percent of the total population of widows, pose the most intractable structural problems. Like other widows, they are assigned to

their husband's heir for "protection"—that is, for political repre-
sentation within the village. A young widow and her children
come under his authority; he will make the marriage negotiations for the children and manage the land and the cocoa farm
until the majority of her oldest son. The old terminology is
used—*a woge ai*, she belongs to—but this no longer entails marriage. She is not inherited as a wife. On the other hand, out of
her own self-interest and in defense of her children's interests,
the widow is not free to leave in another marriage. If the farm is
to be preserved for her son, and if the cocoa income is to be used
on their behalf, she has to be in the village to defend their rights
against the encroachment of the guardian. Such a widow is free
to engage in sexual relations as she pleases, and a few particularly strong-minded women may achieve a kind of "merry
widow" way of life. However, limited to her husband's village, a
young widow often cohabits with her guardian, as would be expected in customary practice. In this case she is in the highly
ambiguous position of being his wife in all but the formal sense
yet having to defend her children's interests against him.

Then there is the question of the status of subsequent children. That "widow inheritance" is a de facto rather than a de
jure transaction means that the children a widow bears are outside the standard rules of descent. Indeed, there are no rules to
deal with this situation because customary law contains no stipu-
lations for an unmarried widow. Unless the guardian recognizes
paternity of the child by entering his name on the birth certificate, the child is without a father. Two examples, one involving
succession and the other inheritance, illustrate the situation. In
the first case, the brother of a deceased village chief was appointed to replace him until his twelve-year-old son reached majority. The chief had one adult son born to him by a young wife
of his father after the latter's death. In nineteenth-century practice this would have been a legitimate inherited marriage and the
son a legitimate heir. Under present conditions he is disqualified
from succession as an illegitimate child. In the second case, a
young widow with three sons and a daughter was assigned to
her husband's brother, who was married and had a son of his
own. Entirely in accordance with traditional expectations, she
bore a child by him. But he, in accordance with current religious

values, never recognized the child. Now adult, this son is in constant conflict with his two groups of half-siblings over inheritance of land. In effect, he belongs to neither group but has been given a very small share by the children of his mother's husband, just to allow him to make a living. In traditional practice he would have been his father's son. There is room in the present system for a guardian to benefit from the widow's domestic economy while avoiding any long-term obligations.

Two summary points can be made. First, the current economy associated with land and cash income as the forms of wealth places emphasis on women's role as workers and as mediators of land transfers between men. With the greater prominence of ties of common descent among men in the inheritance system, situations arise in which widows are an obstacle and an anomaly in men's strategies to increase resource control. At the same time, widows have to be able to make a living and may also, in other circumstances, constitute a valuable source of extra labor. The conjugal estate, with the widow as legitimate heir to her husband, has not developed. Daughters do not inherit from their fathers, nor wives from their husbands; indeed the effort of one widow to claim her deceased husband's land by appeal to the courts resulted in threats of violence from his collateral kin. Thus discussions of, and struggles over, widows' rights are often of a contingent, ad hoc nature. Recourse can be had to claims based on their position as inherited wives; a widow (*nkus*) is a type of married woman with respect to the land tenure system. Recourse can also be had to a narrow interpretation of marriage and legitimacy, particularly with respect to rights in men's income and status. These are rarely shared with the widows and children of collateral kin.

Second, the ground seems to be shifting. In the 1950's the cocoa economy was at the center of personal strategies for accumulation. In the 1970's, as aspirations shifted to formal sector employment, cocoa became a means to an income to finance children's school fees, the search for a job, and bridewealth to ensure a wife. Even if a widow and her children can maintain rights to land, she is often in a poor position to gain access to adult male labor to work it and to maintain independent control of the income. Access to income, distinguished from real property, is dominated by the primary kin relationships within the restricted family. A man's first obligations are to his own and his children's needs, before those of his deceased brother's wife.

The dynamic of this situation seems to lead in two possible directions. Widows, and unmarried women in general, could be endowed as independent farmers with rights in their husband's or father's land and with membership in the cocoa cooperative. Some cases fit this trajectory. Two widowed co-wives who had been "inherited" more than once were allowed by their guardian to operate the farms as they wished and take out cooperative membership in their own names. In 1975 there were 6 women listed out of 119 independent members of the cocoa cooperative in one of the villages. The other, and perhaps more likely, possibility is that the position of unmarried women will become increasingly tenuous in the competition between men in pursuit of their own interests. At the moment many individual outcomes are being shaped, interpreted, and commented on in a vigorous, and often bitter, debate on the rights of men and women in one another's resources and incomes in all the forms these relationships now take.

## Conclusion

Certain of the conclusions in this paper can be presented with some confidence, whereas others represent more tentative forays into problems that, for the moment, are difficult even to conceptualize. Clearly the social practices associated with widowhood are systematically related to other aspects of marriage systems. It is impossible to interpret widowhood without discussing the age at marriage, the extent of polygyny, the value of bridewealth, and the kind of work women do both on their own account and for their husbands. These aspects of marriage systems, as Goody has emphasized (1973, 1976), are implicated in the politics of resource control. In the past century Beti men have been transformed from lords and clients into civil servants and peasants. Formerly wealth was based on wives and affinal ties and a widow was an inheritable asset. Now wealth (such as it is) is based on farms and wage or salaried employment. In this situation widows can be obstacles to their "inheritor's" full enjoyment of the property. A widow is still *nkus* but now struggles to defend her rights to a farm on a guardian's land, rights that in the past embodied inescapable obligations to her inheritor. The transition from the one situation to the other constituted a political battle over many different elements of the resource system, widow inheritance included.

It seems misleading, however, to see two static situations here. Each of the two sets of structural conditions with respect to marriage has itself been realized in varying ways, as I have explored particularly for the nineteenth century. And beyond this variation, there do appear to be historical and cumulative changes throughout the period I have discussed. The monetization of bridewealth, the development of cash-cropping, and the expansion of employment outside agriculture have each separately, and in combination, altered the relative value of resources associated with kinship statuses and the alternative means of acquiring them. The process of monetization is clearly cumulative in that more and more goods and services can be acquired with cash. The central theoretical problems in interpreting the history of kinship lie in relating such apparently cumulative processes to the political structures that only partially control and direct them, and the "practice" through which people continue to redefine their situation under shifting conditions.

# The Widow Among the
# Matrilineal Akan of Southern Ghana

DOROTHY DEE VELLENGA

IN THE MODERN state of Ghana, named after the old Mande empire but quite unrelated to it culturally, many ethnic groups speak languages of the Kwa branch of Congo-Kordofanian. Among these are the Akan speakers, who include the Asante, Fanti, and half a dozen other groups in Ghana and Ivory Coast. The Akan of southern Ghana are matrilineal, tracing descent, inheritance, and succession through the mother's line. This lineage tie, as many observers of matrilineal peoples point out, is often in conflict with conjugal loyalties. As Meyer Fortes notes, among the Asante, although virilocal residence is the ideal, only one-third of all married women actually reside with their husbands, the remainder living with matrilineal kin. In his sample he found 40 to 50 percent of the population residing in female-headed matrilineal households (1950: 262). A high incidence of intravillage marriage—75 percent in Fortes's sample (1950: 279), 74 percent in mine—makes such duolocal residence possible.

This conflict between lineal and conjugal loyalties has been commented on by many observers. As Fortes says, "Ashanti are much preoccupied with this problem and constantly discuss it; and though it has obviously been aggravated by missionary and modern economic influences, there is much evidence to show that it existed in the old days" (1950: 261).

The data presented in this paper were gathered between 1968 and 1976. Research in 1968-69 was sponsored by grants from the American Association of University Women and the African Women's Program of the United Methodist Church. Research in 1972 was supported by a Mack Foundation grant. Research in 1975-76 was supported by a grant from the Social Science Research Council. My survey in 1975-76 owes much to the cooperation of the Cocoa Production Division and my research assistant Ben Fordjour.

Robert Lystad states that men "are at once fathers, sons, matrilineal uncles and nephews. . . . In the traditional society this situation created tensions which had to be resolved by balancing obligations between matrilineal and patrilineal kin groups" (1959: 196). An increase in modern wealth and the desirability of its inheritance heightens this ambivalence felt by individuals, he observes.

Not only is Akan marriage affected by competing loyalties, but it must also be viewed in the context of a system so complex that one archival report listed 24 kinds of heterosexual relationships.[1] The multiplicity of marriage forms may have arisen as an attempt to resolve some of these conflicts, although many theorists think the diversity may be a feature of unilineal systems in general (Gluckman 1950; Herskovits 1938; Ottie 1971).

In addition to the traditional adaptations, there are two significant imported concepts: Christian monogamy and British legal marriage (the latter instituted by the Marriage Ordinance of 1884). The introduction of these Western forms into a matrilineal society with different conceptions of marriage, varied types of conjugal relationships, and different inheritance practices had unanticipated consequences for wives and widows. As a result of the conflicts that emerged, formal and informal legal precedents developed to deal with the mixture of forms. In this paper we shall first examine the implications of traditional marriage forms for widows, and then the impact of Western influence.

Concerns over widows' rights became a focus of the women's movement in Ghana in the late 1950's and early 1960's. Some educated women and men who strongly believed that widows and children were economically disadvantaged in areas with matrilineal descent pressed for legal reform. This topic has been a favorite of the local press for years. Although widows are gener-

---

1. This list of marital forms was found in the Christian Council archives incorporated in a speech given before a church group in Asante in 1960. The name of the speaker is not on the document. I copied the terms and showed them to two elderly informants. One of these men had been a court registrar in Asante in the early part of the century and was himself from a royal family. The other man was a Presbyterian minister and a scholar in the Twi language spoken by the Akan. A table showing the written definitions of the terms and the informants' definitions is found in Vellenga 1975: 52-63.

ally depicted as disadvantaged, my own data suggest that the situation is more complicated. In concluding sections of this paper I shall use data on Akan women cocoa farmers that I collected during 1975-76 to analyze the comparative productivity of widows, wives, and divorced women. I shall also consider how differences in marital backgrounds and rural-urban distinctions relate to widows' situations.

### Traditional Forms of Marriage Among the Akan

The degree of family involvement was one variable in the range of traditional Akan marriage forms. The standard form of marriage required the consent of both families, as well as that of the individuals themselves. Their agreement was symbolized by several stages of negotiations culminating in a final prestation of drinks and a nominal sum of money paid by the man's family to the woman's family. This *ti nsasi* or *tiri nsa* (head drink) legitimized the marriage, gave the husband legal rights to all children of his wife, and entitled him to collect adultery fees. A man's family could later make additional gifts of land, a house, or other property, but these were not necessary to legitimate the marriage. During my fieldwork in 1968-70 this form was still described as the standard "customary marriage."

Considerable family involvement was integral to other forms of marriage as well, such as arranged marriages, child betrothal, and the betrothal of an unborn child—unions in which the primary aim was to link two families. Court records of the 1920's and 1930's, however, suggest that many young people resisted arranged marriages.[2] Modern variants of this practice exist in which an older, wealthier man educates or trains a young girl who eventually becomes his wife.

Cross-cousin marriage, another form that stresses familial involvement, may also serve as a means of reconciling some of the conflicting lineal and conjugal demands. Fortes, writing in the 1940's, noted that older people regarded a cross-cousin as the most satisfactory spouse. But Fortes did not find cross-cousin marriages to be more stable than other forms. Morever, he found that younger men took a different view of such marriages

2. For a discussion of some of these cases involving arranged marriages, see Vellenga 1975: 65-67, 205-8.

from that of their elders. "They say that a cross-cousin is 'too near,' almost a sister, and so she is never as attractive as an unrelated girl." Some young men also argued that such a marriage strengthens the authority of the mother's brother to an "intolerable" degree, since he is now also the father-in-law. Only a small proportion of marriages were with cross-cousins, according to Fortes, and this proportion had been declining during the preceding three or four decades (1950: 281-82).

In concubinage, or *mpena-ware*, families were less involved. In one form of concubinage some drink was given to the women's family, but this was not considered the "head drink." Most money exchanges went directly from the man to the woman. Although traditionally three forms of concubinage were recognized, the subtle differences have been lost in the contemporary scene. Nonetheless, a distinction persists between a concubine or girlfriend and a wife.

If the degree of family involvement is one variable in the variety of marital forms, social stratification is another. Members of the royal lineage had more freedom in marriage choices than commoners did. Royal women, for example, could marry foreigners, craftsmen, or even slaves, and were given considerable freedom to travel and trade, at least in the early days of the empire (Antubam 1947).

There were several varieties of marriage to women of unfree status: a man could marry a war captive, a pawn,[3] a slave, or the descendant of slaves. A slave wife took on the clan of her master and husband. Husbands had more control over slave wives than over other wives who had strong matrilineages backing them. Rattray quotes an old Asante man who said, "I preferred my slave wife and my children by her to my free wife and free children because I had undisputed rights over them" (1929: 23).

3. In Akan society, both persons and land could be given as security for a loan. When the loan was repaid, the person or land would be returned to the original owner. Women could be given to men as pawns in this process. When I showed the term *Ekaano-yere* (debt wife) to my two informants, they defined it as follows: "This may occur if a man goes to a wealthy man and asks for a loan and has difficulty in repaying it, so the lender takes his daughter as temporary payment. If the borrower gets money, he may be able to repay the loan and reclaim his daughter. The family may stand in need of money and send a young girl to a [wealthy] family and the man becomes enamored and marries her. He still has to pay to make the marriage legal."

With the outlawing of domestic slavery and the conquest of the Asante empire in the nineteenth century, the criteria for marriages between people of different status were no longer the same, but stratification continued to affect marriage.

In the 1940's Fortes noted that polygyny was unequally distributed. Although chiefs often had large harems, it was rare, he said, for "commoners to have more than three wives at the same time; 80 percent of all married men have only one wife at a time" (1950: 281). Some years later McCall made the same point, noting that military commanders and heads of large lineages that had accumulated land, pawns, and slaves could provide themselves and men of their lineage with larger numbers of wives than men who lacked these sources of wealth: "very poor men or men out of favor with their lineage heads would be forced to have affairs with unbetrothed girls, risk the penalties of adultery, deal with prostitutes, or arrange an *mpena* elopement" (1956: 27).

Although the terms of stratification have changed, one could speculate that even today, as men acquire more wealth and power, they also acquire more women as wives and concubines. Socioeconomic differentiation is sometimes reflected in modern behavior as well—for example when men father children by domestic servants, or older women of high economic and political standing sponsor attractive young men.

Thus marriage among the Akan was characterized by a variety of different forms, some of which reflected status differences. In some marriages, such as those of chiefs, or marriages with slaves or pawned women, the husband had great control. But in the standard form of marriage between spouses from free families, or in marriages of royal women, the wives were backed by powerful matrilineages to which they retained strong loyalties. Divorce was frequent and wives often continued to live in their matrilineal home. In such situations marriage was a more flexible and temporary institution, compared with the obligatory nature of lineage ties.

## Widows Among the Akan

Clearly, it is difficult to speak of the "typical" Akan widow. A man might be survived by women with whom he had a variety of conjugal relationships. But anthropologists have generally restricted the term "widow" among the Akan to women whose marriages were recognized by the families involved. Such widows were important in the funeral rituals of the deceased husband. Rattray noted in the 1920's that widows had to remain constantly with the dead body until burial: "their position is one of great danger during this period, for it is thought that should the *sunsum* or spirit of the dead man return and have sexual intercourse with them, they will ever after be barren" (1927: 171). Widows were also expected to contribute food and gold, and to wear a particular dress. Such practices to some extent continue today, and complaints about widows' and widowers' rituals occasionally reach the newspapers (eg., Carboo 1960).

Upon a person's death, the family—the matrilineage—meets in council and chooses a successor. The successor does not directly inherit the property of the dead person, but is considered a trustee for the larger family. Succession is not automatic, although there are certain prescribed categories from which to choose the successor. Wives and husbands are never successors to one another since they belong to different matrilineages. Formerly, a man's successor was responsible for the maintenance of his widows and younger children. He might or might not have sexual relations with a widow. If either the widow or the successor did not want to continue the relationship, a public break or "send-off" had to be provided for the widow. In cases where the husband's successor desired the separation, some money or property was given to the widow. If the widow wished to terminate the relationship, part of the marriage payment had to be returned. In other words, a regular divorce procedure had to be enacted to break the tie between the two families.

It is difficult to determine from the literature whether the relationship between a widow and her husband's successor should be classified as the levirate, widow inheritance, or some other form. Rattray, writing in the 1920's, states: "Widows become the property of their late husband's elder brother, i.e., the heir to the property of the deceased." And again: "The matrimonial contract into which they had entered on marriage is not entirely dissolved. . . . Nevertheless I believe this custom in Ashanti is regarded much more in the nature of an obligation than the claiming of a right. Ashanti public opinion would consider it a

disgrace for an heir to succeed to the property but refuse to accept the obligation of taking over the deceased's wives and children, and the *saman* (ghost) of the late husband would be expected to be angry at such neglect." (Rattray 1927: 173, 171n.)
Fortes, writing twenty years later, refers to Akan practices both
as widow remarriage and as the levirate (1950: 257, 271). However, it is not clear from his data whether legal paternity was
vested with the deceased or with the heir. In matrilineal systems, children of course belong to the matrilineage, but the
Akan also emphasize the spiritual bond of father and child.
Thus, the father who names and acknowledges the child, even
one conceived by his wife in adultery, is the legal father.

Fortes's descriptions of Asante practices correspond to those
given by Rattray, but clearly show that these were changing. Fortes notes that the heir inherits not only property, but also debts
and responsibilities. "One of his chief responsibilities as heir, according to traditional custom, is to care for his predecessor's
young children and widow. The simplest way to fulfill this duty
is to marry the widow (*kuna aware*)." He goes on to say that
young people at that time were averse to this practice. "The
women insist just as strongly as the men on freedom to go their
own way after the death of a husband." In his sample of 525
women only 3 percent were inherited wives, and all of these
were over 40. Nonetheless, "the formalities of inviting a widow
to accept her husband's heir still form part of the final funeral
ceremony on the eighth day after burial" (1950: 271).

Contemporary data suggest that the heir's obligation to marry
a widow is weak. Two elderly informants from Akwapim, an
area on the periphery of the Asante empire, defined *kunagyee* or
*kuna aware* (widow remarriage) in terms that suggest an option
rather than an obligation. "A man's successor may or may not
take a widow," said one. The other described *kunagyee* by saying,
"If I die, my wife is a widow. A man may come to marry her. This
is recognized by church and state."

My analysis of court records in Akwapim for the years 1930-31
and 1960 turned up only one case involving the inheritance of
widows. This case was in 1930. A widow sought divorce from
her husband's successor, complaining that he had not treated her
well. Her family had refused to return the marriage payments,

and the man would not give her a divorce. She became involved with another man who paid the husband's successor a fine for adultery. But the successor still refused to divorce the woman. After the court hearing, he finally agreed to a divorce. The case shows that a widow was considered to be married until divorce proceedings were completed.

It is not clear from the literature what happened to widows who might have been in slave, pawn, or *mpena* marriages, or marriages to royalty. What is clear is that widows were entitled to some form of maintenance, which is often described as a life interest in a room in the husband's family house. Thus, although widows could not inherit a husband's property, which went to his matrilineal kin, they did receive some support.

*Western Influences and Their Impact on Akan Widows*

As Ghana became increasingly incorporated in a Western-oriented trade economy, property became more commercialized and individualized. Distinctions, not always clear, began to develop between family property and "self-acquired" property. In the coastal areas that have been part of an international trading system for centuries, this ambiguous relationship between family property and self-acquired property has created conflicts for generations (Priestly 1969). The transformation of self-acquired property such as houses, farms, and businesses into family property was apparently more common than the reverse process of treating family assets as if they were individually acquired wealth. Wives were often helpful in increasing their husbands' individually acquired wealth, and the death of a man brought property conflicts into the open. Wives might also have been helpful in establishing trading stations for their husbands, but when the husband died they would not have an interest in his self-acquired estate. Bosman, writing in 1700, wrote that "on the death of either the man or the wife, the respective relations come and immediately sweep away all, not leaving the widow or widower the least part thereof, though they are frequently obliged to help to pay the funeral charges" (Sarbah 1968: 6).

The Gold Coast became a British colony in 1874, and Europeans' concern for widows and children found expression in legislation during that period. In 1884 a Marriage Ordinance was passed, requiring monogamy for those who married under its provisions, and entitling the widow of such a marriage to receive one-third of the man's estate, with two-thirds going to their children. For those who did not marry under the Ordinance—the vast majority—the traditional rules of inheritance continued to apply. Thus, when a man married under the Ordinance, his lineage could not share in any of his self-acquired property. Such a man, could, however, share in family or lineage property, if he had succeeded to a family headship, and this family property had to be passed on to members of his matrilineage. But as we have noted, the lines between lineage property and self-acquired property could be very unclear. The early interpretation of the Marriage Ordinance was that the widow and children would have rights in property that a man acquired with the help of family property. As N. A. Ollennu, a Ghanaian judge, wrote (1966: 243): "Obviously such a law that a person married under the Ordinance, or issue of such a marriage, may be appointed to succeed a member of his family and hold family property, but his family should not have an interest in his self-acquired property, is against natural justice and good conscience, and is absolutely unfair. But it was not until after some time that people became aware of the implications of this provision in the law." An 1896 court case shows how the new law was applied. A widow married under the Ordinance sued the man's lineage head for rights to his self-acquired property. "Letters of Administration were therefore granted to his widow in preference to his nephew, his successor appointed by his family (lineage) in accordance with customary law" (ibid.).

When these provisions became more widely known, chiefs and lineage heads reacted vehemently. They succeeded in getting the support of some of the churches for a modification in the Ordinance. The Ghanaian lawyer J. M. Sarbah also pressed the governor and attorney general for some changes that would give the lineage a share in the self-acquired property of an individual. Finally, in 1909, the Ordinance was amended so that two-thirds of a man's self-acquired property would devolve by English law to the widow and children and one-third would go by customary law to the matrilineal kin. As Ollennu concludes, "Thus the country won the fight and a compromise was arrived at by which the family (lineage) was restored to its rightful place in Ghanaian society, and which, it was hoped, would help to prevent dissipation of the real estate as far as possible and ensure its preservation as a monument to the member of the family who acquired the same by the sweat of his brow" (1966: 244).

One would suppose that Ordinance marriage would affect only a small minority of people in the colony. The Blue Book of 1909 lists 237 marriages under the Ordinance for that year. But the colony was not large, its estimated population in 1911 being 1,504,000 (Rep. of Ghana 1973: Table 7). Given the complicated network of relationships, even a small number of Ordinance marriages could have widespread implications in terms of property arrangements. One writer suggested in 1935 that the initial Marriage Ordinance did have such implications, and that they were disruptive ("Cousin Frank" 1935):

The Marriage Ordinance of 1884, which favoured the English laws in matters related to inheritance, embittered the relationships between the families of husband and wife and made "church marriage" as it was then, unpopular with the majority. Many families would neither encourage nor consent to their male members contracting such marriages. In 1909 the law was amended, but for the interim customary marriage had assumed an unprecedented rigidity. Up to then there was a mutual recognition of a man's sociological duties as regards his children and vice versa. Today almost immediately after a father's death, his family real or reputed finds some pretence to send his children out of the house, under the name of native custom.

The Presbyterian church, in an attempt to protect the widow who was married under customary law, similarly promulgated a property division in which one-third of a man's self-acquired property would go to the widow, one-third to the children, and one-third to the family. This applied only to church members. It was hoped that the provision would make marriages more stable, by assuring the wife that she would not be rejected at the time of her husband's death. Some variations on this practice were attempted by State Councils but without much success (Garlick 1971: 89; Ollennu 1966: 144-45). During my fieldwork in Akwapim, one clerk who was present during my interview with a subchief offered this description (Adontenhene 1969):

According to Akan custom, if the husband dies intestate, the only right of the woman is to a one-third share of the husband's estate; the children have one-third and the family one-third. But this is not often strictly carried out. It always leads to much litigation. The State Council has prepared commissions to look into this and prepare by-laws many times, but they weren't too consistent. They did this on more than two or three occasions, but there is still no fixed custom in regard to this. Sometimes in the case of illiterate men who marry, the women are sent to the bush (cocoa farms) to work as laborers. When the husbands die, they are driven from the place and don't even get their one-third.

This division into thirds is not precolonial custom. But in Akwapim, where the missions have been active for over a century, their influence has so affected the interpretation of customary law that church regulations have not only become contemporary practice but are regarded as traditional custom. Christian and Ordinance marriage affect only a minority of the population, but when the two are added to the array of traditional Akan forms, the complications multiply. Such marriages also provide an alternative norm emphasizing the conjugal family rather than the lineage.

As more of the population in the interior was drawn into an international economy through the spread of the cocoa industry in the early twentieth century, conflicts arose over the disposition of family and self-acquired cocoa farms. These conflicts often revealed the precarious position of the Akan widow. As noted in the account given by the clerk, a practice has developed whereby wives are expected to work on their husbands' cocoa farms, but unless they are Ordinance or church wives or have some provision made for them during the husband's lifetime, they have no rights to the farms they helped to develop. Sometimes a woman who has helped her husband faithfully for years will be given a gift of a farm or money by the husband, which is witnessed by his matrilineage. This has become established practice and can be cited in legal cases as evidence that the woman is a fully recognized wife (*Yaotey* v. *Quaye* 1961). Such gifts seem to be based on the goodwill of the husband and his relatives, however, and women often feel more secure in developing their own farms by their own efforts, that is, by developing their own matrilineal lands or purchasing land themselves.

Prior to independence, however, legal precedents did not support the position of widows married under customary law who had helped their husbands acquire and develop property. As one lawyer put it: "in the absence of strong evidence to the contrary, any property which a man acquires with the assistance or joint efforts of his wife is the individual property of the husband and not joint property of the husband and wife" (Fiadjoe 1969: 69).

Horror stories circulated about widows and children forced out of their husband's home by his lineage and left with nothing after having served him faithfully. Oppong refers to the prevalence of such stories and images among the women in her sample of a matrilineal, urban, educated elite (1974: 92):

> If an individual builds a house or starts a farm, there may be the expectation on the part of his matrikin that they will be joint benefactors. . . . Thus property a wife helps her husband to establish can eventually be considered to belong to his matrikin, his mother and siblings and maternal nephews. . . . This fear of matrilineal inheritance is perhaps the most deep-seated factor affecting the financial activities of wives. There is a sharp awareness that the practice still continues even among educated urban migrants, far from their natal areas, and even in cases where the wives and orphans in question have resort to the legal protection afforded by the provisions of the Marriage Ordinance. This awareness is continually renewed through the circulation of gossip, giving harrowing accounts of the fate of the conjugal families of deceased educated Akan men. It is also reinforced by observations of the fate of their own rural female kin and affines, whose husbands may have died suddenly, before making any provision for them and their children. Such gossip includes tales of young educated widows, whose in-laws come to seize their deceased husband's clothes and personal possessions and to lay claim to insurance benefits, before even the deceased has been buried; or stories of village widows, whose meagre boxes of possessions have been held and searched by their in-laws, before they have been allowed to return to their family homes with their own few clothes and trinkets.

## Post-Independence Legal Reforms

After independence in 1957, several developments led to a clarification of the legal position of widows in various types of marital relationships. It was increasingly recognized that people do not live in separate sectors of society—either traditional or modern—but in complicated networks where the mixture of systems persists. Thus a man may be married under the Ordinance or in church but also have a wife under customary law and a concubine. What are the implications for his widows when he dies? A few such cases were tried in the courts in the late 1950's and early 1960's and became landmarks.

One case that came before the Supreme Court in 1959 concerned a man who had been involved with three different women. He had had three children under a customary marriage before that was dissolved. Then he wed another woman under the Ordinance, and one child from that union survived. While he was still married, he also cohabited with a third woman, Shang, by whom he had ten children. After his wife died he married Shang under customary law and had the marriage blessed in a Presbyterian church. The man died intestate. The son of the Ordinance marriage claimed that he was the only lawful child and thus was entitled to the two-thirds of the estate that goes to the widow and child under the Ordinance. In a lower court his claim was upheld, but the widow, Shang, appealed the ruling on behalf of the larger family. The Court of Appeals, recognizing the customary marriage, determined that Shang was legally his widow and was thus entitled to two-ninths of the estate. Four-ninths went to the legitimate children—the three children by his first marriage and the son of the Ordinance marriage. However, the ten children of Shang who were born before she married their father were deemed illegitimate and thus not entitled to a share. The remainder of the estate was distributed according to the customary law of the Osu community of Accra. Since this group is patrilineal, all three sets of children shared in this portion of the estate (Ghana Law Reports 1959: 109-11). Woodman, in commenting on this case, notes (1974: 280): "It is worth mentioning a somewhat unexpected result of this reasoning. It means that a customary-law wife, or the child of a customary-law marriage, may be entitled to a portion of a man's estate, not because of any provisions of customary law, but because the man once married someone else under the Ordinance, and is survived by issue of that Ordinance marriage."

Court cases at this level affect only a minority of women. But there is evidence that other avenues are also being pursued by widows seeking a share of their husbands' estates. Data in the

archives of Sunyani, Brong-Ahafo, one of the richest cocoa-
growing regions in the country, indicate that between 1958 and
1960 some widows were bringing cases to the Labour Department, claiming land or compensation from the husband's heirs.[4]
These cases involved both women who were owners of farms
and employers of labor, and women who were employees. Almost all of these "employees" were former wives of the "employers." Four of the thirteen plaintiffs were widows. The others
were divorced women. All felt that they should have been given
a share of the farms they had helped to develop. For the work
they had done, they were claiming either compensation or, if
they were widows, a portion of their husband's estate. Widows
frequently complained that the husband's successor was not taking care of them or their children.

Chiefs were sometimes brought into these arbitrations, but
the involvement of a chief often worked to the disadvantage of
the widow. For example, one chief refused to give a widow more
than a portion of one farm, saying, "It was sufficient. The late
husband had married other women who needed to be maintained." The successor had refuted to the chief's satisfaction the
allegation that he had not maintained the children (Case 955).
When the Labour Officer settled the case, however, the widow
usually got a larger share. Here, then, the Labour Officer emerges
as a new source of arbitration for an old problem.

At about this time—the late 1950's and early 1960's—a women's
movement was organizing in Ghana. The participants were very
concerned about the position of the widow in both matrilineal
and patrilineal areas and the varying statuses of wives—particularly the distinctions between Ordinance and customary wives.
They formed the Federation of Ghana Women in the 1950's. At a
press conference, the general-secretary of the Federation, Dr.
Evelyn Amarteifio, called on the government to pass legislation

4. These labor disputes are complaints lodged by an employee against an employer and are to be settled by a Labour Officer. Between 1952 and 1970, a total of
1,389 such complaints came to the Sunyani office and are now deposited in the
archives there. An analysis of the names of the participants showed that 100
women were involved, either as employers or as employees. For some reason, it
was only in the years 1958 to 1960 that former wives and widows brought complaints about their ex-husbands or their husbands' successors to the Labour
Department.

giving a specified percentage of a man's self-acquired property to his wife or wives upon his death. She also urged that in those areas where existing customs barred a man's children from an inheritance, "the State Councils should ensure that the children received a certain percentage of the property." Finally, she stated that "there should also be a law making it compulsory for fathers to be solely responsible for the upbringing of their children" (*Daily Graphic* 1959).

A test case the group used to dramatize its point is similar to the one cited above. A man died leaving children by two wives. The Ordinance wife had predeceased him, leaving a son. Then under customary law, he married a second wife, by whom he had three children. The son by the Ordinance marriage "rose up to claim the entire inheritance, saying his mother was the only lawful wife" (Wuver 1959). "If native customary marriage was legalized," the Federation felt, "the young man would not have gotten it into his head to cause the stepmother so much heartache. He would have realized that as the eldest child it was his duty to administer the father's estate for the general welfare of his step-brothers and sisters as well as himself." Although the courts might have upheld the claims of the widow and her children, as in the previously cited case, the women were seeking a more comprehensive remedy that would reduce the distinction between Ordinance and customary wives and would obviate the necessity of taking each case to court.

One of the results of their efforts was the appointment of an Inheritance Commission in 1959 to look into how inheritance provisions might be modified. The report of the Commission was never published. Apparently there was dissension within the Commission, but no one I interviewed would give details.

Two years later another attempt was made to change family law so that all children, including children of customary wives and concubines, would inherit part of the estate. But only one "registered" wife would qualify as the widow for purposes of inheritance. Registration would not prevent a man from marrying several women under customary law, but they could not inherit. This change, if adopted, would have eliminated the Marriage Ordinance; there would be no legal provision for monogamy. Women's groups, churches, and legal organizations felt that the proposed law was more detrimental to women than the existing mixture of laws. The bill was eventually voted down (Vellenga 1972: 125-50; Vellenga 1983: 144-55). Since then there have been piecemeal attempts at reform that have benefited the conjugal family at the expense of the lineage, but no comprehensive law has been enacted. As a Ghanaian law professor put it (Bentsi-Enchill 1975: 128):

> Legislation such as the Education Act, 1961, the Maintenance of Children Act, 1965, the Wills Act, 1971, and the Matrimonial Proceedings Act of 1971 contain provisions which, if enforced, would give some added protection to the conjugal unit under customary law and clarify and enforce its obligations to children. But they have yet to pass from the status of the law in the books to that of the law in the lives and actions of the people. . . . For each one case that reaches the courts, thousands do not get breathed about, thousands are settled in accordance with traditional understandings before they reach court; and many of those that reach court are withdrawn for settlement or not prosecuted.

### Rural Akan Women: How Economically Disadvantaged Is the Widow?

Among the educated elite there is the feeling that widows and children are severely disadvantaged under Akan customary law. But most Akan women are in the rural areas. They are farmers and traders. Many are illiterate. To what extent does the image of the disadvantaged widow apply to this population? Although comprehensive data are difficult to obtain, it is evident from the Labour Department cases mentioned earlier that informal mechanisms have evolved to give widows some protection. A survey I conducted in the Sunyani area in 1975-76 throws further light on the position of widows.

Eighty-eight women were interviewed from four towns in the matrilineal cocoa-growing area. The women were not selected randomly; they were farmers who came to meetings in town arranged by the Cocoa Production Division. All of the women grow food, and 66 raise cocoa as well. I obtained information on their farm holdings, the mode of acquisition, patterns of labor utilization, and yields, as well as background data on marital status, village of origin, and number of dependents. For the purpose of this analysis we will compare women by marital status.

My focus in these interviews was on women who were cocoa farmers, but I found that these women raise food for cash as well. Indeed, profits from the sale of food are the largest single source of capital for investment in cocoa farms. The husbands or ex-husbands of most these women (47 out of 63 who responded) are local men. Thus these women could work on both their own matrilineal lands and the lands of their husbands.

Although most women have only one farm, some women have multiple holdings, as is seen in Table 1. A greater proportion of divorced women are without cocoa farms than married women. Widows are least disadvantaged in this respect. For those women who have cocoa farms and reported annual yields, it is interesting to note (see Table 2) that widows average the highest yields. When these yields are related to both age and marital status, it is clear (see Table 3) that older women generally are more productive, and that widows and older divorced women have a decisive edge.

Widows are also fairly independent in the means by which they acquire farms. As Table 4 shows, almost half their farms are acquired through their own efforts. This means that profits from other enterprises—trading, food farming, food processing—are used to acquire land and labor to set up a cocoa farm.

Husbands are also important as sources of farms for widows, though not as important as for married women. Three widows who obtained farms from their husbands stated that after the man's death the family agreed that the widow and children should keep the farms so that they might maintain themselves, and because of the services they had performed for the man and his family. One woman, however, stated that after her husband died, his relatives came and took the farm from her. The other six widows who had obtained farms from their husbands did not state when or under what conditions they had obtained them. Widows may have the best of both worlds in terms of productivity. Their husbands helped them to establish farms, yet they are no longer required to work on their husbands' farms and thus have the time and resources to establish farms of their own.

Widows also appear to have access to the fullest range of labor available. Table 5 is based only on the answers of cocoa farmers and tabulates the number of times a particular form of labor is

TABLE 1

*Number of Cocoa Farms Owned, by Marital Status*

| Marital status | Number of farms | | | | | Total |
|---|---|---|---|---|---|---|
| | 0 | 1 | 2 | 3 | 4+ | |
| Married | 15 | 15 | 13 | 2 | – | 45 |
| Divorced | 5 | 4 | – | 3 | 1 | 13 |
| Widowed | 1 | 9 | 7 | 2 | – | 19 |
| Unknown | 1 | 4 | 4 | 1 | 1 | 11 |

TABLE 2

*Average Yield of Cocoa Farms by Marital Status*

| Marital status | Average number of 60-lb. loads per year |
|---|---|
| Married ($N = 26$) | 30.94 |
| Divorced ($N = 6$) | 33.10 |
| Widowed ($N = 16$) | 45.00 |
| Unknown ($N = 7$) | 41.50 |

TABLE 3

*Productivity by Marital Status and Age*

| Age | Marital Status | | | |
|---|---|---|---|---|
| | Married | Divorced | Widowed | Unknown |
| 60+: No. of women | 7 | 3 | 9 | 2 |
| Loads produced | 34.28 | 47.33 | 45.77 | 34.00 |
| 40-59: No. of women | 14 | 1 | 6 | 2 |
| Loads produced | 23.81 | 20.00 | 49.33 | 15.00 |
| 20-39: No. of women | 4 | 0 | 0 | 2 |
| Loads produced | 14.00 | – | – | 6.25 |
| Unknown: No. of women | 1 | 2 | 1 | 1 |
| Loads produced | 175.00 | 18.50 | 4.00 | 180.00 |

mentioned. The *abusa* laborer is a sharecropper who takes one-third of the profits, a day laborer works for a set daily fee, and a contract or annual laborer works for a yearly fee. From this table, it appears that children are a more important source of labor assistance for both widows and divorcées than for married women. This may mean that when a woman is married, both she and her

TABLE 4

Source of Women's Farm Ownership by Marital Status

| Marital status | Source of farm | | | | | Total farms acquired |
|---|---|---|---|---|---|---|
| | Self | Husband | Father | Woman's lineage | No answer | |
| Married | 16 | 18 | 4 | 5 | 1 | 44 |
| Divorced | 11 | — | 1 | 6 | – | 18 |
| Widowed | 14 | 10 | – | 4 | 1 | 29 |
| Unknown | 12 | 5 | – | 3 | – | 20 |

TABLE 5

Forms of Labor on Women's Farms by Marital Status of Owner

| Marital status | Form of labor | | | | | Total |
|---|---|---|---|---|---|---|
| | Abusa | Self | Day | Contract | Child | |
| Married | 17 | 12 | 16 | 3 | 4 | 52 |
| Divorced | 4 | 4 | 4 | – | 2 | 14 |
| Widowed | 11 | 12 | 12 | 2 | 7 | 44 |
| Unknown | 7 | 1 | 4 | – | 2 | 14 |

children are expected to work on the husband's farm. When no longer married, a woman may have more access to her children's labor and more freedom to work on her own farms. Also, the children of the divorced women and widows in this sample are probably older.

Although these samples are small and not representative, and there are problems of reliability for self-reported yields, the tables suggest a pattern. It would appear that the position of the rural Akan widow does not conform to the popular stereotype. (A parallel survey I did in a patrilineal Ewe area showed the same order of productivity on cocoa farms, with widows averaging 34.57 loads per year, divorced women 27.07 loads, and married women 14.07.) Some widows are acquiring farms that they helped develop, by a variety of mechanisms such as the Labour Department, churches, and family agreements. A consensus appears to be emerging that it is unfair for a widow who has helped her husband acquire farms not to benefit after his death. But there is still the threat that the lineage will not honor these informal norms and mechanisms.

As Oppong reported in her survey of urban, educated Akan wives (1974: 92-93):

Some wives readily admit that they maintain their own resources separately from those of their husbands, sometimes refusing to assist the latter in their efforts because of a definite feeling of alienation from the husband and his matrikin, at least as regards financial matters, and the very real fear that at possible widowhood only a very small part of any household property will be theirs. Even, as a wife married under the Ordinance, a woman's due share of her husband's property at his death intestate amounts only to two-ninths, unless she has legal evidence that her rights are more extensive, as they may in fact be if she has worked and earned a salary throughout her married life and added her resources to his.

In our survey of rural women, this tendency to develop one's individual resources is at least as strong as it is among the urban elite. Both divorced and widowed women have more time to devote to their own enterprises and are more successful than married women in developing farms by using their own resources. Marriage means that the husband's farms have priority. It *may* mean that when the man dies, the widow can benefit by inheriting, but this is problematic. Women feel more secure when they set aside some resources to acquire farms of their own. It may well be that in the rural, matrilineal setting it is easier for women to find these independent sources of income through food farms, crafts, and trade than it is for women in an urban setting to do so.

As Oppong has suggested, the educated, urban Akan wife has become more dependent on her husband. Although she is more likely to be married under the Ordinance or in a church, in reality she may be less secure than her rural counterpart who has maintained more of her economic independence. This has definite implications for widows. The rural widow is more likely to have developed her own resources. In addition she may have benefited from her marriage. The urban Akan widow may be much more vulnerable. With more pressure on her to pool her income with her husband's, she has less opportunity to develop her own resources. After her husband's death, she may find that the traditional norms of matrilineal inheritance assert themselves, and unless she is married under the Ordinance and willing to fight a court battle, she is left with nothing.

If the wave of the future in Ghana is toward greater emphasis on the conjugal bond as the society becomes more individualized, urbanized, and educated, then it will be necessary to strengthen the positions of wives and widows. It would be ironic if, in this process, the wife becomes more dependent on her husband and the traditional independence of the Akan wife is compromised. If, however, the direction of the future is toward more female-headed households and networks of extended kin struggling to survive in economic crisis, it might be more prudent to look for ways to strengthen the individual resources of women as independent producers and consumers rather than simply as wives and widows.

# Contradictions, Constraints, and Choices: Widow Remarriage Among the Baule of Ivory Coast

MONA ETIENNE

THE PURPOSE of this paper is to examine the contradictions, constraints, and choices that characterize the position of widows among the Baule of Ivory Coast, especially as they affect widow remarriage to a husband's kinsman. This practice is by no means systematic, and its frequency is subject to regional and local variations, but it corresponds to a norm in the sense that propriety requires the kin group of the deceased to make the widow an offer, which she may accept or refuse.[1] The prohibitive rules

I am grateful to the Ivory Coast government and the Wenner-Gren Foundation for Anthropological Research, who made possible the research on which this paper is based. The principal source of my data is fieldwork in 1962-63 among rural Baule of the Bouaké region, sponsored by the Ivory Coast Ministère du Plan. Other data were provided by a research project among urban Baule of Abidjan in 1974-75, supported by grant no. 3067 from the Wenner-Gren Foundation and authorized by the Ivory Coast Ministère de la recherche scientifique and the Institut d'ethno-sociologie of the Ivory Coast National University in Abidjan. I thank my field assistants, Kouamé Kodjoua Christine and Kouassi Affoué Yvonne, for their tireless collaboration, and my many Baule informants for their patient and intelligent responses to endless questions. I also thank, for their comments and suggestions, Alma Gottlieb, and Betty Potash, who has been a most helpful and patient editor.

1. My rural research was limited to four villages: Diamelassou, Andobo-Alluibo, Ngatakro, and Abouakro. They belong to different subgroups but are all in the northern half of the Baule region. Between and within these villages there was great variability in the acceptance and the practice of widow remarriage to husband's kin. It is likely that other areas and villages would present other variations, possibly even a total absence of the norm and the practice. Although I have basic matrimonial data for the quasi-total female population of three villages and of one neighborhood in the fourth and much larger village (Andobo-Alluibo), along with more detailed case histories of a smaller sample of women, it is the latter material, not the quantitative analysis, that proved meaningful. It is

of the matrimonial system, however, should logically preclude the very possibility of such a marriage. There is, in effect, a fundamental contradiction between the formal rules governing matrimonial alliance in general and the legitimacy of widow remarriage to the kinsman of a deceased spouse. This contradiction will be examined, and then explained in terms of structural factors that determine competition for descendants among Baule kin groups.

Because kin group membership and residence are by no means clearly ascribed, a widow, insofar as she represents a means of retaining children, may become the focus of this competition. The very flexibility and mobility that engender competition for descendants among kin groups also leave considerable space for individuals, both women and men, to enhance their social and economic status by strategic choices, both in ordinary circumstances and in crises such as that represented by the death of a kinsman or a spouse. Individual strategies affecting the actual practice of widow remarriage will therefore also be examined, as will the interplay between individual interests and motivations and those of the kin groups involved. Although somewhat more attention will be given to the strategies of women, these cannot be understood without understanding the strategies of men— potential husbands of the widow, other kinsmen of the deceased, and kinsmen of the widow herself. The complexity of these strategies is compounded by the total life histories of the individuals involved, notably by factors affecting their status in their kin groups, and, for women, their status in the conjugal kin group. It would be impossible to unravel these complexities by detailing all the pertinent variables, but an attempt will be made to define those most likely to influence the matrimonial destiny of the widow.

The contradictions and complexities of widowhood and widow remarriage are deeply embedded in more fundamental contradictions and complexities of the society itself. It will therefore be necessary first to present an overview of Baule society, with close attention to the aspects most relevant to the issues exam-

---

the whys and wherefores, not the actual frequency of occurrence, that are relevant to my concerns. For this reason, statistical data are not presented.

ined here. The analysis that follows addresses basic tendencies of Baule society, which, though subject to the vicissitudes of history and played out differently in changing socioeconomic contexts, present a certain continuity. It is this continuity that will be my focus. Some directions of change will, however, be discussed.

## The Baule: An Overview

The Baule are a population of approximately one million in the east-central Ivory Coast. Although often classified as Akan, they are in fact of heterogeneous origin, the product of encounters between immigrants from the Akan groups in what is now Ghana (notably Denkyira and Asante) and earlier occupants of the present Baule area—Mande-Dyula, Voltaic, and Kru—who still inhabit the neighboring areas. Although war and conquest played a role in Baule history, the peaceable intermingling of populations largely contributed to the present form of Baule society and to the elaboration of a culture that in spite of variations of custom from region to region, from village to village, and even within villages, has a certain homogeneity and a specificity that distinguish the Baule from their neighbors, both Akan and non-Akan.

Early attempts by Akan immigrants to establish their hegemony ultimately failed, and effective centralization of authority was limited in scope and short-lived. There exist territorial units, and, within these units, a hierarchy of villages based on identification with founding ancestors and primacy of origin, but this hierarchy implies prestige rather than authority, and each village is largely autonomous. A village is composed of localized kin groups (*awlɔmu*; sing., *awlɔ*),[2] with membership determined cognatically. In other words, individuals may belong to an *awlɔ* by matrilateral or patrilateral links.[3] *Awlɔmu* have no names and are

2. The transcription of Baule terms is based on Carteron 1972, the only changes being the use of ɔ instead of ô and ɛ instead of ê; and the omission of tones, unnecessary here. Pending the publication of a more authoritative study of the Baule language, Carteron's work, in spite of its imperfections and limitations, is the only common standard of reference for authors on the Baule.

3. As is usual in societies with cognatic descent, kinship terminology is "Hawaiian," i.e., based on distinctions of sex and generation only (P. & M. Etienne 1967).

referred to only by the name of the living elder (*kpengben*). This, along with the principle of cognatic descent, makes their survival precarious. Each *awlɔ*, however, is represented by a sacred treasure (*adya*), which embodies the kin group's genealogy (see below) and serves to perpetuate its identity. The *kpengben* of the founding *awlɔ* of the village is generally also the village chief. His—or her—authority is limited to decisions involving the village as a whole and is based on the consensus of all elders.[4] Succession to the position of *kpengben*, also guardian of the *adya* of the *awlɔ*, is generally restricted to uterine descendants of the founding ancestor. A uterine descendant is called *bla ba* (pl., *bla bamu*), "child of a woman," in contradistinction to *yasua ba*, "child of a man"—a term that designates both agnates and cognates, including, for example, the child of a woman who is herself *yasua ba*. Besides being used in reference to descent from a founding ancestor and a living *kpengben*, these terms may be used to specify descent from any living person, usually but not necessarily a head of household. For example, a man or a woman's sister's child is his or her *bla ba*.

Subsistence farming land, which belongs to the village, is accessible to all residents, *yasua ba* as well as *bla ba*; coffee and cocoa farms, representing durable wealth, are transmitted matrilineally, although a father may bequeath in vivo such a farm to a son when the son has contributed to planting it. A *yasua ba* is, of course, a *bla ba* elsewhere, but full rights in an *awlɔ* are associated with effective residence.[5] It is important to note that the exclusion of the *yasua ba* from succession is not necessarily as disadvantageous as it may seem. Elders may benefit by the labor of juniors but cannot systematically coopt their surplus product, and adult dependents enjoy considerable economic autonomy. Individual wealth therefore coexists along with the sacred trea-

4. The term *kpengben* is used to designate both the head of the *awlɔ* and elders in general. Baule sometimes avoid confusion by using *awlɔ kpengben* for the former. I prefer to make the distinction by using *kpengben* here and the word *elder* for elders in general. The term *famien*, "chief," is used only at a level above that of the village (i.e., to designate the head of a regional subgroup).

5. The criterion of residence for succession to office is variable. In some villages, the *kpengben*, especially if he is also to be chief of the village, must be someone raised in the village, because, otherwise "he (she) does not know our customs." In other villages, it is acceptable to bring in as heir to office a person who has been raised elsewhere.

sure that embodies the *awlɔ*'s identity and continuity. It too is transmitted matrilineally, except for in vivo bequests such as that noted above. An enterprising *yasua ba* can, however, accumulate his own wealth, and, over time, attract his own uterine kin, such as sisters' children, thus constituting a subgroup within the *awlɔ* that may eventually form a new *awlɔ* with its own *adya* and of which he will become the founding ancestor. Slaves (sing., *kanga*) and their descendants (sing., *kanga ba*) complete the membership of the *awlɔ*. Today, with a few exceptions, only the latter remain. Intermarriage, traditions of discretion concerning their origin, and socioeconomic change may obscure their identity, but slave ascent is the object of rigorous matrilineal reckoning and therefore tends to persist in the case of uterine descendants of slaves. In the past, slaves played an important role in both production and reproduction and their descendants still do, to some extent (M. Etienne 1976). This will be made clear below.

Colonization by the French, involvement in the world economy, and modern political structures have introduced new factors of stratification, but differences in wealth and prestige could, even in the past, be considerable. Agriculture, with the yam as a staple crop, was the basis of subsistence, and all Baule were agricultural producers. Agricultural surplus, crafts (notably cloth production), gold-prospecting, and trade were sources of wealth (M. Etienne 1980). The economy was, with vicissitudes and regional variations, a prosperous one, especially in the late precolonial period. During the last decades of the nineteenth century, an already thriving trade with neighboring societies was enhanced by the indirect effects of coastal societies' trade with Europeans, and by an influx of low-priced slaves from the war-ridden northern fringes of Ivory Coast. Today, the Baule continue to be a relatively prosperous West African people, maximizing opportunities to accumulate wealth by cash-cropping—including coffee and cocoa farming on their own lands and on better-situated lands of southern neighbors—and by wage labor, seasonal and permanent. Differences in wealth and prestige, both between *awlɔmu* (kin groups) and between individuals, were and to a great extent still are determined by entrepreneurship and the ability to mobilize labor in the form of dependents: junior kin, sometimes affines, and, especially in the past, *kanga* and *kanga ba* (slaves and slave descendants). Even slaves had a share in the product of their labor, but on their death any accumulated wealth reverted to their owner, and, if he or she was *kpengben*, to the *adya* (treasure) of the *awlɔ*. Other dependents retain their share in the product, but elders nevertheless benefit by their labor.

All Baule are preoccupied with becoming wealthy, but this preoccupation must be understood to reflect a concern with both the ancestors and the individual's own future as an ancestor. The *adya* represents the ancestors and the history of the *awlɔ*: each item in it can be identified with the ancestor who contributed it. The *kpengben* is therefore particularly committed to increasing the *adya*, both to honor the ancestors (who are powerful and vindictive) and to ensure his or her own survival as an ancestor. To leave nothing is to be forgotten. Others in the line of succession to the office of *kpengben* are likely to share this commitment, but those who know they cannot succeed to office are not. In order to be remembered, the latter must become ancestors in their own right by accumulating wealth and transmitting it to their descendants. Eventually, they may become known as founding ancestors of an *awlɔ*, but in any case their memory will survive. For any inherited estate always has a sacred character; it must be maintained, increased if possible, and retransmitted along with the specification of its origin. Dependents contribute to an elder's wealth and thus to the building of an estate. At the same time, having wealth without descendants to receive the inheritance and to remember one's name would be meaningless. The Baule illustrate what has been noted for many other African societies: wealth is people and people are wealth; the two are inseparable. Because even the very young share these values and these concerns, wealth attracts dependents; for although the latter receive only a share of what they produce, the more prosperous the elder, the greater this share is likely to be.

## Gender Relations in Marriage and Kinship

A wife's labor is also an asset to her husband, but her position is not that of a junior dependent. The conjugal relationship is perceived as a partnership between a man and a woman for purposes of production and reproduction, with both partners having rights in the fruits of their productive and reproductive labor. Today, economic and social changes have disrupted the fragile and complex equilibrium of this relationship, generally to the disadvantage of women (M. Etienne 1980, 1983). The fundamental principles that determine women's status as adult participants in the social, economic, and political spheres nevertheless persist.

Marriage itself is not the object of overt arrangements between kin group elders. Although they may influence choices, must be called to sanction them, and are involved in the prolonged and multiple phases of matrimony, elders can neither control the initial choice of a spouse by a woman or a man, nor impose ultimate compliance with a choice that may be the result of their manipulations. Such manipulations are themselves hindered by custom: a clandestine sexual liaison (*sɔman*) is considered to be the initial phase of the premarital relationship, and should this liaison result in pregnancy, elders cannot legitimately oppose conclusion of the marriage. Although both ideology and practice support freedom of choice in marriage, the influence of elders, through both kin group solidarity and their moral authority over juniors, may play a role. As we shall see, however, free choice in marriage is but one expression of a system that favors individual enterprise and effectively limits the power of elders.

Gerontocratic control over marriage is further precluded by the absence of bridewealth, properly speaking. Gifts, primarily of consumable goods such as meat and drink, or, today, small amounts of money meant as a substitute, are given to the woman's kin, but the most valuable and durable goods, for example cloth and gold, go to the woman herself. Brideservice exists, but it is less important than in the past and in any case tends to be formulated as a diffuse and ongoing obligation to aid affines.

The practice of child betrothal, although it was never systematic and now has almost disappeared, may seem to contradict the above observations. But such an arrangement, usually based on an agreement between individual parents (especially mothers), even though underwritten by years of brideservice by the groom or his elder, could later be broken without penalty by a refusal—normally the girl's—that had only to be formulated in terms of lack of affection. In effect, whatever other considerations may intervene, marrying for love is by no means foreign to the Baule; and, indeed, love is generally the reason given for a marriage.[6]

Conjugal residence is virilocal, and, although the mutual rights and obligations of spouses tend toward an egalitarian balance, virilocality effectively restricts the full realization by women of the rights they otherwise enjoy. This is most notable in the political sphere, since access to the position of *awlɔ kpengben* (and, a fortiori, that of village or regional chief), otherwise open to both women and men, is contingent on residence in one's own village and compound. This political obstacle is also a social and economic one, because it limits access to dependents of one's own (other than offspring) and thus to a share in the product of their labor. An enterprising woman can nevertheless attract dependents in the form of junior kin, notably by means of adoption, which will be examined below. In the past, slaves of her own were an important asset to the socioeconomic status of a married woman (M. Etienne 1976).

The constraints of virilocality are also mitigated in other ways. First of all, marriage is such a gradual process that early conjugal residence is practically duolocal, and permanent residence with the husband may not occur until one or several children are born. Before a husband can request that a wife take up permanent residence with him, he must build a house for her. In the past, this meant demonstrating his ability to mobilize labor. Today, new—and government-imposed—housing norms require cash, causing delays that aggravate the traditional difficulty of concluding a marriage. Meanwhile, a woman can move back and forth between her kin and her husband, and her stays with the

---

6. There did exist in the past another form of arranged marriage, called *atonvlɛ*, which does stand in clear-cut opposition to all the rules of ordinary marriage. It represented a binding alliance between two high-ranking families or between a high-ranking family (that of the husband) and a low-ranking one (that of the wife). *Atonvlɛ* marriage involved bridewealth and gave the man and his kin inalienable rights in children. The woman had little freedom to refuse or to divorce, nor could she or her children return for visits (spend the night) among her kin. However, although such marriages appear to have been widespread, at least in the area studied (northern Baule), they were by no means commonplace. Moreover, they had practically disappeared well before colonization, probably in connection with the growing availability of slaves and the similarities between *atonvlɛ* and marriage to a female slave.

latter may be considered "visits" though they may last for years. This means, of course, that the marriage process has not been completed, since virilocal residence is the juridical norm. A frequent argument at divorce hearings in customary courts, used especially by women and their kin, is that there really was no marriage, because the woman, although she may have been living with the man for twenty years, was "just visiting." Divorce is frequent; exactly when it is concluded is unclear, but it is usually initiated by the wife's departure.[7] Even without an intention to divorce, however, a fully married woman may make frequent and prolonged stays among her kin, where, no matter how long she has been there, she is then "just visiting."

Such mobility and indetermination of residential status are made feasible by the rights a woman retains among her own kin, rights she can reactivate at any time, whether or not she has been "completely" married. The same model that governs the productive relationship of wife and husband also applies to the relationship between an adult woman in residence and her male kinsmen. Just as a husband must clear and help cultivate farming land for her needs and those of her children, so must the kinsman—usually a brother, but possibly a father, son, or uncle. Like a husband, he controls surplus yams, which are the product of their cooperative labor, but she has usufructuary rights in the cultivated plot and controls whatever she produces by intercropping and subsequent planting of other crops. A very young woman or a woman in residence only temporarily may work as a junior dependent with a mother, older sister, or other kinswoman, sharing in the labor and the product of that woman's farming plot; but an adult woman in residence for at least a full agricultural cycle has the right to farming land and male labor in proportion to her needs—including those of any children accompanying her—and her own ability to work.

7. Partly because they can take the decisive step of leaving the conjugal residence, divorce is easier for women than for men. If a man wants to divorce, he will usually make life so unpleasant for his wife that she will leave. The Baule are polygynous, but neither the rate nor the frequency of polygyny is high. Further, when a man is observed to have, for example, three wives (more are extremely rare), it may be just an appearance; he may be only beginning to marry the third, and, at the same time, may be getting divorced by at least one of the two others. Except for one village chief who had married several elderly widows of kinsmen, the only high rates of polygyny I observed (three or more) were in town.

Although a resident wife may resent the loss of a husband's labor to his kinswoman when it diminishes her own productive advantages, the inalienability of sisters' and sisters' children's rights is so firmly established that no wife would consider contesting them. Further, as suggested above, the relationship between affines, both as individuals and as groups, is governed by a general principle of mutual support and assistance. It can nonetheless be affected by personal likes and dislikes, and it is always fraught with tensions, of which the potential animosity and rivalry of sister and wife are but one instance. The reasons for these tensions will be made clear in the following section.

### Kin Group Competition and Individual Autonomy

The inalienability of a woman's rights in her own kin group favors her autonomy vis-à-vis her husband and his kin, facilitating temporary separation, divorce, and rejection of a marriage proposal following widowhood. The autonomy specific to women, however, reflects a more general tendency toward individual autonomy that must be examined at the structural level if we are to understand the choices and constraints of widows, their kin, and their affines.

Cognatic descent, as it is played out among the Baule, creates competition among awlɔmu (kin groups) for descendants, as well as a potential for considerable differences in wealth and status among these kin groups, according to their success or failure in this competition. At one extreme, an awlɔ can become impoverished for lack of labor, can shrink and even disappear for lack of descendants and heirs; at the other extreme, an awlɔ can become populous and prosperous by retaining children of both wives and sisters. The process is self-perpetuating, since, as noted above, wealth attracts people and people produce wealth. The system is skewed, however, by a matrilineal bias, which not only privileges uterine descendants with regard to inheritance and succession, as noted, but also affirms stronger and deeper ties to one's maternal awlɔ than to one's paternal awlɔ,[8] even

8. I use the terms *maternal* and *paternal* because in a cognatic system, a person may be a first-generation uterine descendant in his or her mother's kin group if the mother herself is *yasua ba*; or, a person may be a first-generation agnate in his or her father's kin group, if the father is *bla ba*. "Matrilineal" and "patrilineal" would therefore be inappropriate here.

though informants may insist that children (except married daughters) should reside with the father. The *awlɔ* where one is *bla ba* is the locus of one's ancestors, creating bonds that go beyond secular time and the contingencies of specific interpersonal relationships. Thus it is said that a person can "return" among maternal kin, even as an adult who has always resided elsewhere, whereas membership in the paternal kin group is contingent on effective continuity of residence and a specific relationship to an elder, especially the father himself. As a result, trading on their potential mobility, men and women generally enjoy considerable autonomy vis-à-vis their elders and may, in fact, change residence more than once in a lifetime. In practice, possibilities are generally limited, on the father's side, to the *awlɔ* in which the father himself has become integrated. On the mother's side, one may become integrated in the mother's father's *awlɔ* if she herself maintained this integration, but rights in the mother's mother's *awlɔ* nevertheless tend to be retained.[9]

Although changes in residence can occur late in life, and then generally in the form of "returning" to one's matrikin, residential mobility is greatest in the case of young people and children. Even very young children may change residence voluntarily. Most frequently, however, the residence of a child is determined by that of the mother. Babies and very young children will almost always accompany a woman whenever she returns to her kin, whether on a visit or otherwise; often, older daughters will do so too. A mother's kinswoman is considered an appropriate substitute for an absent mother, but a co-wife is not. Nor is a father's kinswoman, unless she has a close personal relationship with the mother or has received the child in fosterage or adop-

9. If the mother's mother was *yasua ba* in her *awlɔ*, other matrilineal ties sometimes may be maintained. But if an individual can trace descent in the uterine line through two or three generations of women who remained in their mother's *awlɔ*, it is probable that the *yasua ba* status of the grandmother or great-grandmother will by that time have been obscured and that she or her brother will have become the founding ancestor of a new *awlɔ*. In effect, among the *awlɔmu* of a village, some, because their founder was a *yasua ba*, may be *yasua ba* in relation to the founding *awlɔ*. The matrilineal members of such an *awlɔ*, founded by "the child of a man," would nonetheless be *bla ba* in the *awlɔ* and would usually consider themselves *bla ba* in the village, although they might specify that their *awlɔ* is *yasua ba* and might be able to refer to their links to an *awlɔ* in another village that has *bla ba* status there.

tion, as may happen (see below). The departure of the child may be considered only temporary, a necessity of nurturing, but various dilatory maneuvers can delay its return indefinitely, and the longer the residence with matrikin, the less likely it is that a father—or, a fortiori, the kin of a deceased father—will be able to activate his rights.

In sum, the structures of Baule society are marked by extreme flexibility, leaving much leeway for groups as well as individuals to manipulate the system to their advantage. This they do with considerable finesse, resolute pragmatism, and an acute consciousness of the contradictions of their society. This is perhaps not unusual in societies with cognatic descent, but here matrilineal bias further complicates relations.

*Widows and Widowers: Ritual as Paradox*

There is a certain indifference to gender that permeates Baule ideology and is also present in many aspects of material relations (M. Etienne 1979b, 1980). It is exemplified, on the symbolic level, by the ritual of bereavement that follows the death and burial of a married person. Observances for widows and widowers are identical. During the period of mourning, which formerly lasted as long as a year but now may last only three months, the surviving spouse must wear special clothing, fast during the day, weep each day at sunup and sundown, remain confined to the conjugal compound, abstain from contact or conversation with any but a previously widowed person, and observe other fastidious restrictions. (For details, see Guerry 1970.) Like a widow, a widower must maintain sexual abstinence, and this even though he may have other wives. Both a widow and a widower must submit to evening visits from affines, often accompanied by insults, and weep all the louder to placate them. Any property belonging to the deceased must be turned over to his or her kin.[10]

10. Some data, mainly from one Baule informant, a townswoman originally from the southeast, present a less egalitarian picture of bereavement ritual, depicting hazing of the widow and appropriation of her personal property by in-laws. Closer examination suggested, however, that, although this report may reflect a regional variation, distortion by the informant was also probable. Notably, ritual expressions of resentment on the part of in-laws seemed to be interpreted literally and emphasized in their application to widows, even though they also apply to widowers.

When the rites that terminate the period of bereavement have been completed, the widow or widower is not yet quite ready to return to the world of the living. Before resuming normal sexual relations, he or she must first have a sexual encounter with a stranger. This observance, say the Baule, is dictated by fear of the ghost of the deceased, whose jealousy may kill the widow or widower's sexual partner. Relations with wives (for a polygynous widower) or with potential conjugal partners can then be resumed or undertaken. It is significant that fear of the ghost, which also underlies other elements of bereavement ritual, is not the object of gender distinctions. Like female and male ancestors, female and male ghosts are equally powerful.

The material realities of widowhood are nonetheless very different from those of widowerhood. Detailed consideration of the latter is beyond the scope of this chapter. Briefly, although the loss of a wife affects a man's life, especially insofar as it can mean the loss of children to the deceased wife's kin—as a result of bad feelings, or the maintenance of good feelings by "compensating" them for the loss of their daughter, or for other reasons related to matrilineal bias—the rich and complex dimensions of strategy and choice that affect widows do not apply to widowers. A widower, as we shall see, can never remarry into his wife's kin group, and his remarriage is in any case not an issue, whereas the remarriage of a widow is a very important one for all concerned. Thus the ritual equivalency of widow and widower constitutes a paradox with reference to the radical disparity in their actual status. In effect, both the principle of virilocality and the descent system, as described above, put the widow in a very different structural position from that of the widower. It is this difference that explains the contradiction, for widows but not for widowers, between remarriage possibilities and the formal rules that govern all other marriages, a contradiction we will now examine.

*Breaking the Rules: The Logical Inconsistency of Widow Remarriage*

Unlike related Akan societies, such as the Asante, and like other societies with cognatic descent, the Baule have a system of marriage prohibitions that preclude both restricted and gener-

alized exchange. They formulate this system explicitly, with regard to restricted exchange, by saying that "we do not exchange
women," and, with regard to generalized exchange, by specify-
ing the interdictions that oppose the duplication of matrimonial
ties. In other words, an individual does not marry twice into the
same awlɔ, simultaneously or successively, and two or more
members of the same awlɔ, especially if they are closely related,
do not marry related members of another awlɔ. The qualification
"related" or "closely related" is necessary here because of the
heterogeneous composition of these kin groups and the presence of kanga ba (slave descendants), both of which leave the formal prohibition open to numerous exceptions. It is not, however, these exceptions that are my focus with regard to widow
remarriage. Sororal polygyny and the sororate, as well as marriage with the real or classificatory sister of a divorced wife, are
the object of particularly rigorous prohibitions and would be
considered incestuous, just as would sexual relations between
these partners or between close kin (P. Etienne 1975). Because
sexual relations and marriage are closely identified, the prohibitions governing both are identical.

   Logically, widow remarriage with a husband's kinsman should
also be prohibited; it is not permitted in other societies with cognatic descent and a similar set of interdictions, such as Gonja
(E. N. Goody 1962). Further, the Baule themselves regard it with
ambivalence, and in keeping with the variability and pragmatism that characterize both their norms and their practice, some
elders say, "It is wrong; in our awlɔ we don't do that." By and
large, however, this ambivalence is resolved by a compromise:
the suitor must be a kinsman, but not too closely related. Remarriage with a husband's brother, maternal uncle, uterine
nephew, or even son (by a co-wife) does occasionally occur, but
is looked upon askance. Sometimes, a falsified genealogy—
especially the misrepresentation of a slave relationship—may
explain what appears to be a remarriage with such a close kinsman.[11] The usual solution, by simultaneously affirming and

   11. Further, the kin status of a kanga ba (always determined matrilineally)
presents an often convenient peculiarity: kin relations on the father's side that
would otherwise constitute an obstacle to marriage can be ignored—annulled,
so to speak—by the stronger value of slave descent. Questioning informants

denying the duplication of matrimonial ties in the case of widow remarriage, stands in opposition to the more logical consistency of both the matrilineal Asante, among whom the nephew and heir must marry the widow (Rattray 1969), and the cognatic Gonja, who eschew remarriage to a dead husband's kinsman (E. N. Goody 1962).[12]

By its denial of identity between the new husband and his dead kinsman, the Baule compromise implies a dissociation between the two marriages. In effect, the new marriage can by no means be considered leviratic. Rights and obligations of the spouses are the same as in any other marriage. Procedure is also similar, but, for widow remarriage, a specific ritual must first be observed, whether or not the new husband is related to the deceased: the dead husband's elders must "discover" the couple in the act of "clandestine" love-making and demand compensation for this simulated adultery in the form of a propitiatory sacrifice to the ghost of the deceased. It is particularly revealing that a kinsman, albeit one designated by the kin group, must, like any other man, obtain permission from the deceased to marry his widow.

It should be clear that the new husband will be the recognized *pater* of any children he fathers. In any case, the Baule do not institutionally dissociate biological and social paternity (although they may cheat on the system, as we do). The new husband's obligations to existing children are those of any stepfather, and also

---

about a case of cross-cousin marriage (normally prohibited) in which a man had married his father's sister's child, I was told by the man himself, "But I am their [my wife's] *kanga ba*, so it doesn't matter [that I am closely related through my father]." In another *awlɔ*, where three generations of men had married the widows of fathers (co-wives of their mothers), the men explained, "Well, our father and his father did it and it worked for them." They gave the additional justification that the women were all *kanga* or *kanga ba*; otherwise these marriages would not have been possible. Unusual circumstances may account for other instances of normally prohibited widow remarriage, as in the case of the maternal uncle who married his nephew's widow because she was the beneficiary of a pension (discussed below).

12. Alma Gottlieb, in a recent dissertation on the Beng, neighbors of the Baule who have a system of double descent, shows that, like the Baule, the Beng prohibit the kind of duplication one finds in generalized exchange, i.e., men of one kin group systematically marrying women of another. Unlike the Baule, the Beng are logically consistent in also prohibiting widow remarriage to a husband's kinsman (Gottlieb 1983).

those of a father's kinsman—which he would have even had he not married the mother. Both a stepfather and a kinsman must contribute to children's subsistence, and to their other needs if called upon—although the contribution of the stepfather tends more to be mediated by his support of their mother. Both a stepfather and a kinsman, if they wish to consolidate relations with the children or the mother, may go beyond the minimal support required, but this is more likely to occur if the stepfather is also a kinsman.

To understand why the Baule practice a type of marriage that contradicts their own rules and is distasteful to them, it is necessary to refer to critical aspects of the kinship system, as described above. It is perhaps the combination of the formal factors of cognatic descent and matrilineal bias that is decisive in producing this contradiction. Comparative evidence is provided by Gonja, which presents a patrilineal bias and where individuals are also extremely mobile, but sons are said usually to return among their fathers' kin in late adulthood (J. R. and E. N. Goody 1967).

Baule fathers and patrikin have no such assurance. Although it is often said that children "belong to the father," that in exchange for procreation and nurturing they should reside and work with him, paternal rights are always precarious and contingent on specific circumstances that make integration in the paternal group either advantageous or disadvantageous. Even while the father is alive and his marriage to the mother intact, a child, a young man or woman, or even an older person may go to live among maternal kin. Mothers themselves, however, play a decisive role in influencing the residence and kin group membership of their children. This influence weighs most heavily on young children, but may also affect adults. Whereas divorce or temporary separation poses a threat to paternal kin rights over descendants, the death of a father can produce a veritable crisis, given the importance of the father-child personal relationship in binding individuals to the paternal kin group.

Although the father-child relationship may be expressed in terms of sentiment, it can be fully understood only in the light of the principle of matrilineal succession. A father may make in vivo bequests to his children of any wealth that is the product of his or their labor—and, in hopes of retaining them, he may be very generous indeed—but a man's son or daughter is not his heir. There may be a closeness to the father's brother and sometimes an expectation of being treated by him as by the father, but, cognatic links notwithstanding, the father's sister's child, who most often inherits wealth and succeeds to office, is practically a stranger. Personal animosity and rivalry between children of wives and children of sisters may be compounded by the animosity and rivalry between their mothers, as noted above. Whereas an adult *yasua ba* who has already established himself as a prosperous head of household may choose to remain in the *awlɔ* after the death of his father, a younger and less integrated son, or a daughter, generally will not. Small children will normally accompany the mother in any case, but even they are remarkably aware of the pros and cons of residence choices.

Therefore, the institution of widow remarriage to a husband's kinsman, although other reasons may intervene in specific cases, reflects a fundamental concern with retaining children. The contradictions between this institution and formal rules of alliance are rooted in the deeper contradictions of the kinship system itself. As we shall see, the contradictions do not stop here; they appear at every level of actual practice. One might expect, for example, that widows most likely to remarry in the husband's kin group would be relatively young women with young children. The data, however, do not bear this out. At one extreme, there are elderly women, sometimes childless, who marry a husband's kinsman; at the other extreme, many women, widowed young and with young children, remain unmarried for long periods of time and/or remarry men unrelated to the husband. What effectively happens after a man's death and determines whether or not his widow will remarry into his kin group is a function of conflicting interests and motivations, not only between the affinal kin groups and between individual affines, but also between members of the same kin group, for the concerns of the group and those of each individual member do not necessarily coincide. All the parties involved have choices and are limited by constraints. To understand the discrepancies between principle and practice, it is necessary to examine the real meaning of these choices and constraints, first for the kin group and the individual kin of the deceased, then for the widow and her kin group. Their respective points of view will be the focus of each of the two following sections, even though it will not always be possible to dissociate rigorously the analysis of one point of view from that of another.

*Constraints and Choices: The Dead Man's Kin*

The risk that an *awlɔ* may lose a dead kinsman's children to their maternal kin is made particularly acute by the procedure that normally follows the death. When the period of bereavement is terminated, the widow must return among her own kin (or "be returned," since the husband's elders must accompany her). She will take with her any young children and perhaps one or more unmarried daughters. According to some informants—especially those who eschew widow remarriage to the husband's kinsman—these children should in any case be returned at some later date to their patrikin, but, according to the majority, "you cannot take the child and leave the mother." As a normative statement, this remark expresses the principles of both kin group solidarity and solidarity between affinal groups: a man's kin must show that they love and respect his widow. It also expresses a related practical concern: what affines would otherwise want to give up a daughter's children to her husband's kin, and what children would otherwise want to live with the kin of their dead father? However this may be, it is in fact unlikely that, if they do not reintegrate the widow, the dead man's kin group will ever reintegrate her children, who meanwhile are growing up elsewhere. Therefore, her return must be the object of a formal request, which may be accepted or refused. It is particularly significant, as we shall see, that no time limit is specified for this request.

Independently of its concern for retaining descendants, the kin group of the deceased is obliged, by the code of proper behavior and by respect for his ghost, to request the return of his widow. To neglect this obligation not only would antagonize the widow, her children, and her kin, but might damage their reputation as affines in general, and also anger the ghost himself. The constraint is particularly strong in the case of an old woman widowed after a long marriage. They may also be genuinely fond of the woman, since a durable marriage often means a good relationship with affines. The initial request, formulated in terms of affection on the part of the whole kin group, does not necessarily mention marriage and should be made whether or not marriage is intended. In effect, one may occasionally find an aged unremarried widow residing with her dead husband's kin, generally as a member of the household of an adult son or other descendant, and sometimes, although less frequently, as a dependent of a husband's kinsman, such as the son of one of his other wives or even his sister's son. In such cases, especially of the latter type, the widow may in fact be an *awlɔ bla*, or "*awlɔ* wife"—that is, a woman married in her own *awlɔ*—for if the kin relationship is distant enough, individuals belonging to the same *awlɔ* may marry. Or, and this is even more likely, she may be a *kanga ba* of her husband's *awlɔ* (also called *awlɔ bla*). Because slave origin is reckoned matrilineally and never lost, however much it may be obscured by generations of intermarriage with free men and residence elsewhere, a wife who is *kanga ba* in her husband's *awlɔ* would also be a member of this *awlɔ* in her own right, even if she had never resided there before marriage and had patrikin or matrikin in other *awlɔmu*. When a widow is *awlɔ bla*, her status as a kinswoman may be invoked, by herself or others, to justify continued residence among her affines.

Only unusual circumstances, however, would motivate a widow belonging to another *awlɔ* to reside unmarried among affines, and only a very old woman can be expected not to remarry. It would be unrealistic, in most cases, to expect a widow to return and remain without finding her a husband. A request for the widow's return, therefore, if it is to be more than pro forma, must usually be backed up by a marriage proposal. In the case of a middle-aged or elderly woman, the reasons that motivate such a proposal may be much the same as those that motivate the reintegration of an elderly woman without marriage. Children may not be involved, the widow may even be barren, but she may be valued not only as a person and as an affine, but also as a wife, for her companionship and, if she is not too old, for her labor. Well-integrated in the *awlɔ*, she may have adopted children and other dependents from her kin group whose contribution to the life and labor of her conjugal kin group is appreciated; she and these dependents may be poles of attraction for future dependents and potential marriage partners. If she has received adoptees from her husband's kin, her departure would pose a problem, since her rights over such children would conflict with those of the kin group. Indeed, gifts of children to a kinsman's wife are often an expression either of her strong integration in the affinal group or of a concern with effecting such an integration. Thus it is not surprising that such women often remarry among their affines.

At the other extreme is the young widow with children who does not return among her affines and eventually remarries elsewhere. Whatever the reasons, which will be discussed below, a frequent explanation given by women and their kin is that she was not asked. This may mean that the pro forma request was not backed up with a serious offer and very often, since no deadline is specified, that the affines simply did not move quickly enough. The longer they wait, the more likely it is that, once she is freed of the restrictions that mark the bereavement period and has returned among her kin, the widow will become involved with another man and want to marry him. If she does, her affines can block the marriage for a while by refusing the ritual "discovery" of the liaison and the propitiatory sacrifice to the dead husband's ghost, but they must eventually accept, since a clandestine sexual liaison sooner or later is publicly acknowledged, and then it is practically a de facto marriage, which cannot be contested by refusal of sanctions, especially if it should result in pregnancy.

The widow's explanation that her affines did not ask for her in marriage, usually formulated to suggest that they did not want her, although sometimes valid, may be misleading. The request in marriage cannot be made in the name of the group, but must refer to a specific individual, and so must be delayed until an appropriate suitor can be found. This is often no simple matter. Because Baule society is anything but gerontocratic and an autocratic elder runs the serious risk of finding himself (or herself) without dependents, a man cannot be designated and forced to propose if no one really wants to marry the woman. Personal likes and dislikes effectively play a role in the ease or difficulty of finding a husband for the widow. More relevant to our analysis, however, are the constraints that limit the *awlɔ*'s choice and the possibly conflicting interests of those involved.

Most concerned with retaining the widow in order to retain her children are the *awlɔ kpengben* (elder) and the dead man's heir. (If the deceased was himself *kpengben*, his heir would succeed to this office, and the two would then be one and the same person.) The heir, however, as we have noted, would be too close a kinsman to marry the widow himself, as would the *kpengben*, even though not the heir, if he is a brother or maternal uncle of the deceased.

Marriage to the widow of a uterine nephew, a maternal uncle, or a brother is considered particularly indecent. A less distantly related man, most likely a *yasua ba* ("child of a man"), would be the appropriate candidate; but, precisely, the interests of such a man are least likely to coincide with the interests of the heir or the *kpengben* and the higher interests of the group as a whole. This "catch-22" may be resolved if there is a solidly integrated *yasua ba* in whose interest it may be to support the *awlɔ* in which he has elected residence. In the past, the ideal prospective husband might be a *kanga* (slave) or *kanga ba* (slave descendant), solidly integrated if only for lack of the option to elect membership elsewhere. Today, the *kanga ba* still occupies a privileged position as a marriage partner in these circumstances and in others, notably when prohibitions based on kinship conflict with the tendency to favor unions that are for all intents and purposes endogamous.[13]

But what if the deceased was himself *yasua ba* or *kanga ba*? In this case, the interests of the *kpengben*, representing the *awlɔ* as a whole, and of the prospective new husband are more likely to coincide insofar as the elder himself or any of his closely related uterine kinsmen are likely to be in a position to marry the widow,

13. The logic described above (note 11), which allows an otherwise cognatic system to ignore patrilateral kinship in the case of slave descent, reflects a more general characteristic of *kanga* and *kanga ba* status: in a society where wealth and prestige are achieved by maximizing options based on potential membership in more than one *awlɔ*, the *kanga* does not enjoy such options. As for the *kanga ba*, even when fathered by a freeman, he (or she) is bound to the maternal *awlɔ* like a fatherless child. Indeed, a "fatherless" *bla ba* (usually an individual whose mother has refused to recognize or have any connection with the father), even if he (or she) is the nephew of a chief, may be considered deprived and "like a *kanga ba*" because of his (or her) lack of options.

with the exception, of course, of the dead man's father or father's brother (too closely identified with the father). Other than these latter, the elder—necessarily a *bla ba*—and his brothers and other close kin might well be distantly enough related to the deceased to become the widow's husband. The concern with remarrying the widow, however, would be all the greater the closer the kin relationship between the deceased and the *kpengben*, for the children of a too distantly related man would be most likely to leave, and might have other options, even among other paternal kin, e.g., their father's matrikin. Again, a decisive factor would be the degree of integration of the *yasua ba*, this time in the position of deceased kinsman and father.

If the deceased was a *kanga* or *kanga ba*, his own integration in the *awlɔ* was perhaps even stronger than that of a *bla ba*, but his children do not inherit his status, and their attachment to the paternal *awlɔ* might be so weak that remarriage with their mother would be unlikely to prevent them from returning to their maternal kin—assuming the mother was a free woman, or even a *kanga ba* of another *awlɔ*. If the widow herself is *awlɔ ba*, i.e., a "daughter," *kanga* or *kanga ba* of her husband's *awlɔ*, the latter might be concerned with remarrying her to a husband's kinsman, but more with an eye to retaining future offspring than through a preoccupation with retaining the progeniture of the deceased, since these children, called "children of the *awlɔ*" (*awlɔ bamu*) would have no other options.

As we see, not only is there likely to be a disparity between the interests of those who are especially concerned with remarriage of the widow in the *awlɔ* and those in a position to marry her, but it is precisely in those cases where remarriage in the *awlɔ* is least problematic that it may also be least critical in determining a hold on children. This alone could explain delays in offering marriage to the widow. Moreover, assuming that circumstances make such an offer feasible and desirable, there is no assurance that, in the long run, it will be worth the effort. Although a dead man's kinsmen may enhance their chances of retaining his children by remarrying his widow, they have no guarantee that, on the occasion of a divorce, or even with the new marriage still intact, the children may not one day rejoin their maternal kin. This eventuality was concretely expressed by one disgruntled informant who complained that he had married a kinsman's widow only to keep the children. Now he had lost them to their maternal kin and was stuck with the woman. Thus, how the kinsmen of the deceased gauge their chances of effectively retaining his children may have a decisive effect on how assiduously they pursue remarriage with the widow. If they do not particularly like the woman and fear they will eventually lose the children anyway, they may neglect their obligation to request her return, or may make a pro forma request that is not followed up by any specific proposal, knowing that their insincerity will be understood, and that, in any case, a still marriageable widow would not long reside unmarried among her husband's kin.

*Constraints and Choices: The Widow and Her Kin*

The factors that determine the widow's matrimonial destiny are perhaps even more complex. To understand them fully, it will be necessary to consider in some detail a dimension only touched upon when we examined the choices and constraints of her husband's kinsmen: that of the long-term strategies involved in achieving status as a kinsperson and an affine. Indeed, both husband and affines, by nurturing good relations with a woman and by promoting her integration among them, may diminish the risk of losing her and her children if she is widowed. The long-term strategies of a woman, on the other hand, go rather in the opposite direction, for they involve reinforcing her kin ties and establishing a certain autonomy vis-à-vis her husband and her affines. Further, they are perhaps more essential to her future prosperity than are the complementary strategies of affines to theirs, for the status a woman has thus achieved can substantially enhance the choices open to her as a widow. How women "prepare for the future" will be examined in the following section. First, our analysis, as in the previous section, will focus on choices and constraints more in terms of abstract possibilities, based on the workings of the system and the structural positions of the parties.

As suggested above, a widow's options are limited by an initial constraint: she can return among her husband's kin only if they request it, and remarry among them only if she receives an offer.

A woman cannot propose formally to a man, and a widow is no exception to this rule. She can, if sought out by a man of her husband's *awlɔ* on his individual initiative—perhaps provoked by discreet encouragement on her part—engage in a clandestine liaison with him without the consent or knowledge of elders, hoping that this relationship will eventually be approved and sanctioned. It may be, or it may not. In one case, the kinsman with whom the widow became involved was not the one the elders wanted her to marry, for reasons having to do with the respective positions of the two men in the kin group, and they effectively created enough obstacles for the couple to prevent the marriage, although she did not marry the other man either. Without any such personal involvement, and knowing that her husband's kin do not really want her, a woman would be most unlikely to want to return among them. She may of course have a well-integrated adult son who is head of household, and in that case would have rights in his labor and would be more at home than if she had to depend on the labor of a male affine. Because of the proscription against duplication of matrimonial ties, especially rigorous with regard to kinsmen marrying related women, she would be unlikely to have a daughter married in her deceased husband's *awlɔ*. If she did, she might live with her, since one always has rights in a daughter's labor as well as a son's, but because the head of household, the daughter's husband, would be an affine rather than a kinsman, such an arrangement would tend to be only temporary. Were it observed to be durable, it would be necessary, as in the case of a widow directly dependent on an affine, to look for reasons in her relationship with her own kin group. This will be made clear below.

Having specified the limited possibilities a widow has to elect residence with her affines on her own initiative, we will now assume that she has received an offer and consider the factors that determine her response, examining together the variables that influence her choice and those that may influence her kin group elders to exert pressure on her in one direction or the other.[14] Again, it should be remembered that, for women as for men, in-

14. I use the term *elders* (plural) rather than *elder* (singular) or *kpengben* here because, in the case of the widow, it is her parents, parent, or older sibling who would be most directly concerned and involved, although none of these may be the *kpengben* of the *awlɔ*.

dividual and group interests do not necessarily coincide and elders do not exercise absolute authority over juniors. Although far from being in themselves decisive, the widow's age and the ages of her children, if any, are important variables. We will therefore examine first the options of elderly widows, then those of younger women.

As explained above, persons can always return among their maternal kin and women retain rights in the labor of their kinsmen. A woman might, of course, have been raised and integrated in her father's *awlɔ*. Depending on the relations her mother had maintained with her own kin group, the widow might have the option of returning either among them or among her father's kin. In the latter case, it is nevertheless possible that she would have uterine kinsmen residing there—brothers, sisters' children, and perhaps others. In one case or the other, however, her prosperity and her status in her kin group would be contingent on the possibilities of effectively mobilizing the labor of a close kinsman, for closeness of the kin relationship, even between uterines, is important in validating rights and obligations that otherwise may be more abstract than real.

For an elderly woman, such possibilities may be limited. If she is still able to work, land would be made available to her, but male labor might be more problematic. Her elders—father, maternal uncle, etc.—would be deceased or too old, as might her peers—brothers, first cousins, etc. It is therefore among her juniors that she must find support. Most appropriate to provide this support are own sons or classificatory sons such as sisters' children. A woman may take up residence with a daughter residing in the *awlɔ* and work with her or be supported by her, but this solution also supposes the presence of a close male kinsman on whose labor the daughter depends. Should the widow have adult adopted children among her kin, their obligations to aid or support her would be the same as that of biological offspring. (This eventuality will be discussed in detail below.) If no such juniors are available, the widow might find herself dependent on a distantly related kinsman with whom she has had little personal contact. She would usually be taken care of, but perhaps grudgingly, and would have somewhat the status of a poor relative—or a *kanga* (slave). Such a situation might reflect the posi-

tion of her kin group. If the *awlɔ*'s descendants have repeatedly
been lost to competing *awlɔmu*, it may even have disappeared.
She might then find a place in a related *awlɔ*, but her relationship
to its members (not counting kinswomen who are wives) would
surely be very distant. On the other hand, the more her *awlɔ* has
prospered, the more likely it is that close junior kin will be available to her. And she may even be in a position to assume the
office of *kpengben*, having been prevented from doing so as long
as she resided elsewhere as a wife. Moreover, as we shall see, the
widow herself may have largely contributed to determining both
her own status among her kin and the status of her kin group.

The more favorable an elderly widow's status in her own kin
group the more probable it is that she will choose to reside there.
But if she must face the prospect of depending on remote and
perhaps unwilling kinsmen in an *awlɔ* where, for lack of young
people, labor may already not be easily available, she is likely to
opt for remarriage with a kinsman of her husband or, if she is
very old, even for remaining among them without remarrying.
This she will do all the more readily if her marriage has been
a long and solid one and her integration among affinal kin is
strong. Such may well be the case precisely when conditions for
her return among her kin are unfavorable, for the close junior
kin who are absent there may well be her own children, who
have remained and become integrated among her husband's kin,
and perhaps adoptees, especially any received from her affines.
Although fortunate and enterprising women may build strong
social networks among both kin and affines, it more generally
happens that one set of relations is nurtured at the expense of
the other. This will become clear as we look at the choices and
constraints of younger widows.

A childless young or middle-aged woman may receive a remarriage offer from her husband's kin, but such cases, since
bridewealth is not an issue, tend to reflect strong social ties between the two affinal groups or a personal attraction between
the woman and her suitor. However this may be, it is the widow
with children who is most likely to receive an offer, and it is her
situation that most concerns us here. Personal inclination—her
feelings for both the prospective husband and her other affines—may well influence her to accept or refuse, but her decision is likely to be affected by strategic considerations.

In principle, a refusal weakens her claim on her children. The affines have acted properly, she has refused, they have the right to claim their dead kinsman's children. Whether or not they will succeed in doing so, however, is contingent on specific circumstances, including the age and sex of each child, its present residence, the relative prosperity of the two *awlɔmu*, and, in connection with this, the probability that a child will prefer integration in one or the other of the two kin groups. One *awlɔ* may also be in a position to retain or obtain children by exerting pressure on the other. If a woman believes that some or all of her children will effectively be kept or reclaimed by their paternal kin, she is more likely to accept remarriage. If, on the other hand, she is confident that any young children or daughters who have left with her will remain with her, and perhaps even that older children who have remained with their paternal kin will eventually rejoin her, she is less likely to accept. Her predicament is, in a sense, the mirror image of the predicament described above for the kinsmen of the deceased: if she gauges the situation badly, she may accept an undesired marriage needlessly or jeopardize her future by refusing it. For the children may remain or return among their matrikin even with their mother remarried among their patrikin; or, even with their mother returned among their matrikin or remarried elsewhere, they may ultimately become integrated in their paternal *awlɔ*. In the former case, the widow could, of course, eventually divorce and rejoin her children. In the latter case, she could eventually join the household of an adult son, but she might then have been better off to accept the marriage offer. Even though the deck is stacked, so to speak, in favor of a child's residence with mother and matrikin when the father is deceased, anything can happen in a given case. It should be noted, moreover, that although the residence of one child, especially an older son, tends to influence the residence of others, siblings do not always reside in and belong to the same kin group. Indeed, some informants suggest "sharing" as a mode of resolving contradictory rights in children. Where this does occur, a widow with several children would have more flexible options.

A widow's decision to accept or refuse an offer of remarriage will of course be affected by her kin group—not only by their status and the possibilities they offer her and her children, but also by the influence they may try to exert on her directly, especially if she is a young woman with children. Like the prospective husband, she cannot be coerced. Since the children in question are her own, her interests are more likely to coincide with those of her elders than are his, but this is not necessarily the case. They may want her to remarry the husband's kinsman, even though it means losing the children—perhaps to maintain a good relationship with the affinal group, which may, for example, be superior in power and prestige, or for other reasons unrelated to her concerns for herself and her children. They may want her to refuse remarriage because of similarly unrelated conflicts with the affines, or because they are more concerned than she is with integrating the children in their *awlɔ*. Even when the concerns of the widow and her elders do coincide, they may gauge the situation differently, perhaps disagreeing on the probability of retaining the children, and therefore taking different positions with regard to the offer of remarriage.

A young widow's own kin position in her *awlɔ* will also be a factor in her decision and the pressure exerted on her. This is also true of the prospective husband in his kin group, but the two situations are not easily comparable. If the widow is *bla ba* (a uterine descendant), she and her children may be in the line of succession to the office of *kpengben*. Their reintegration would then be particularly desirable, and in any case the children would be valued as uterines and she, as a producer of uterine descendants, would also be valuable to her *awlɔ*. The widow may of course be *yasua ba* (child of a man), but if she at all considers her paternal kin group to be her *awlɔ* and has returned among them rather than among her matrikin, she is probably strongly integrated there, perhaps through association with a brother who is head of household. Although he too is *yasua ba*, his sister is for him the source of uterine descendants: her children are his *bla bamu* and eventually may make him the *kpengben* of his own *awlɔ* and, over the generations, a founding ancestor.

If a woman is *kanga ba* in her *awlɔ*, her value as a source of descendants is equivalent to that of a *bla ba*, perhaps greater, because of the heavy emphasis on matrilineality in determining the membership of slaves and their descendants. For this reason, she is more vulnerable to pressure than a freewoman, and pressure not to accept a remarriage offer is more likely to be exerted on her. If, on the other hand, she is *kanga ba* among her affines and *yasua ba* in the *awlɔ* where she was born and raised, the affines can exert considerable pressure to accept remarriage on both her and her patrikin. Moreover, the latter might offer little resistance, because her children would be both *kanga ba* and *yasua ba* in her husband's *awlɔ* and the affinal group would have exceptionally strong claims over them.

*Preparing for the Future: Widows and Their "Children"*

Whether integrated in her maternal or paternal *awlɔ*, a woman generally has this in common with a male *yasua ba*: her status in the kin group, in contrast with that of a male *bla ba*, tends to be a function more of achievement than of ascription. For like the *yasua ba*, she can strengthen her position in the *awlɔ* by accumulating her own dependents. The same is true of her position in her conjugal *awlɔ*. In the past, a woman could have her own slaves. A slave child might be given her by an elder when she married, to accompany her and remain with her in the conjugal residence. An enterprising woman might also acquire her own slaves, both before and after marriage (M. Etienne 1976, 1979b). Although this possibility no longer exists, today as in the past the institution of adoption gives women a means of building their own constituency of dependents.

I have thus far avoided expanding on references to adoption, precisely because it deserves special attention. A detailed analysis of the workings of this institution, not possible here, has been the object of other publications (M. Etienne 1979a, 1979b). It is, however, essential to understand how the giving and receiving of children can bring a woman prestige and autonomy, both as a kinswoman and as a wife, and thus enhance the choices open to her in the eventuality of widowhood. The strategies involved imply foresight; they must be elaborated from the very beginning of marriage, perhaps even before marriage, for even a young unmarried woman can receive a child in adoption.

Let us examine the possibilities first from the point of view of the recipient of adoptees. It has been noted above that a woman may receive a child from her husband's kin. In this case, widowhood, like divorce, would create a dilemma, for her kin group is not the child's, and the latter's ties to its adoptive mother would conflict with ties to its own kin group were she to leave. But such adoptions are in fact infrequent, and generally occur when the woman is an older, perhaps barren wife who seems to enjoy an especially solid marriage and the affection and esteem of her affines. Most frequent are adoptions of kin, mostly children of kinswomen (especially sisters), but also children of kinsmen (especially brothers). Such adoptees are important for a barren woman, but also for a woman who bears children, for a husband has rights in the children he has fathered with a wife, but not in those she has received in adoption. Like a stepfather, he may wish to win their affection and thus reinforce ties with both them and his wife, but a child is given to one person, not to a couple, and he is no more than a stepfather. He would lose the children if his wife were to leave, and if he were to die, his kin would have no rights whatsoever in them. As noted above, their presence may contribute to the prosperity of the awlɔ, and for that reason the elders would be all the more anxious to keep the widow. She, on the other hand, would be able to leave without having to face the prospect of losing these children and the support she may receive from them in the future. Once grown, they may already have returned among her kin, facilitating her reinsertion there.

It is important to understand that although Baule adoption does not imply the obliteration of links to biological parents or of obligations toward them, it does create indissoluble links and identical obligations to the adoptive parent.[15] A woman will rarely have more than one or two adoptive babies or young children at a time, but she may receive and nurture many, including offspring of adoptees, throughout her life span and thus for a period unlimited by the contingencies of fecundity. An old woman, even though barren, may therefore have a considerable number of adult "children." All owe her the affection and support due a biological mother. Among them may be a uterine

15. For this reason, and contrary to habitual usage among Africanists (but not Oceanists), I use the term *adoption* rather than *fosterage*. Fosterage is also practiced, but its temporary nature and other criteria justify the distinction (M. Etienne 1979b). Because it creates stronger ties, only adoption is dealt with here, although some of my observations about adoption also apply to fosterage.

kinswoman or kinsman she has chosen as heir, ensuring her status as ancestor for this kinsperson and his or her uterine descendants.

Similar advantages are to be gained by giving children to kinswomen or, more rarely, to kinsmen. In order to give a child in adoption, a parent must have the other parent's consent. Understandably, a husband may be unwilling to lose children to his wife's kin, but it is selfish and improper to systematically refuse the gift of a child to one's affines. The ability to give children, unlike the ability to receive them, is of course contingent on fecundity, and a woman with many children is most expected and most likely to make such gifts. It is not unusual, however, for a woman to give her firstborn baby to a kinswoman, especially if she herself was raised as that woman's adoptee.[16] Although the child's labor is temporarily lost to the mother, she can expect future gains, for, as noted above, both kinship links and filial obligations persist. To understand the long-term advantage of giving children, we need only look again at the advantages of receiving them: should the adoptive mother, if she is married, subsequently be widowed or divorced, the child would end up among her kin, who are also the biological mother's. Even if the adoptive mother remained married, these children, once grown, would be unlikely to remain in an *awlɔ* where they have no kin ties other than to a woman married there. Moreover, assuming again that the child has been given to a kinswoman of the biological mother and raised either among the kin of both these women or in the former's conjugal household, ties to the child's paternal kin group would be weak and it would be unlikely ever to take up residence there.

We have seen that children both given to and received from a woman's own kin are likely in adulthood to become integrated members of her kin group and, if she herself returns, will contribute to her support. At least as important as these specific

16. Although a woman *may* give a child to her biological mother "to replace herself and thank the mother for raising her," this practice is frequently presented as a *systematic obligation* of an adoptee toward her (or his) adoptive mother—it being further specified that the gift should be of a firstborn. Since this adoptee's child incurs the same debt to the adoptive mother, one may find, in the case of a very old woman, duplication of the adoptive tie over as many as three, even four, generations, i.e., 60 to 70 years (M. Etienne 1979b).

benefits are the more general advantages to be gained by the practice of adoption. The gift of a child tends to maintain and consolidate social networks among kin for both the donor and the recipient. However close their kin relationship may or may not be, a special bond is established between them, drawing them closer not only to each other, but also to those who are close to each of them. This makes it possible for a woman to return among her kin in her old age without the onus of being a "poor relative" for lack of close ties to others who have remained or returned, a quasi-dependent herself for lack of junior dependents.[17] A woman who invests too heavily in her conjugal relationship and her affinal network at the expense of kin relations may have a closer marriage and a more solid integration in her husband's kin group, but she is likely to be among the aged widows, with or without children, who remarry or even remain unmarried among their affines. Although treated with affection and respect, she cannot have the same status as an elder that she would among her own kin, where her ancestors reside and where she herself, over the generations, may become an honored ancestor.

*The Impact of Socioeconomic Change on Widows' Choices*

The Baule remain strongly attached to the goals and values of their culture. For historical reasons related to the balance of power in France at the time of conquest (1898-1911) and to the preoccupations of the colonial government in the early 1900's, Christian missionary activity played a minor role in the colonization of Ivory Coast. Further, the Baule, in comparison with other peoples, have demonstrated strong resistance to religious conversion, and Christians represent a small minority of the rural population. In town, Christianity is more widespread, but it is often adapted in such a way as to accommodate elements of traditional religion—especially those beliefs and practices that express the essential and indestructible connection between the living and the dead, and, thus, the power of the ancestors and

17. E. N. Goody (1962) describes in a similar way the role of fosterage for Gonja women, who practice what she calls "terminal separation," systematically ending marriage by returning among their kin in old age. This practice is fairly frequent among the Baule, but appears less systematic than among the Gonja.

the importance of becoming an ancestor. The persistence of these concerns is such that the most orthodox of Christians, even though they themselves abstain from sacrifices to the ancestors, may on special occasions request that a kinsperson fulfill this obligation in their place. Such arrangements, generally between a townsperson and rural kin, also contribute to maintaining kin group solidarity.

The persistence of basic family structures was facilitated by colonial policy in Ivory Coast. Indeed, the French colonial administration was generally as unconcerned with imposing a transformation of family structures as it was with imposing Christianity. The same cannot be said of the postindependence Ivory Coast government. In the past twenty years, considerable efforts, through both propaganda and legislation, have been devoted to promoting the patriarchal nuclear family. For example, campaigns against "le parasitisme familial" (i.e., support of the less fortunate by their more fortunate kin), against matrilineal inheritance, and against excessive funeral expenditures—along with the encouragement of statutory marriage under a community property regime—converge toward the same goals: consolidation of the nuclear family to the detriment of the extended kin group, individualization of property rights, and concentration of wealth by the restriction of its transmission to direct descendants.

Should these goals ever be attained, one could predict radical changes in the patterns of widow remarriage. Indeed, without the concerns specific to the Baule system of cognatic kinship and matrilineal inheritance, the raisons d'être of widow remarriage to a husband's kinsman would no longer exist. Government policy with regard to the family, however, has thus far had a limited impact. It mainly affects the urban elite and, to some extent, petty civil servants and salaried workers—especially insofar as statutory marriage establishes rights to fringe benefits. But even among these categories, family structures have not been fully transformed. Among the rural population and the urban nonelite, the effects of new legislation and official policy have been for the most part superficial—in the sense that they have not altered basic structures—and sometimes paradoxical.

For example, in one of the villages studied, a man had married his uterine nephew's widow. Normally, remarriage to such a close kinsman of the husband would be prohibited. The justification given was that the deceased had been a government employee and the marriage statutory. His widow therefore qualified for a pension, which could be paid only to her. For the kinsmen of the deceased, however, the pension represented an inheritance that belonged to the kin group, and the only way to ensure their appropriation of this form of wealth was for one among them to marry the beneficiary, a point of view the widow did not contest.

This case is exemplary rather than anecdotal, for it shows how unexpected the effects of partial change can be. In this instance, as in others, new laws and global structures create circumstances that are interpreted and acted upon in the light of unchanged values and extremely resistant microstructures. The result may be very different from that intended by the legislators, even diametrically opposed to their intentions. Given the complexity of this interaction between the new and the old, which compounds the already complex constellation of factors that affect widow remarriage, it would be unrealistic even to speculate concerning a specific direction of change, e.g., to suggest a diminishing (or increasing) frequency of remarriage to husbands' kinsmen. The constraints and choices that govern widow remarriage may take new forms, but these forms themselves are unpredictable, and the outcome in terms of actual behavior is even more so.

There is, however, an area of change that lends itself to analysis: the overall impact that socioeconomic transformations affecting women in general are likely to have on the *quality* of the choices open to widows. We have seen that building a constituency of personal dependents is a decisive means by which women establish their autonomy and affirm their status among both kin and affines, thus enhancing their options in the eventuality of widowhood. The key element in this process is the practice of adoption. We have also seen, in the introductory section of this paper, that wealth and dependents are inseparable. They are the underpinnings of Baule spirituality and indispensable to the attainment of full personhood as a potentially powerful ancestor. Moreover, each in relation to the other is the means to an end: dependents contribute to an elder's wealth, and wealth attracts dependents. This is true in the case of adoption, as it is in other forms of dependency. It is necessary, therefore, to consider the ways in which changes in women's access to economic resources, by affecting their opportunities to give and receive children, may affect their eventual options as widows. Although the focus on adoption emphasizes one element among several that might serve to depict the changing condition of widows, it is hoped that this focus will give insight into the more global picture.

As suggested above, the persistence of traditional structures and values, especially among the nonelite, is such that one cannot make categorical distinctions between rural and urban behavior with regard to widow remarriage. Indeed one cannot make categorical distinctions between rural and urban Baule, for urbanization is most often temporary, and even when it is of long duration and apparently permanent, geographical separation does not preclude continued insertion in the rural kin group. This is especially true for women. In analyzing changing access to resources and changing access to dependents, it will nevertheless be necessary to take into consideration the impact of urban migration.

When a child is given in adoption, important motivations, in addition to those examined in the preceding section, are the child's welfare and future prosperity—and the resulting benefits to the biological parents, especially the mother, in old age. Even when a child is given to a young unmarried or newly married woman, the fact that she is enterprising and likely to become prosperous is taken into account. An old woman who is miserable and barely able to take care of herself may receive a child helper from a daughter or other close relative, but she is unlikely to receive adoptees, with the permanent commitment true adoption implies, even from a dutiful daughter, and much less from more distant kin. As noted above, differences in wealth existed in the past. For women, these differences depended partly on the prosperity of their kin group or their conjugal kin group insofar as it affected the resources made available to them. For example, a woman whose husband or brother commanded the labor of numerous males, whether junior kin or slaves, could, with their collaboration in male tasks, increase her own productivity. But a woman's prosperity was also largely a function of her own diligence in agricultural and craft production and of her ability to invest the surplus in entrepreneurial pursuits, such as gold-prospecting and trade. These pursuits, in turn, might permit her to purchase slaves of her own, who would further contribute to both production and other activities. Elderly informants frequently tell of grandmothers and great-grandmothers who set out on trading and gold-prospecting expeditions with perhaps a few pieces of cloth and ultimately accumulated considerable estates.

Today, Baule women continue to seek prosperity, but colonial and postcolonial involvement in the world economy, even while opening up new areas of entrepreneurial activity that, to some extent, replace those that have disappeared, has had the long-term effect of restricting women's access to economic resources. Cash-cropping, now the principal source of wealth for rural Baule, has developed in such a way that it primarily benefits men. At the same time, it absorbs the available labor of both women and men, leaving little time for other productive activity beyond that indispensable to subsistence. Subsistence itself is contingent on cash, for the Baule must buy many goods they no longer produce, but cash is generally more accessible to men than to women (M. Etienne 1980). In especially prosperous villages, persistent and enterprising women may obtain a substantial share in the wealth. Where, for instance, coffee farm profits and other income are considerable, men may pay laborers to do work otherwise required of wives and sisters. In some instances, they may even hire laborers to replace themselves in making a contribution to the production of women's crops, thus giving the women the opportunity to profit by the sale of large quantities of surplus produce (condiments, peanuts, cassava, rice) on local markets. In much of the Baule hinterland, however, even with cash-cropping, families barely eke out a living. Urban and seasonal rural migration (to southern coffee and cocoa farms) by men brings some return in cash to their kin groups, but deprives the village—especially village women—of the male labor necessary to produce agricultural surplus. As a result, rural women, by and large, are at a disadvantage in building the kind of prosperity and prestige that attracts dependents.

One response to this situation has been widespread urban migration by women. Indeed, among the Baule population of Abidjan, women slightly outnumber men. In town, a woman can hope to accumulate wealth, by trade and other activities, sometimes prostitution, and by investment of profits in assets such as urban real estate, taxicabs, and coastal coffee and cocoa farms. Some succeed, in varying degrees; others fail. It is questionable, in the light of repercussions of the ongoing world recession on the Third World and in the context of changing urban structures, whether the hopes of today's unschooled young townswomen will materialize as they have for their elders, whose "success stories" so often serve as a model. As noted, urbanization among the nonelite is rarely definitive, and this is especially true for women. Not only do young women come and go frequently, but many older women, whatever their present residence, have lived for long periods in both town and village, often with several changes over a lifetime. These changes in residence sometimes correspond to those of husbands, but they are often undertaken by single women before, after, and between marriages. Widowhood may be a reason for urban migration, insofar as it can facilitate resistance to demands of remarriage, or it may be simply an occasion to try one's luck as a single townswoman. The widow may be one of the many women who have returned to the village, married, and remained there because they failed to prosper in town. In this case, she sometimes may return as a "visitor," that is, a dependent of a kinsperson, often a more fortunate kinswoman, and may or may not establish herself as a long-term and successful urban resident. Success is unlikely, however, if she is elderly and has not already established a solid foothold in town.

Although one or several marriages may figure in their life histories, successful townswomen tend to be unmarried and heads of their own households. Even they may return to the village when very old, but generally with the intention of remaining unmarried. In any case, they maintain their rural ties, making frequent visits, often selling in town products from their village, sometimes from "their" farm cultivated by junior kin or by wage labor. Probably their most frequent major investment is to build a house in the village, establishing a presence that is both material and symbolic. In these and other ways, a prosperous townswoman will nurture her relations with her kin. For, once again, wealth alone is meaningless; the ultimate goal is to achieve status as an elder and as an ancestor. Consolidating rural-urban networks, especially those that involve junior kin, is essential to this pursuit.

Because of the opportunities, real or imagined, of city life, a townswoman, especially if she is prosperous—but sometimes even if she is not—attracts rural kin as dependents and notably as adoptees. Both parents and the children themselves hope that the child will share in the elder's prosperity and learn by her achievements. For the townswoman, in addition to consolidating links with rural kin, a foster child or adoptee, especially a girl, is an economic asset by her contribution to domestic labor, trade, and other profitable activities. Sending a child to school (which is more common when the child is male) may represent a financial burden, but nevertheless one with potential long-term advantages, for if the child is successful, the adoptive mother can hope to receive compensation in the form of a solid and durable tie to a member of the modern elite. Growing unemployment among elementary school and even among high school graduates makes such hopes more and more illusory, but examples still abound of illiterate old women whose "children" have become high-ranking government employees, even ministers, and the realization that ongoing class formation will make such achievements unlikely in the future has not yet been fully grasped.

Urban men also receive rural children as dependents, although more often in fosterage than in adoption. Indeed, insofar as wage labor and, a fortiori, well-paying salaried positions, are more accessible to men than to women, there has been an increasing tendency among rural parents to seek out successful urban kinsmen rather than kinswomen as sponsors for their children. The detailed analysis of this shift and its ramifications is, however, beyond the scope of this chapter (but see M. Etienne 1979b). What is important here is the overall effect of urban fosterage and adoption, whether by women or by men: a drain, so to speak, of children away from the villages that operates to the detriment of the rural economy and, more specifically, to the economic and social detriment of rural women. The urban migration of children may have long-term advantages for some individual rural parents, but the resulting loss of labor—and children often leave precisely at the age when they become productive—seriously affects the rural economy in general. Since girls and younger boys usually work with their mothers, this loss is felt more acutely by women than by men and compounds the economic disadvantages of rural women described above. Moreover, it is not the biological mother alone who is at a disadvantage, for the children given in adoption or fosterage to urban kinswomen (or kinsmen) are children not available for rural kinswomen.

The same strategies and values that once allowed women to build their own constituency of dependents continue to operate today, but in a different context and with different consequences. Inequalities in wealth and status that were largely a function of individual enterprise and position within the framework of relatively homogeneous traditional structures are now set in the global context of the urban-rural imbalance. This imbalance introduces an additional dimension that must be considered in examining the choices open to widows. A rural wife who has maintained a durable marriage and worked hard all her life may have little to show for it, for access to economic resources and access to dependents mutually reinforce one another, and she has been deprived of both. As an aged widow, she is likely to be among those who have restricted options. True, her children given in adoption to a townswoman may have become prosperous and be able to support her, but what if they have failed, as so many do? Children she might otherwise have received in adoption have been given to townswomen, and because of this her ties to them may be even weaker than if they had remained with their parents, her rural kin. Aware of the possible consequences, women are often reluctant to become or remain involved in lasting rural marriages, which, however comfortable, may lead to a very uncomfortable old age. Rather, concerned with their future as elders and as ancestors, they see urban migration as a means to this end. Once established as wealthy and independent women, they may marry or remarry—in the village or in town—but if widowed, they would not have to choose between the status of a dependent affine and that of a "poor relative." Thus aspirations that superficially may appear to reflect new values and goals in fact reveal the foresight with which Baule women adapt old values and old goals to new circumstances. At the same time and somewhat paradoxically, the solution perpetuates the problem: as a prosperous townswoman and a pole of attraction for rural kin and, especially, their children, the successful urban migrant inevitably contributes to the conditions of rural life and marriage she herself has sought to escape.

## Conclusion

The practice by the Baule of widow remarriage to a husband's kinsman contradicts the logic of a matrimonial system that otherwise prohibits both restricted and generalized exchange and therefore normally precludes marriages that duplicate ties of alliance between kin groups. Other such marriages—for example, the sororate and sororal polygyny—are in effect the object of rigid interdictions. The Baule also appear unusual by comparison with other societies that have a system of cognatic descent and similar matrimonial rules but do not practice widow remarriage to a husband's kinsman. The Baule themselves regard their practice with ambivalence and attempt to dissociate the two marriages by choosing as a second husband to the widow a kinsman who, although well-integrated in the local kin group, is not too closely related to the deceased. The new marriage is by no means leviratic; it entails all the rights and obligations of an ordinary marriage, as well as a ritual specific to the remarriage of a widow, a propitiatory sacrifice to the ghost of the deceased husband, which must be accomplished whether or not the new husband is his kinsman.

The contradiction between general rules governing marriage and widow remarriage to husband's kinsman can be understood only by reference to the competition for descendants that characterizes Baule society. Cognatic descent combined with matrilineal bias creates conditions whereby paternal kin are in constant danger of losing dependents to maternal kin. A decisive factor determining residence in one group or the other is the residence of the mother. Children are frequently acquired by maternal kin following a divorce, but the death of a father makes it even more likely that a mother's departure will mean the departure of her children. Since women retain full rights in their own kin group, it is always feasible and often advantageous for a widow to return among her kin, whether or not she will eventually remarry.

Although it is incumbent on the kin of the deceased to offer remarriage to his widow, such a marriage is no guarantee that they will retain his children. Moreover, disparities between the interests of kin group members eligible to marry the widow and their elders may make it difficult to designate a prospective husband and effectively conclude the marriage. Delays facilitate the refusal of an offer by the widow, and in any case she is free to refuse, remaining with her kin or remarrying elsewhere. The widow's decision may be influenced by her elders, but her interests, like those of the prospective husband, do not necessarily coincide with those of the elders. As a result, complex strategies are involved in determining the real meaning of constraints and choices for the widow and her kin on the one hand, and the kin of the deceased on the other.

The complexity of the strategies that affect widow remarriage reflect more fundamental characteristics of Baule society and, especially, of a kinship system that makes kin group membership extremely flexible and open to manipulation by both elders and juniors. The kin group (*awlɔ*) is not a monolithic unit composed of the elder (*kpengben*) and of juniors who are all direct dependents of the elder. All adults, women as well as men, can build their own constituencies of dependents within their *awlɔ*—and, for women, within the conjugal *awlɔ*. This pursuit, related to the pursuit of wealth, is essential to the ultimate goal of all Baule: to become a powerful and honored ancestor. It is especially important to women, whose access to power is limited by virilocality, and who, as widows, may otherwise have restricted options. The practice of adoption, by allowing women to build their own constituency of dependents, largely contributes to their status among both kin and affines and enhances the options open to them should they be widowed.

In spite of postindependence efforts to modify family structures, these structures and corresponding beliefs and values remain very much intact among rural Baule and among the urban nonelite. In both groups, people adapt to new legislation in sometimes unexpected ways. Therefore, it is not possible to make predictions or even to speculate about changes in patterns of widow remarriage. It is, however, possible to examine the impact socioeconomic change has had on women's access to resources and, consequently, on the potential quality of widows' choices.

The cash economy has developed to the general disadvantage of rural women, making it difficult for them to accumulate the wealth that attracts dependents. At the same time, because of the real or imagined prospects of urban prosperity, many children are being given in adoption or fosterage to town dwellers. Children are a particularly important economic and social resource for rural women, and their absence compounds the effects of other changes. Therefore, although these transfers of children may have advantages, albeit uncertain, for individual parents, including mothers, they operate to the general detriment of rural communities, which are deprived of children's contribution to production. The resulting lack of opportunities motivates urban migration on the part of women themselves.

Urbanization is rarely definitive, but women are increasingly reluctant to become entrenched in lasting rural marriages. Those who do may be among the elderly widows with limited options, forced to become a "poor relative" among their kin or to accept an undesired remarriage, perhaps even to reside as an unmarried dependent among their affines. In town, a woman may become wealthy and the head of her own household. The successful townswoman generally maintains her kin relations. By wise investments and support of kin, especially adoptees, she seeks to consolidate her rural networks, to establish her status as an elder, and eventually to become an honored ancestor. The "success stories" of a few become models for many, who, in the context of ongoing class formation and changing urban structures, are less and less likely to succeed. Paradoxically, their response to their discontent tends to perpetuate its causes.

# References

# References

*Slater: Foreword*

Bohannan, Laura. 1966. "Shakespeare in the Bush." *Natural History*, 75: 8.

Hart, C. W. M., and Arnold Pilling. 1966. *The Tiwi of North Australia*. New York: Holt, Rinehart & Winston.

Kluckhohn, Clyde. 1949. *Mirror for Man*. New York: McGraw-Hill.

Lévi-Strauss, Claude. 1971. "The Family," in Harry L. Shapiro, ed., *Man, Culture and Society*. London: Oxford Univ. Press.

Slater, Mariam K. 1976a. *African Odyssey*. New York: Doubleday Anchor Books; and Bloomington: Indiana Univ. Press.

———. 1976b. *The Caribbean Family: A Case Study in Martinique*. New York: St. Martin's Press.

*Potash: Widows in Africa*

Abrahams, R. G. 1973. "Some Aspects of Levirate," in Jack Goody, ed., *The Character of Kinship*. Cambridge: Cambridge Univ. Press.

Bay, Edna G., ed. 1982. *Women and Work in Africa*. Boulder, Colo.: Westview Press.

Bledsoe, Caroline H. 1980. *Women and Marriage in Kpelle Society*. Stanford: Stanford Univ. Press.

Caldwell, J. C. 1976. *The Socio-economic Explanation of High Fertility: Papers on the Yoruba Society of Nigeria*. Changing African Family Project Series. Canberra: Dept. of Demography, Australian National Univ.

Cohen, Abner. 1969. *Custom and Politics in Urban Africa*. Berkeley: Univ. of California Press.

Cohen, Ronald. 1971. *Dominance and Defiance*. Anthropological Studies No. 6. Washington, D.C.: American Anthropological Assoc.

Colson, Elizabeth. 1951. "The Plateau Tonga of Northern Rhodesia," in Elizabeth Colson and Max Gluckman, eds., *Seven Tribes of British Central Africa*. Oxford: Oxford Univ. Press.

Comaroff, J. L., ed. 1980. *The Meaning of Marriage Payments*. New York: Academic Press.

Etienne, Mona. 1979. "The Case for Social Maternity: Adoption of Children by Urban Baule Women." *Dialectical Anthropology*, 4.

Evans-Pritchard, E. E. 1951. *Kinship and Marriage Among the Nuer*. Oxford: Clarendon Press.

Fallers, L. A. 1957. "Some Determinants of Marriage Stability in Busoga: A Reformulation of Gluckman's Hypothesis." *Africa*, 27.

Fallers, Margaret Change. 1960. *The Eastern Lacustrine Bantu*. Ethnographic Survey of Africa. London: International African Institute.

Firth, Raymond. 1951. *Elements of Social Organization*. London: Watts & Co.

Fortes, Meyer. 1949a. *The Web of Kinship Among the Tallensi*. London: Oxford Univ. Press.

————. 1949b. "Time and Social Structure: An Ashanti Case Study," in Meyer Fortes, *Social Structure*. London: Oxford Univ. Press.

Gluckman, Max. 1959. "Kinship and Marriage Among the Lozi of Northern Rhodesia and the Zulu of Natal," in A. R. Radcliffe-Brown and Daryll Forde, eds., *African Systems of Kinship and Marriage*. Oxford: Oxford Univ. Press.

————. 1971. "Postscript to 'Marriage Payments and Social Structure Among the Lozi and Zulu'" (excerpt from 1959 article), in Jack Goody, ed., *Kinship*. Harmondsworth: Penguin.

Goody, Esther. 1971. "Forms of Pro-parenthood: The Sharing and Delegation of Parental Roles," in Jack Goody, ed., *Kinship*. Harmondsworth: Penguin.

————. 1973. *Contexts of Kinship*. Cambridge: Cambridge Univ. Press.

————. 1982. *Parenthood and Social Reproduction: Fostering and Occupational Roles in West Africa*. Cambridge: Cambridge Univ. Press.

Goody, Jack. 1967. *The Social Organization of the LoWiili*. London: Oxford Univ. Press. 2d ed. (Original edition 1956.)

Gravel, Pierre Bettez. 1968. *Remera: A Community in Eastern Ruanda*. The Hague: Mouton.

Gray, Robert F. 1964. "Introduction," in Robert F. Gray and Philip Gulliver, eds., *The Family Estate in Africa*. Boston: Boston Univ. Press.

Gulliver, Philip. 1964. "The Arusha Family," in Robert F. Gray and Philip Gulliver, eds., *The Family Estate in Africa*. Boston: Boston Univ. Press.

Guyer, Jane I. 1981. "Household and Community in African Studies." *African Studies Review*, 24.

Hafkin, Nancy J., and Edna G. Bay, eds. 1976. *Women in Africa*. Stanford: Stanford Univ. Press.

Kirwen, Michael C. 1979. *African Widows*. Maryknoll, N.Y.: Orbis.

Klima, George. 1970. *The Barabaig*. New York: Holt, Rinehart & Winston.

Kopytoff, Igor. 1964. "Family and Lineage Among the Suku of the

Congo," in Robert F. Gray and Philip Gulliver, eds., *The Family Estate in Africa*. Boston: Boston Univ. Press.

———. 1977. "Matrilineality, Residence and Residential Zones." *American Ethnologist*, 4 (3).

Kottak, Conrad Phillip. 1974. *Anthropology: The Exploration of Human Diversity*. New York: Random House.

Lallemand, Suzanne. 1977. *Une Famille Mossi. Récherches Voltaiques* (Paris), 17.

Leach, E. R. 1957. "Aspects of Bridewealth and Marriage Stability Among Kachin and Lakher." *Man*, 57.

LeVine, Robert A. 1964. "The Gusii Family," in Robert F. Gray and Philip Gulliver, eds., *The Family Estate in Africa*. Boston: Boston Univ. Press.

Lopata, Helena Znaniecki. 1979. *Women as Widows: Support Systems*. New York: Elsevier–North Holland.

Mair, Lucy P. 1934. *An African People in the Twentieth Century*. London: Routledge.

———. 1953. "African Marriage and Social Change," in A. Phillips, ed., *Survey of African Marriage and Family Life*. London: Oxford Univ. Press.

Marris, Peter. 1958. *Widows and Their Families*. London: Routledge and Kegan Paul.

Meillassoux, Claude. 1981. *Maidens, Meal and Money* (trans. from the French). Cambridge: Cambridge Univ. Press.

Mitchell, J. Clyde. 1951. "The Yao of Southern Nyasaland," in Elizabeth Colson and Max Gluckman, eds., *Seven Tribes of British Central Africa*. Oxford: Oxford Univ. Press.

———. 1956. *The Yao Village*. Manchester: Manchester Univ. Press.

Mullings, Leith. 1976. "Women and Economic Change in Africa," in Nancy J. Hafkin and Edna G. Bay, eds., *Women in Africa*. Stanford: Stanford Univ. Press.

Obbo, Christine. 1976. "Dominant Male Ideology and Female Options: Three East African Case Studies." *Africa*, 46.

Oboler, Regina Smith. 1980. "Is the Female Husband a Man?: Woman/ Woman Marriage Among the Nandi of Kenya." *Ethnology*, 19.

O'Brien, Denise. 1977. "Female Husbands in Southern Bantu Societies," in Alice Schlegel, ed., *Sexual Stratification: A Cross-Cultural View*. New York: Columbia Univ. Press.

Okeyo, Achola Pala. 1980. "Daughters of the Lakes and Rivers: Colonization and the Land Rights of Luo Women," in Mona Etienne and Eleanor Leacock, eds., *Women and Colonization*. New York: Praeger.

Oppong, Christine, ed. 1983. *Female and Male in West Africa*. London: George Allen and Unwin.

➝Pittin, Renée. 1983. "Houses of Women: A Focus on Alternative Life-Styles in Katsina City," in Christine Oppong, ed., *Female and Male in West Africa*. London: George Allen and Unwin.

Poewe, Karla O. 1978. "Religion, Matriliny and Change: Jehovah's Witnesses and Seventh-Day Adventists in Luapula, Zambia." *American Ethnologist*, 5 (2).

Reiter, Rayna R. 1975. *Towards an Anthropology of Women*. New York: Monthly Review Press.

Richards, Audrey. 1950. "Some Types of Family Structure Amongst the Central Bantu," in A. R. Radcliffe-Brown and Daryll Forde, eds., *African Systems of Kinship and Marriage*. Oxford: Oxford Univ. Press.

———. 1951. "The Bemba of North-Eastern Rhodesia," in Elizabeth Colson and Max Gluckman, eds., *Seven Tribes of British Central Africa*. Oxford: Oxford Univ. Press.

———. 1969. *Bemba Marriage and Present Economic Conditions*. The Rhodes-Livingsone Papers No. 4. Manchester: Manchester Univ. Press. (First published 1940.)

Robertson, Claire. 1976. "Ga Women and Socioeconomic Change in Accra, Ghana," in Nancy J. Hafkin and Edna G. Bay, eds., *Women in Africa*. Stanford: Stanford Univ. Press.

Rosaldo, Michelle Zimbalist, and Louise Lamphere, eds. 1974. *Women, Culture, and Society*. Stanford: Stanford Univ. Press.

Sacks, Karen. 1982. *Sisters and Wives: The Past and Future of Sexual Inequality*. Urbana: Univ. of Illinois Press.

Schildkrout, Enid. 1978. "Age and Gender in Hausa Society: Socio-Economic Roles of Children in Urban Kano," in J. S. LaFontaine, ed., *Sex and Age as Principles of Social Differentiation*. New York: Academic Press.

Schlegel, Alice. 1977. *Sexual Stratification*. New York: Columbia Univ. Press.

Spencer, Leon P. 1973. "Defence and Protection of Converts: Kenya Missionaries and the Inheritance of Christian Widows, 1912-31." *Journal of Religion in Africa*, 5 (2).

Steady, Filomina Chioma, ed. 1981. *The Black Woman Cross-Culturally*. Cambridge, Mass.: Schenkman.

Stenning, Derrick J. 1959. *Savannah Nomads*. London: Oxford Univ. Press.

Turner, Victor W. 1957. *Schism and Continuity in an African Society*. Manchester: Manchester Univ. Press.

Ware, Helen. 1983. "Female and Male Life-Cycles," in Christine

Oppong, ed., *Female and Male in West Africa*. London: George Allen and Unwin.

Wellesley Editorial Committee. 1977. *Women and National Development: The Complexities of Change*. Chicago: Univ. of Chicago Press.

Winans, E. V. 1964. "The Shambala Family," in Robert F. Gray and Philip Gulliver, eds., *The Family Estate in Africa*. Boston: Boston Univ. Press.

Yanagisako, Sylvia Junko. 1979. "Family and Household: The Analysis of Domestic Groups." *Annual Review of Anthropology*, 8.

*Potash: Widows in a Luo Community*

Crazzolara, J. P. 1950-53. *The Lwoo*. Verona: Missioni Africane. 3 parts.

Economic Commission for Africa. 1974. "The Data Base for Discussion on the Interrelations Between the Integration of Women in Development, Their Situation and Population Factors in Africa." New York: United Nations Economic and Social Council, E/CN.14/SW/37. Mimeo.

Fearn, Hugh. 1961. *An African Economy: A Study of the Economic Development of the Nyanza Province of Kenya, 1903-1953*. Oxford: Oxford Univ. Press.

Hay, Margaret Jean. 1976. "Luo Women and Economic Change During the Colonial Period," in Nancy J. Hafkin and Edna G. Bay, eds., *Women in Africa*. Stanford: Stanford Univ. Press.

Mboya, Paul. n.d. *Luo kitgi gi timbegi*. Kendu Bay, Kenya: African Herald Publishing House. 3d printing 1965.

Ocholla-Ayayo, A. B. C. 1976. *Traditional Ideology and Ethics Among the Southern Luo*. Uppsala: Scandinavian Institute of African Studies.

Ogot, B. A. 1967. *A History of the Southern Luo Peoples, 1500-1900*. Vol. 1. Nairobi: East African Publishing House.

Okeyo, Achola Pala. 1980. "Daughters of the Lakes and Rivers: Colonization and the Land Rights of Luo Women," in Mona Etienne and Eleanor Leacock, eds., *Women and Colonization*. New York: Praeger.

Parkin, David. 1978. *The Cultural Definition of Political Response: Lineal Destiny Among the Luo*. New York: Academic Press.

Potash, Betty. 1978. "Some Aspects of Marital Stability in a Rural Luo Community." *Africa*, 48.

Stichter, Sharon. 1982. *Migrant Labor in Kenya: Capitalism and African Response, 1895-1975*. Harlow, Essex: Longman.

Whisson, Michael. 1964. *Change and Challenge: A Study of the Social and Economic Changes Among the Kenya Luo*. Nairobi: National Christian Council of Kenya.

*Oboler: Nandi Widows*

Gluckman, Max. 1950. "Kinship and Marriage Among the Lozi of Northern Rhodesia and the Zulu of Natal," in A. R. Radcliffe-Brown, ed., *African Systems of Kinship and Marriage*. London: Oxford Univ. Press.

Langley, Myrtle. 1979. *The Nandi of Kenya: Life Crisis Rituals in a Period of Change*. New York: St. Martin's Press.

Oboler, Regina Smith. 1977. *Work and Leisure in Modern Nandi: Preliminary Results of a Study of Time Allocation*. Working Paper No. 324. Nairobi: Institute for Development Studies.

————. 1980. "Is the Female Husband a Man?: Woman/Woman Marriage Among the Nandi of Kenya." *Ethnology*, 19: 69-88.

————. 1985. *Women, Power, and Economic Change: The Nandi of Kenya*. Stanford: Stanford Univ. Press.

Snell, G. S. 1954. *Nandi Customary Law*. London: Macmillan.

*Obbo: East African Widows*

Barth, Frederick. 1966. *Models of Social Organization*. Royal Anthropological Institute Occasional Paper No. 23. London.

Elam, Yitzchak. 1973. *The Social and Sexual Roles of Hima Women: A Study of Nomadic Cattle Breeders in Nyabushozi County, Ankole, Uganda*. Manchester: Manchester Univ. Press.

Evans-Pritchard, E. E. 1945. *Some Aspects of Marriage and the Family Among the Nuer*. Rhodes-Livingstone Paper No. 11 (originally published in 1938 in *Zeitschrift fur Vergleichende Rechwissenschaft*).

Fearn, Hugh. 1961. *An African Economy: A Study of the Economic Development of the Nyanza Province of Kenya, 1903-1953*. London: Oxford Univ. Press.

Kirwen, Michael C. 1979. *African Widows: An Empirical Study of the Problems of Adapting Western Christian Teachings on Marriage to the Leviratic Custom for the Care of Widows in Four Rural African Societies*. Maryknoll, N.Y.: Orbis.

Low, D. A. 1971. *The Mind of Buganda: Documents in the Modern History of an African Kingdom*. Berkeley: Univ. of California Press.

Marris, Peter. 1958. *Widows and Their Families*. London: Routledge and Kegan Paul.

Mukwaya, A. B. 1953. *Land Tenure in Buganda: Present Day Tendencies*. Kampala: East Africa Inst. of Social Research.

Muthiani, Joseph. 1973. *A Kamba from Within: Egalitarianism in Social Relations*. New York: Exposition Press.

Ndisi, John W. 1974. *A Study of the Economic and Social Life of the Luo of Kenya*. Uppsala: Scandinavian Institute of African Studies.

Obbo, Christine. 1976. "Dominant Male Ideology and Female Options: Three East African Case Studies." *Africa*, 46: 4.

———. 1980. *African Women: Their Struggle for Economic Independence.* London: Zed Press.

Ocholla-Ayayo, A. B. C. 1976. *Traditional Ideology and Ethics Among the Southern Luo.* Uppsala: Scandinavian Institute of African Studies.

Potash, Betty. 1978. "Some Aspects of Marital Stability in a Rural Luo Community." *Africa*, 48: 380-96.

*Landberg: Swahili Widows and Divorced Women*

Anderson, J. N. D. 1970. *Islamic Law in Africa.* London: Frank Cass and Co. Reprint of Colonial Research Publication No. 16, H.M.S.O., London, 1955.

Arens, W. 1975. "The Waswahili: The Social History of an Ethnic Group." *Africa*, 45 (4): 426-37.

Bujra, J. M. 1968. "An Anthropological Study of Political Action in a Bajuni Village in Kenya." Diss., Univ. of London.

———. 1977. "Production, Property, Prostitution: 'Sexual Politics' in Atu." *Cahiers d'Etudes Africaines*, 65: 13-39.

Caplan, Ann Patricia. 1968. "Non-Unilineal Kinship on Mafia Island, Tanzania." Diss., Univ. of London.

———. 1969. "Cognatic Descent Groups on Mafia Island, Tanzania." *Man*, n.s., 4 (3): 419-31.

———. 1975. *Choice and Constraint in a Swahili Community: Property, Hierarchy, and Cognatic Descent on the East African Coast.* London: Oxford Univ. Press.

Cohen, Ronald. 1971. *Dominance and Defiance: A Study in Marital Instability in an Islamic African Society.* Anthropological Studies No. 6. Washington, D.C.: American Anthropological Association.

Eastman, Carol M. 1971. "Who Are the Waswahili?" *Africa*, 41 (3): 228-35.

———. 1976. "Ethnicity and the Social Sciences: Phonemes and Distinctive Features." *African Studies Review*, 18 (1): 29-38.

Gulliver, P. H. 1955. *Labour Migration in a Rural Economy.* East African Studies No. 6. Kampala: East African Institute of Social Research.

Hemedi El-Buhuriy, Sheik Ali bin. 1959. *Kitabu cha Nikahi.* Dar es Salaam: Government Printer. In separate volume, translated into English by J. W. T. Allen, as *Nikahi* (Dar es Salaam: Government Printer, 1959).

Johnson, Frederick. 1939. *A Standard Swahili-English Dictionary.* London: Oxford Univ. Press. Reprinted 1964.

Landberg, Leif C. W. 1975. "Men of Kigombe: Ngalawa Fishermen of Northeastern Tanzania." Diss., Univ. of California, Davis.

Landberg, Leif C. W., and Pamela L. Weaver. 1974. "*Maendeleo*: Economic Modernization in a Coastal Community of Northeastern Tanzania," in John J. Poggie, Jr., and Robert N. Lynch, eds., *Rethinking Modernization*. Westport, Conn.: Greenwood Press.

Landberg, Pamela. 1977. "Kinship and Community in a Tanzanian Coastal Village (East Africa)." Diss., Univ. of California, Davis.

Lienhardt, Peter. 1968. *The Medicine Man*. Oxford: Clarendon Press.

Mascarenhas, Adolfo C. 1970. "Resistance and Change in the Sisal Plantation System of Tanzania." Diss., Univ. of California, Los Angeles.

Middleton, J. 1961. *Report on Land Tenure in Zanzibar*. Colonial Research Studies No. 33. London: H.M.S.O.

Middleton, John, and Jane Campbell. 1965. *Zanzibar: Its Society and Its Politics*. London: Oxford Univ. Press.

Prins, A. H. J. 1967. *The Swahili-Speaking Peoples of Zanzibar and the East African Coast*. Ethnographic Survey of Africa: East-Central Africa, Part 12. London: International African Institute.

Roberts, D. F., and R. E. S. Tanner. 1959-60. "A Demographic Study in an Area of Low Fertility in Northeast Tanganyika." *Population Studies*, 13: 61-80.

Strobel, Margaret. 1979. *Muslim Women in Mombasa: 1890-1975*. New Haven: Yale Univ. Press.

Swartz, Marc J. 1982. "The Isolation of Men and the Happiness of Women: Sources and Use of Power in Swahili Marital Relationships." *Journal of Anthropological Research*, 38 (1): 26-44.

Tanner, R. E. S. 1962. "The Relationship Between the Sexes in a Coastal Islamic Society: Pangani District, Tanganyika." *African Studies*, 21 (2): 70-82.

———. 1964. "Cousin Marriage in the Afro-Arab Community of Mombasa, Kenya." *Africa*, 34 (2): 127-38.

Trimingham, J. Spencer. 1964. *Islam in East Africa*. Oxford: Clarendon Press.

Wijeyewardene, Gehan. 1959. *Kinship and Ritual in the Swahili Community*. East African Institute of Social Research Conference Paper No. 108. Kampala: Makerere College.

———. 1961. "Some Aspects of Village Solidarity Among Ki-Swahili Speaking Communities of Kenya and Tanganyika. Diss., Cambridge Univ.

*Schildkrout: Widows in Hausa Society*

Adamu, M. 1978. *The Hausa Factor in West African History*. Ibadan: Oxford Univ. Press.

Bargery, G. P. 1934. *A Hausa-English Dictionary and English-Hausa Vocabulary*. London: Oxford Univ. Press.

Cohen, R. 1971. *Dominance and Defiance: A Study of Marital Instability in an Islamic African Society*. Anthropological Studies No. 6. Washington D.C.: American Anthropological Association.

Goody, E. 1973. *Contexts of Kinship: An Essay in the Family Sociology of the Gonja*. Cambridge Studies in Social Anthropology No. 7. Cambridge: Cambridge Univ. Press.

Hill, P. 1969. "Hidden Trade in Hausaland," *Man* 4 (3): 392-409.

———. 1972. *Rural Hausa: A Village and a Setting*. Cambridge: Cambridge Univ. Press.

Lopata, H. Z. 1972. "Role Changes in Widowhood: A World Perspective," in D. O. Cowgill and L. D. Holmes, eds., *Aging and Modernization*, pp. 275-303. New York: Appleton-Century-Crofts.

Nwogugu, E. I. 1974. *Family Law in Nigeria*. Ibadan: Heinemann.

Pittin, R. 1979. "Marriage and Alternative Strategies: Career Patterns of Hausa Women in Katsina City." Ph.D. diss., School of Oriental and African Studies, London.

———. 1983. "Houses of Women: A Focus on Alternative Life-Styles in Katsina City," in C. Oppong, ed., *Female and Male in West Africa*, pp. 291-303. London: George Allen and Unwin.

Raynaut, C. 1977. "Aspects socio-economiques de la préparation et de la circulation de la nourriture dans un village hausa (Niger)." *Cahiers d'Etudes Africaines*, 68 (XVII-4): 569-97.

Schildkrout, E. 1978. "Age and Gender in Hausa Society: Socio-Economic Roles of Children in Urban Kano," in J. S. LaFontaine, ed., *Sex and Age as Principles of Social Differentiation*, pp. 109-37. New York: Academic Press.

———. 1979. "Women's Work and Children's Work: Variations Among Moslems in Kano," in S. Wallman, ed., *Social Anthropology of Work* (A.S.A. Monograph 19), pp. 69-85. London: Academic Press.

———. 1981. "The Employment of Children in Kano," in G. Rodgers and G. Standing, eds., *Child Work, Poverty and Underdevelopment*, pp. 81-112. Geneva: International Labour Office.

———. 1983. "Dependence and Autonomy: The Economic Activities of Secluded Hausa Women in Kano," in C. Oppong, ed., *Female and Male in West Africa*, pp. 107-27. London: George Allen and Unwin.

Smith, M. 1954. *Baba of Karo: A Woman of the Muslim Hausa*. London: Faber and Faber.

Smith, M. G. 1955. *The Economy of the Hausa Communities of Zaria*. Colonial Research Studies No. 16. London: H.M.S.O.

*Salamone: Dukawa Widows*

Bohannan, Laura. 1949. "Dahomean Marriage." *Africa*, 19: 273-87.

Bohannan, Paul. 1959. "The Impact of Money on an African Subsistence Economy." *Journal of Economic History*, 19: 491-503.

Beidelman, Thomas O., ed., 1971. *The translation of culture*. London: Tavistock.

Cohen, Ronald. 1971. *Dominance and Defiance*. Washington, D.C.: American Anthropological Association.

Divale, William Tulio, and Marvin Harris. 1976. "Population, Warfare, and the Male Supremacist Complex." *American Anthropologist*, 78: 521-88.

Etienne, Mona. 1979a. "The Case for Social Maternity: Adoption of Children by Urban Baoulé Women." *Dialectical Anthropology*, 4: 237-42.

———. 1979b. "Maternité sociale, rapports d'adoption et pouvoir des femmes chez les Baoulé (Côte d'Ivoire)." *L'Homme*, 19: 63-108.

Evans-Pritchard, E. E. 1951. *Kinship and Marriage Among the Nuer*. Oxford: Clarendon Press.

Fox, Robin. 1972. "Alliance and Constraint," in *Sexual Selection and the Descent of Man*, B. G. Campbell, ed. Chicago: Adline.

Goldschmidt, Walter. 1959. *The Anthropology of Franz Boas*. San Francisco: Chandler Press.

Goody, Esther N. 1978. "Some Theoretical and Empirical Aspects of Parenthood in West Africa." Changing African Family Project Series No. 4, Part 1, 227-72.

Greenberg, Joseph. 1966. *The Languages of Africa*. Bloomington: Indiana Univ. Press.

Hammond, Dorothy, and Alta Jablow. 1973a. "Women: Their Economic Roles in Traditional Societies." Reading, Mass.: Addison-Wesley.

———. 1973b. *The Africa That Never Was*. New York: Library of Social Science. Reissued in 1977 as *The Myth of Africa*.

———. 1976. *Women in Cultures of the World*. Menlo Park, Calif.: Cummings.

Harris, Marvin. 1977. "Why Men Dominate Women." *N.Y. Times Magazine*, Nov. 13, pp. 46ff.

Leacock, Eleanor Burke. 1981. *Myths of Male Dominance*. New York: Monthly Review Press.

Lévi-Strauss, Claude. 1969. *The Elementary Structures of Kinship*. Boston: Beacon Press.

MacBride, D. F. M. 1935. "The Rijau Report." Ms. Archives of Univ. of Birmingham, England.

Mahdi, Adamu. 1968. "A Hausa Government in Decline: Yawuri in the

Nineteenth Century." M.A. Thesis, Dept. of History, Ahmadu Bello University, Zaria.

Mathieu, Nicole-Claude. 1977. "Paternité biologique, maternité sociale," in Andrée Michel, ed., *Femmes, sexisme et société*. Paris: Presses universitaires de France.

Meillassoux, Claude. 1981. *Maidens, Meals, and Money: Capitalism and the Domestic Community*. Cambridge: Cambridge Univ. Press. Trans. from the French (1975).

National Archives of Nigeria (NANK) at Kaduna K 6099. Vol. 1 (*Kontagora Province: Portion of the Dukawa Tribe in Yauri Emirate*) and vol. 2 (*Kontagora Province: Transfer of, to Rijau District*).

Paulme, Denise, ed. 1963. *Women of Tropical Africa*. Berkeley: Univ. of California Press. First published 1960.

Persell, Nancy. 1983. *Understanding Society*. New York: Harper & Row.

Poewe, Karla. 1980. "Universal Male Dominance: An Ethnological Illusion." *Dialectical Anthropology*, 5: 111-25.

Prazan, Ceslaus, O. P. 1977. *The Dukkawa of Northwest Nigeria*. Pittsburgh: Duquesne Univ. Press.

Rossi, Ino, ed. 1974. *The Unconscious in Culture: The Structuralism of Claude Lévi-Strauss in Perspective*. New York: Dutton.

Sacks, Karen. 1981. *Sisters and Wives*. Westport: Greenwood Press.

Salamone, Frank A. 1972. "Structural Factors in Dukawa Conversion." *Practical Anthropology*, 19: 219-25.

———. 1974. *Gods and Goods in Africa*. New Haven: HRAFlex.

———. 1976. "Structures, Stereotypes, and Students: Implications for a Theory of Ethnic Interaction." *Council on Anthropology and Education Quarterly*, 8: 6-13.

———. 1978a. "Children's Games." *Ethnicity*, 5: 203-12.

———. 1978b. "Dukawa *Wakar Gormu* (Wedding Songs)." *Research Bulletin*, Univ. of Lucknow.

———. 1979a. "Children's Games as Mechanisms for Easing Ethnic Interaction." *Anthropos*, pp. 201-10.

———. 1979b. "Dukawa-Kamberi Relationships of Privileged Familiarity: Implications for a Theory of Play." *Ethnicity*, 6: 123-36.

———. 1979c. "Epistemological Implications of Fieldwork and Their Consequences." *American Anthropologist*, 81: 146-60.

———. 1983. "The Clash of Indigenous, Islamic, Colonial, and Postcolonial Law in Nigeria." *Journal of Legal Pluralism*, 21: 15-60.

——— and Charles Swanson. 1979. "Identity and Ethnicity." *Ethnic Groups*, 2: 167-83.

*Muller: Widows' Choices Among the Rukuba*

Chalifoux, J. J. 1979. "Polyandrie et dialectique communautaire chez les Abisi du Nigéria," *Anthropologie et Sociétés*, 3 (1): 75-127.

————. 1980. "Secondary Marriage and Levels of Seniority Among the Abisi (Piti) of Nigeria," in "Women with Many Husbands: Polyandrous Alliance and Marital Flexibility in Africa and Asia," special issue of *Journal of Comparative Family Studies*, 11 (3): 325-34.

Collard, C. 1979. "Mariage 'à petits pas' et 'mariage par vol': Pouvoir des hommes, des femmes et des chefs chez les Guidar," *Anthropologie et Sociétiés*, 3 (1): 41-74.

Juillerat, B. 1971. *Les bases de l'organisation sociale chez les Mouktélé (Nord Cameroun)*. Paris: Institut d'Ethnologie.

Meek, C. K. 1931. *Tribal Studies in Northern Nigeria*, Vols. 1 and 2. London: Trench, Trubner and Kegan Paul.

Muller, J. C. 1976. *Parenté et mariage chez les Rukuba (Etat Benue-Plateau, Nigéria)*. Paris: Mouton.

————. 1980. "On the Relevance of Having Two Husbands: Contribution to the Polygynous/Polyandrous Marital Forms of the Jos Plateau," in "Women with Many Husbands: Polyandrous Alliance and Marital Flexibility in Africa and Asia," special issue of *Journal of Comparative Family Studies*, 11 (3): 359-69.

————. 1981. *Du bon usage du sexe et du mariage: Structures matrimoniales du haut plateau nigérian*. Paris: L'Harmattan.

Richard, M. 1977. *Traditions et coutumes matrimoniales chez les Mada et les Mouyeng*. St-Augustin: Anthropos Institut.

Sangree, W. H. 1969. "Going Home to Mother: Traditional Marriage Among the Irigwe of Benue-Plateau State, Nigeria." *American Anthropologist*, 71: 1046-57.

Sangree, W. H., and N. Levine. 1980. "Conclusion: Asian and African Systems of Polyandry," in "Women with Many Husbands: Polyandrous Alliance and Marital Flexibility in Africa and Asia," special issue of *Journal of Comparative Family Studies*, 11 (3): 385-410.

Smith, M. G. 1953. "Secondary Marriage in Northern Nigeria." *Africa*, 23 (3): 298-323.

*Guyer: Beti Widow Inheritance and Marriage Law*

Alexandre, P., and J. Binet. 1958. *Boulou-Beti-Fang: Le Group dit Pahouin*. Paris: Presse Universitaire Française.

AN (Archives Nationales, Section Outre Mer), Paris.

AR (Annual Report of the Government of Cameroon to the Permanent Mandate Commission of the League of Nations), Geneva.

Assoumou, J. 1977. *L'Economie du Cacao*. Paris: Jean-Pierre DeLarge.

Bertaut, M. 1935. *Le Droit coutumier des Boulous*. Paris: Domat Montchrestian.

Binet, J. 1956. *Budgets familiaux des planteurs de cacao au Cameroun*. Paris: Office de la Recherche Scientifique et Technique, Outre-Mer.

CNA (Cameroon National Archives), Yaoundé.

Comaroff, J., and S. Roberts. 1977. "Marriage and Extra-marital Sexuality: The Dialects of Legal Change Among the Kgatla." *Journal of African Law*, 21 (1): 97-123.

de Thé, M. P. 1965. "Influence des femmes sur l'évolution des structures sociales chez les Beti du Sud-Cameroun." Mémoire, Ecole Pratique des Hautes Etudes, Paris.

————. 1970. "Des Sociétés secrètes aux associations modernes: La femme dans la dynamique de la société Beti 1887-1966." Diss., Université de Paris.

Douglas, M. 1967. "Primitive Rationing: A Study in Controlled Exchange," in R. Firth, ed., *Themes in Economic Anthropology*. London: Tavistock.

Goody, J. 1973. "Bridewealth and Dowry in Africa and Eurasia," in J. Goody and S. J. Tambiah, *Bridewealth and Dowry*. Cambridge: Cambridge Univ. Press.

————. 1976. *Production and Reproduction: A Comparative Study of the Domestic Domain*. Cambridge: Cambridge Univ. Press.

Guyer, J. I. 1978. "The Food Economy and French Colonial Rule in Central Cameroun." *Journal of African History*, 19 (4): 577-97.

————. 1981. "The Depression and the Administration in South-Central Cameroun." *African Economic History*, 10: 69-79.

Hopkins, A. G. 1973. *An Economic History of West Africa*. New York: Columbia Univ. Press.

JOC (Journal Officiel du Cameroun), Cameroon National Archives, Yaoundé.

Kuczynski, Robert. 1939. *The Cameroon and Togoland: A Demographic Study*. London: Oxford Univ. Press.

Laburthe-Tolra, P. 1977a. *Minlaaba*. Paris: Honoré Champion.

————. 1977b. "Charles Atangana," in C. A. Julien, ed., *Les Africains*, vol. 5. Paris: Editions Jeune Afrique.

————. 1981. *Les Seigneurs de la forêt*. Paris: Publications de la Sorbonne.

Lloyd, P. C. 1968. "Divorce Among the Yoruba." *American Anthropologist*, 70 (1): 67-81.

Meillassoux, C. 1964. *Anthropologie Economique des Gouro de Côte d'Ivoire*. Paris: Mouton.

———. 1978. "The Economy in Agricultural Self-Sustaining Societies: A Preliminary Analysis" (trans. from the French), in D. Seddon, ed., *Relations of Production*, pp. 127-57. London: Frank Cass.

Ngoa, H. 1968. "Le Mariage chez les Ewondo." Diss., Sorbonne, Paris.

Ogbu, J. 1978. "African Bridewealth and Women's Status." *American Ethnologist*, 5 (2): 241-62.

Owono Nkoudou, J. R. 1953. "Le Problème du mariage dotale au Cameroun Français." *Etudes Camerounaises*, 6 (39/40): 41-83.

Parkin, D. 1980. "Kind Bridewealth and Hard Cash: Eventing a Structure," in J. Comaroff, ed., *The Meaning of Marriage Payments*, pp. 197-220. London: Academic Press.

Quinn, F. 1970. "Changes in Beti Society, 1887-1960." Ph.D. diss., Univ. of California, Los Angeles.

———. 1980. "Beti Society in the Nineteenth Century." *Africa*, 50 (3): 293-304.

Radcliffe-Brown, A. R., and D. Forde. 1950. "Introduction," in *African Systems of Kinship and Marriage*, pp. 1-85. London: Oxford Univ. Press.

RFC (Republique Federale du Cameroun). 1970. "La Population de Yaoundé: Résultats définitifs du recensement de 1962." Yaoundé: Ministry of Planning.

Sahlins, M. D. 1961. "The Segmentary Lineage: An Organization of Predatory Expansion." *American Anthropologist*, 63 (2, pt. 1): 322-45.

Spencer, P. 1980. "Polygyny as a Measure of Social Differentiation in Africa," in J. C. Mitchell, ed., *Numerical Techniques in Social Anthropology*, pp. 117-60. Philadelphia: Institute for the Study of Human Issues.

Tabi, I. 1971. "L'Eglise au Cameroun 1884-1935." Mémoire. Faculté des Lettres et Sciences Humaines, Lyon.

Tardits, C. 1970. "Femmes à crédit," in J. Pouillon and P. Maranda, eds., *Exchanges et communications: Mélanges offertes à C. Lévi-Strauss*. Paris: Mouton.

Tessman, G. 1913. *Die Pangwe*. Berlin: Ernst Wasmuth.

Vincent, J. F. 1976. *Traditions et Transitions. Entretiens avec des femmes Beti du Sud-Cameroun*. Paris: Office de la Recherche Scientifique et Technique, Outre-Mer.

*Vellenga: The Widow Among the Akan*

Adontenhene of Akwapim. 1969. Interview.

Antubam, Kofi. 1947. "Cultural Contributions of the Queen-Mothers of Bono-Manso-Tackyiman and the Reigns of Bono Kings from the Middle of the 16th Century Onward." Institute of African Studies, Legon. Typescript.

Bentsi-Enchill, K. 1975. "Some Implications of Our Laws of Marriage and Succession," in Christine Oppong, ed., *Changing Family Studies* (Legon Family Research Papers No. 3), pp. 125-28. Legon: Institute of African Studies.

Carboo, Patience. 1960. "Okuna: It's So Archaic and Brutal." *Sunday Mirror* (Accra), Sept. 15.

"Cousin Frank." 1935. *Catholic Voice*. Accra: Catholic Church of Ghana.

*Daily Graphic* (Accra). 1959. "Protect Future of Children," Apr. 18.

Fiadjoe, A. 1969. "Notes and Comments: Matrimonial Property." *Review of Ghana Law*, vol. 1, no. 1 (May).

Fortes, Meyer. 1950. "Kinship and Marriage Among the Ashanti," in A. R. Radcliffe-Brown and Daryll Forde, eds., *African Systems of Kinship and Marriage*, pp. 252-84. London: Oxford Univ. Press.

Garlick, P. 1950. *African Traders and Economic Development in Ghana*. Oxford: Clarendon Press.

Gluckman, Max. 1950. "Kinship and Marriage Among the Lozi of Northern Rhodesia and the Zulu of Natal," in A. R. Radcliffe-Brown and Daryll Forde, eds., *African Systems of Kinship and Marriage*, pp. 166-200. London: Oxford Univ. Press.

Gold Coast. 1910. *Gold Coast Colony Blue Book: 1909*. Accra: Government Printing Office. C.O. 100/59.

Greenberg, Joseph H. 1963. "The Languages of Africa." *International Journal of American Linguistics*, 29.

Herskovits, Melville J. 1938. *Dahomey*. New York: Augustin.

Lystad, R. 1959. "Marriage Among the Ashanti and Agni," in W. R. Bascom and M. J. Herskovits, eds., *Continuity and Change in African Cultures*, pp. 187-204. Chicago: Univ. of Chicago Press.

McCall, Daniel. 1956. "The Effect on Family Structure of Changing Economic Activities of Women in a Gold Coast Town." Ph.D. diss., Columbia Univ.

Ollennu, N. A. 1966. *The Law of Testate and Intestate Succession in Ghana*. London: Sweet and Maxwell.

Oppong, Christine. 1974. *Marriage Among a Matrilineal Elite*. London: Cambridge Univ. Press.

Ottie, O. 1971. "Processes of Family Formation Among the Urhobo of Midwestern Nigeria." *International Journal of Sociology of the Family*, vol. 1, no. 2 (Sept.): 125-36.

Priestly, M. 1969. *West Africa and Coast Society: A Family Study*. London: Oxford Univ. Press.

Rattray, R. 1927. *Religion and Art in Ashanti*. Oxford: Clarendon Press.

————. 1929. *Ashanti Law and Constitution*. Oxford: Clarendon Press.

Republic of Ghana. 1959. *Ghana Law Reports*. Accra: General Legal Council.

―――. 1973. *Statistical Yearbook 1969-70.* Accra: Government Printing Office.

Sarbah, J. M. 1968. *Fanti Customary Laws.* London: Frank Cass. Original edition 1897.

Vellenga, D. D. 1972. "Attempts to Change the Marriage Laws in Ghana and the Ivory Coast," in P. Foster and A. Zolberg, eds., *Ghana and the Ivory Coast: Perspectives on Modernization,* pp. 125-50. Chicago: Univ. of Chicago Press.

―――. 1975. "Changing Sex Roles and Social Tension in Ghana: The Law as Measure and Mediator of Family Conflict." Ph.D. diss., Columbia Univ.

―――. 1983. "Who Is a Wife? Legal Expressions of Heterosexual Conflict in Ghana," in Christine Oppong, ed., *Female and Male in West Africa,* pp. 144-55. London: Allen and Unwin.

Woodman, G. 1974. "The Rights of Wives, Sons, and Daughters in the Estates of Their Deceased Husbands and Fathers," in Christine Oppong, ed., *Domestic Rights and Duties in Southern Ghana* (Legon Family Research Papers No. 1), pp. 268-84. Legon: Institute of African Studies.

*Yaotey* v. *Quaye* in the High Court, Accra. 1961. Univ. of Ghana Law School, Legon. Mimeo.

Wuver, Edith. 1959. "Edith Wuver Hears the Voice of Ghana—So Strong and Exciting." *Sunday Mirror* (Accra), Apr. 19.

*Etienne: Widow Remarriage Among the Baule*

Carteron, Michel. 1972. "Etude de la langue baoulé." Bocanda, Ivory Coast. Mimeo.

Etienne, Mona. 1976. "Women and Slaves: Stratification in an African Society." Paper presented to the 75th Annual Meeting of the American Anthropological Association, Washington, D.C.

―――. 1979a. "The Case for Social Maternity: Adoption of Children by Urban Baule Women (Ivory Coast)." *Dialectical Anthropology,* 4 (3): 237-41.

―――. 1979b. "Maternité sociale, rapports d'adoption et pouvoir des femmes chez les Baoulé (Côte d'Ivoire)." *L'Homme,* 19 (3-4): 63-107.

―――. 1980. "Women and Men, Cloth and Colonization: The Transformation of Production-Distribution Relations Among the Baule (Ivory Coast)," in Mona Etienne and Eleanor Leacock, eds., *Women and Colonization: Anthropological Perspectives,* pp. 214-38. New York: J. F. Bergin/Praeger.

―――. 1983. "Gender Relations and Conjugality Among the Baule," in

Christine Oppong, ed., *Female and Male in West Africa*, pp. 303-19. London: George Allen and Unwin.

Etienne, Pierre. 1975. "Les interdictions de mariage chez les Baoulé." *L'Homme*, 15 (3-4): 5-29.

Etienne, Pierre, and Mona Etienne. 1967. "Terminologie de la parenté et de l'alliance chez les Baoulé." *L'Homme*, 7 (4): 50-76.

Goody, Esther N. 1962. "Conjugal Separation and Divorce Among the Gonja of Northern Ghana," in Meyer Fortes, ed., *Marriage in Tribal Societies*, pp. 14-54. Cambridge: Cambridge Univ. Press.

Goody, Jack R., and Esther N. Goody. 1967. "The Circulation of Women and Children in Northern Ghana." *Man*, n.s. 2 (2): 226-48.

Gottlieb, Alma. 1983. "Village Kapok, Forest Kapok: Notions of Separation, Identity and Gender Among the Beng of Ivory Coast." Ph.D. diss., Dept. of Anthropology, Univ. of Virginia, Charlottesville.

Guerry, Vincent. 1970. *La vie quotidienne dans un village baoulé*. Abidjan: Institut africain pour le développement économique et social.

Rattray, R. S. 1969. *Ashanti Law and Constitution*. Oxford: Clarendon Press.

# Index

segmentary          affine
agnate              affinity / alliance
cognate

Library of Congress Cataloging-in-Publication Data
Main entry under title:

Widows in African societies.

Bibliography: p.
Includes index.
1. Widows—Africa, Sub-Saharan—Addresses, essays,
lectures.   2. Ethnology—Africa, Sub-Saharan—Addresses,
essays, lectures.   3. Africa, Sub-Saharan—Social
life and customs—Addresses, essays, lectures.
I. Potash, Betty, 1933–
GN645.W48   1986      305'.90654'0967      85-26054
ISBN 0-8047-1299-9